TIP-OFF

TIP-OFF

How the 1984 NBA Draft
Changed Basketball Forever

FILIP BONDY

DA CAPO PRESS
A Member of the Perseus Books Group

Designed by Brent Wilcox
Set in 10.75 point Janson Text by The Perseus Books Group

Library of Congress Cataloging-in-Publication Data
Bondy, Filip.
    Tip-off : how the 1984 NBA draft changed basketball forever / Filip Bondy.
        p.   cm.
    Includes bibliographical references and index.
    ISBN-13: 978-0-306-81486-0 (hard cover : alk. paper)
    ISBN-10: 0-306-81486-2 (hard cover : alk. paper)
    1. Basketball draft.   2. Basketball players—United States—Recruiting.
3. National Basketball Association.   I. Title.
GV885.514.B65 2007
796.323'640973—dc22

                                                                    2006035572

Published by Da Capo Press
A Member of the Perseus Books Group
http://www.dacapopress.com

Da Capo Press books are available at special discounts for bulk purchases in the U.S. by corporations, institutions, and other organizations. For more information, please contact the Special Markets Department at the Perseus Books Group, 11 Cambridge Center, Cambridge, MA 02142, or call (800) 255-1514 or (617) 252-5298, or e-mail special.markets@perseusbooks.com.

1 2 3 4 5 6 7 8 9

For Gus, Luke, and Max

CONTENTS

PROLOGUE *The Flip*   ix

1 *The View from Chapel Hill*   1
2 *Decision Time*   15
3 *The Achilles Shin*   31
4 *Out of Africa, Into Texas*   45
5 *The Well-Rounded Recruit*   65
6 *Spokane Man*   75
7 *Trial by Knight*   83
8 *Embracing Defeat*   101
9 *Finishing the Picasso*   109
10 *Liking Mike*   121
11 *The Safe Pick*   135
12 *The Imperfect Fit*   145
13 *Sweet Sixteen*   155
14 *Portland Selects Sam Bowie*   165
15 *Not Twins at All*   181
16 *After the Fall*   193

17 *A Different Kind of Star*   203

18 *Far from Eden*   217

19 *Charles in Charge*   225

20 *The Player's Player*   237

EPILOGUE   247

ACKNOWLEDGMENTS   263

BIBLIOGRAPHY   267

INDEX   271

PROLOGUE

The Flip

On the late morning of Tuesday, May 22, 1984, two opposing groups of thoroughly superstitious team officials converged on the NBA offices in Manhattan to pray for good fortune, to flip a coin, and to redraw the league's burgeoning road map for decades to come. They all hoped to win the big prize in the "Olajuwon lottery," though there were certainly some intriguing alternatives. College basketball in 1984 was chock full of individual genius, a bushel of seasoned, polished upperclassmen eager to impact the league in their rookie professional season. Consider some of the players who had just been showcased in the forty-eight-team NCAA tournament, whetting appetites for NBA fans: Patrick Ewing, playing center, helped Georgetown capture the title. And while Ewing decided to remain a Hoya for another year, Hakeem Olajuwon (he was still "Akeem" back then, at least to the public) chose to leave school early and declare for the draft. He had played fearlessly in that same tournament for the University of Houston, leading the Cougars to the final. Sam Bowie and Mel Turpin, two talented big men, reached the Final Four with Kentucky. Michael Jordan and Sam Perkins at North Carolina were brilliant at times but lost unexpectedly early on to Indiana. And while Auburn could not quite measure up to these other top basketball schools, its star, Charles Barkley, was a hurricane force out of the Southeast Conference.

These players, and their arrival at this special moment in time, would mean the birth of a new National Basketball Association, the modern NBA. The league that was waiting anxiously for this wave of saviors was very different from the one that exists today, at a crossroads in so many ways. The NBA in 1984 had only recently turned the corner from its darkest days, from the budget deficits affecting seventeen of twenty-three franchises and the kind of rampant substance abuse that was coming to light through the well-publicized plights of Micheal Ray Richardson and Quintin Dailey. In 1983, the NBA and its Players Association adopted their first drug program, aimed particularly at those societal scourges: cocaine and heroin. A system of testing, based on "reasonable cause" for suspicion, was put into place, and a series of penalties was introduced in three steps—a period of rehabilitation, without loss of pay, for the first voluntary admission of drug use; a suspension without salary during the rehab period for the second violation; and a permanent league ban for a third violation. A relatively rumpled league attorney, David Stern, accepted the reins from a well-connected, hands-off politician, Lawrence O'Brien, who had been more at ease as campaign manager of John F. Kennedy than as keeper of the flame for Bob Cousy and Bill Russell. Stern inherited a stagnant business from O'Brien, and the new commissioner envisioned an aggressive marketing strategy to turn the league around with assistance from salary controls.

The transition at the top heralded the start of a hands-on regulation era. Earlier, as aggressive point men for the league, Stern and his lieutenant, future NHL commissioner Gary Bettman, won a salary cap in 1983 during collective bargaining negotiations with the players' union. The nascent NBA once had a cap in the 1940s but abandoned it after just one season. Groundbreaking for professional sports, the new system would go into effect for the 1984–85 season, basing the cap on 55 percent of the league's total revenues. The maximum combined player payroll would be set at $3.6 million for each team. Twenty-one years later, for the 2005–06 season, the cap number was $49.5 million, and many franchises were well over that number because of rule exceptions. The average salary of players in 1984 was $340,000 and would grow to $4.28 million within two decades.

"The things we worried about then . . . ," Stern said, looking back. Most of all, the league fretted about getting its product on television. No network wanted any part of the NBA in prime time, so Stern found himself scheduling playoff games on back-to-back Saturday and Sunday afternoons, just so they would be broadcast live. "Even later, the year the NFL was on strike [1987], CBS would rather put on a St. John's–Yugoslavia game," Stern said. "They wanted $50,000 from us to get our games on. We were begging them to get on."

Ironically, the NBA was in its competitive and artistic heyday at this time. The playoffs that spring of 1984 produced incredible basketball, dramatic matchups that ended in a sublime, seven-game victory by the Boston Celtics over the Los Angeles Lakers in the finals. Larry Bird and Magic Johnson were incomparable bicoastal rivals. And yet these stars were still not transcendent in a global marketing sense. They were most famous for their passes, for their championships, not for their dunks or for their shoes or for their off-court trash talk. Playoff games finally were being shown live, instead of on tape, but networks were just beginning to bid for rights.

So this would be a brave new world, and the class of rookies would be its founding fathers. Fresh, exciting dynamics were suddenly in place. Stern was leading the charge toward competitive parity with his crusade, the salary cap. Younger players were leaving college before their graduation, offering yet another layer of suspense to the draft: Will he stay, or will he go? As the stakes grew, players looked to maximize their marketing power. Family friends and lawyers no longer afforded adequate representation. Super agents with big firms and impressive client lists would soon determine the very composition of the league and its teams. And then there were the sneakers, the fast food chains, the soft drinks. Endorsements and television money were about to change all the rules, forever.

The league in 1984 was in its last throes of a stubborn plutocracy, dominated by a powerful ruling triumvirate: the Boston Celtics, the Los Angeles Lakers, and the aging Philadelphia 76ers. The rosters of too many other teams were paper-thin in marketable stars. The coin flip to determine the first draft pick on May 22 represented a chance for either the Houston Rockets or the Portland Trail Blazers to change all that, to transform the trio of elite teams into a quartet. Olajuwon wasn't a particularly glamorous figure. He wasn't even American. But the Nigerian star figured to have an immediate impact. He was big, smart, and agile. He owned surprising court savvy despite his inexperience. Title teams were built around such centers, guys like Kareem Abdul-Jabbar and Robert Parish. Olajuwon looked like a franchise player who figured to win a championship or two.

The two sides, Houston and Portland, did not arrive empty-handed to this coin flip in midtown Manhattan, for that surely would invite disaster. Ray Patterson, president of the Houston Rockets and an Irish-American to the core, considered himself an exceedingly lucky man who knew all about this courtship of the coin-flip gods. As president of the Milwaukee Bucks in 1969, he once won the flip for Lew Alcindor, later to become the incomparable NBA superstar Kareem Abdul-Jabbar. And in 1983, with a different league commissioner but in the same office with windows looking down on the spires of St. Patrick's Cathedral, Patterson had won another flip for the first pick and the right to draft Ralph Sampson.

This time, the Rockets would be flipping against the Trail Blazers for Olajuwon, the surest of sure things. The Sampson flip, a year earlier, served as a model for success, and the Houston representatives would repeat every ritual. On the eve of the flip, they gathered again at the renowned Jimmy Weston's bar on Manhattan's East Side to drink Irish whiskey late into the night. Weston knew Jim Foley, the Rockets' public relations director, from the late '60s, when Foley was working at Marquette University. Anybody who was a friend to Al McGuire, the personable coach and bon vivant at Marquette, was a friend of Weston. So not only did Weston host these good-luck eves for the Rockets, he ordered a worker at the saloon to grab a pair of giant shears and to snap a chain that tethered an odd-looking clock to the barroom wall. This clock was in the shape of Ireland, with twelve Irish coins in a circle to represent each hour. This would be Weston's gift to the Rockets, and it was guaranteed by the proprietor himself to assure success in the coin flip for Sampson, for Olajuwon, for anybody.

To this fateful meeting in May, the Rockets also brought a couple of certified bearers of good luck: Liz Patterson, Ray's daughter, and Tracy Thomas, the daughter of the Rockets' owner, Charles Thomas. Tracy, a twenty-one-year-old senior at Texas A & M, had suggested in 1983 that her father call "heads" for the Sampson flip, but cried in panic as then-commissioner O'Brien prepared to flip the coin. "Oh, Daddy," Tracy screamed suddenly. "Why did you listen to me? Please don't blame me!"

That coin bounced twice, hit the wall, and turned up heads. Charles Thomas turned proudly toward Ray Patterson, the Rockets' owner. Tracy was correct, allowing Houston to choose first in the draft and to pick Sampson, College Player of the Year from the University of Virginia. "I would have jumped out the window if his daughter was wrong," Ray Patterson said. The Indiana Pacers were stuck with Steve Stipanovich at number 2, who was the worst sort of consolation prize. Afterward, before heading back to Houston, Rockets' personnel, family, and friends consumed five bottles of Dom Perignon at Weston's. A few more bottles were left unopened, gifts to their gracious host, Jimmy.

Funny thing, though: the Rockets kept right on losing games in 1983–84, even with Sampson. They were back in the coin flip, and this time the stakes were arguably even greater. Most experts believed that Hakeem "The Dream" Olajuwon was a purer pro center than Sampson and therefore an even bigger catch. Patterson was convinced again that all lucky omens were pointing in Houston's direction, even though the Irishman, O'Brien, had been replaced by a Jewish attorney, David Stern. Larry Weinberg, the owner of the Portland Trail Blazers, knew he faced a tough coin-flip opponent in Patterson and didn't trust his own karma that day. He dragged along a friend from an entirely different walk of life, a guy known to others only as "Lucky," because of a serendipitous personal history. Lucky would advise Weinberg on the coin flip. Mainly, he would stand around and be lucky.

Stern, the new commissioner, performed this famous flip in his office. Jimmy Weston's clock was again present. It was held for a bit by Steve Patterson, Ray's son, who would much later become president of the Trail Blazers—a touch of bittersweet irony. First, there was a coin flip to decide who would call the real coin flip. The Blazers won this flip, the wrong flip. They then made the call: "tails." The coin landed heads. Foley tore off his jacket and dress shirt, like Clark Kent crammed into a phone booth, to reveal a T-shirt underneath that proclaimed in large block letters "AKEEM." There was much hugging and kissing. Bill Fitch, the Rockets' coach, remembered that Weinberg growled only one thing after his own crushing defeat: "C'mon, Lucky, let's get out of here!" The victorious Houston crowd headed to Weston's for more celebrating. The Blazers' officials departed New York in a huff, terribly disappointed they had lost Olajuwon and now had only Michael Jordan, Sam Perkins, Charles Barkley, John Stockton, and a pack of other future NBA stars to choose from.

Fitch, meanwhile, sneaked away just ten minutes after the victorious flip, placing a clandestine phone call to someone in North Carolina.

The View from Chapel Hill

Nearly twenty-two years after receiving Fitch's courtesy call, Dean Smith sits in a cluttered office in the nether regions of an arena that was named for him when it opened in 1986. The room is little more than a broom closet inside the Smith Center. A few books are scattered about, along with loose papers on a desk. There is not a trophy in sight, no photos of glorious bygone days on the walls. A bust of Smith sits in the lobby of the building, down the hall and up an elevator flight. But those who know the retired coach best say he isn't even aware of the statue.

Back in 1984, Smith's office was elsewhere, what had previously been the athletic director's office adjacent to Carmichael Auditorium, where the University of North Carolina Tar Heels were playing and winning virtually all their games. That office was where Smith received the phone call from Bill Fitch, who told him that the Houston Rockets had won the flip and that they would take Hakeem Olajuwon with the pick. Fitch had become one of Smith's many friends in the business, forging a symbiotic relationship in which each man would reach out and help the other whenever possible. Smith thrived on these NCAA-to-NBA contacts, on this sort of networking. Billy Cunningham, Larry Brown, Doug Moe, Donnie Walsh—they were all Tar Heel alums. They were all Smith's friends, part of his growing network. The coaches wanted scouting reports, films, and deep personality background checks on players. Smith wanted to know exactly what was happening in the pro league so he could better advise his players about their future plans. He also was not above manipulating the system to the advantage of his own players, which he felt was only right. "I tried," Smith said, with an impish grin. "The best one ever was George Lynch."

Lynch would come into the NBA draft after his senior year in 1993. He'd just won a national championship, and Smith loved the guy. Lynch was a leader, a worker. But nobody was calling Smith to find out information, and Lynch's stock was slipping precariously, right out of the first round. So Smith picked up that well-worn phone receiver, called Jerry West, and asked the Los Angeles Lakers' general manager to help. "I know you're drafting 12, you're not drafting George, but how about bringing him out there to L.A. for a workout and let some of the other teams notice?" Smith asked him. West was accommodating, and soon Lynch was being invited to come work out for the teams drafting 13, 14, 15, on and on. Word got out. There were only a few men in the league with that kind of respect, but West was one of them. Then the night before that 1993 draft, West and Mitch Kupchak, the assistant GM, called Smith to tell him the next plot twist. They were going to draft Lynch.

Weeks before the 1984 coin flip, Smith had called Fitch and was told straight out that if the Rockets lost that first pick, they were going to draft Michael Jordan at the number 2 spot. It made perfect sense for Houston, because the Rockets already owned a big man in Ralph Sampson, and they were not about to take a chance on any giant other than the sure thing, Olajuwon. Smith then called Stu

Inman, the general manager in Portland, who said the Trail Blazers were set to take a big man, probably Sam Bowie, at number 2. Smith shook his head in disbelief. How could they pass up Jordan? How could they do that? But Inman said he would. "We love Jordan, but we think we need some size," Inman told Smith. "We'll take Bowie if we lose the flip and Olajuwon if we win." The madness would stop there, Smith figured. Rod Thorn loved Jordan in Chicago. Thorn was a pal of Billy Cunningham, and Cunningham thought Jordan was a transcendent star. So Smith figured Jordan as a certain top-three pick, and postulated that the Tar Heels' other top player, Sam Perkins, would go 4 or 5.

It was now time for some decision making, and that process no longer seemed very difficult. Smith would advise Jordan to come out early, before his senior year. "We really have a rule here: We do what's best for the player out of season and what's best for the team in season," Smith said. He had another rule: if a player was going to be drafted in the top five, he might as well come out early because he would be financially set for life. By the '90s, as salaries in the NBA ballooned to unfathomable levels, Smith would revise his guidelines and advise any player projected as a top-ten pick to hustle out of college—with one big caveat. Smith had reputations to protect, his own and that of the university. He wanted these players to become examples to those recruits who would follow. So he elicited a promise from each of these early-leavers that they would return and earn their degrees. "If you have an opportunity to have a college degree, it doesn't mean you're going to live happily ever after," Smith explained. "But I think that's why they came here, I hope." Before Jordan, Smith had advised only two of his players to leave early—James Worthy and Phil Ford. Ford rejected Smith's advice, strangely enough, which only increased Smith's affection and respect for the playmaking guard. Near the end of his head coaching reign, Smith had the opportunity to recruit a couple of strong impact players who told him they intended to play just one season at North Carolina. Smith turned them both down. Of the nine who jumped to the pros during Smith's thirty-six-year tenure from 1961 to 1997, Smith proudly reported, seven returned to finish their degree requirements, and Bob McAdoo was still flirting with classes at the advanced age of fifty-four.

Among the coaches in his generation, Smith was arguably the most respected across all groups—his peers, the media, the players. He had his share of critics, nonetheless, and there were those who will always argue that Smith did not allow Michael Jordan to shine in his full glory, and perhaps cost that North Carolina team a second NCAA title. Smith reluctantly allowed Jordan to start as a freshman, but when *Sports Illustrated* asked to put the Tar Heels' starting five on the cover of its magazine, the coach told editors they could only have four. "Not the freshman," he said. Smith told Jordan directly that he hadn't earned such publicity yet, and even later Smith refused to anoint this amazing athlete as anything more than another member of the team. A riddle would become extremely popular in the years to come: Who was the only man who could hold Jordan to less than 20 points per game? The answer was Dean Smith, because even in his senior season Jordan managed only 19.9 points per game. But at North Carolina, friends of Smith will tell you this is not quite so, that Jordan actually averaged 20 points that last year, 1983–84. The Atlantic Coast Conference (ACC) was experimenting with the three-point arc, not yet officially recognized in NCAA statistics. If you counted Jordan's three-pointers, as the ACC did, then the riddle didn't hold. And Smith, famous for his stodgy, four-corner offense before the forty-five-second shot clock became NCAA law in 1985, was less vulnerable to such statistical disdain.

The way that Smith figured this Jordan thing, his player would be drafted number 2 or number 3 that June. If Jordan stayed at North Carolina for another season, he would be number 1 or number 2 in the 1985 draft, when Patrick Ewing graduated. But there was no guarantee because an injury was always a possibility. The coach remembered how James Worthy, midway through his freshman year, had suffered a broken ankle that required an internal pin to hold it together. When Worthy joined the Lakers, he broke his ankle again. "That was definitely in my mind," Smith said. There were other factors, too. This was an unusual draft: the teams with the top-five draft picks were all attractive homes for a rookie. There wasn't a San Diego Clippers franchise among them. Houston and Chicago were losing teams, but they both had large, untapped markets and decent potential. Portland, Philadelphia, and Dallas, already top contenders, happened to own the draft picks of much worse and less alluring franchises. Smith grimaced whenever the name "Clippers" came into play, but they weren't the only homely possibility. Such traditionally horrid teams as the Pacers and the Cleveland Cavaliers, perennial losers at the time, stood little chance of near-future success. Salary considerations were another factor. The NBA planned to implement its new salary cap during the 1984–85 season, and the ramifications of that new system were difficult to predict. One rule would severely limit the amount of money paid to any rookie, as little as $75,000, if the team were already over the cap. One year later, that player could make his fortune as a free agent, but again this would introduce new risk factors into the equation.

The coach thought this was a pretty clear-cut case, that Jordan should come out now, even though it would possibly cost the coach a run at another national title. Other opinions were decidedly mixed. Smith's assistants at the time were not so supportive of this early departure plan. Smith knew that Jordan's father, James, a General Electric plant supervisor from Wilmington, North Carolina, wanted Michael to turn pro. Smith also knew that Michael's mother, Deloris, a customer service representative for United Carolina Bank, didn't want him to leave North Carolina. The coach called an

agents' meeting, which he did almost every year. It would be a conference with Michael, his parents, and a few carefully chosen business agents to discuss the matter. Sam Perkins and his guardian,
Herb Crossman, were also there to get information, and Matt Doherty would sit in, too. Doherty was a senior, the team captain; he
wasn't expected to be drafted until the third or fourth round.

"We sat there and Mrs. Jordan certainly wanted him to finish his
degree," Smith said. "His dad thought it would be a good time to
turn pro. You could see Michael wanted to turn pro, too. I told
Michael to go back, think about it."

When the NCAA tournament had begun in March 1984, the North
Carolina Tar Heels on paper appeared to be virtually unbeatable.
They were 14–0 in the ACC, entered the tourney 27–2, were ranked
number 1 in the country, and were seeded first in the region. They
had enormous talent and experience to boot. Several players had
been part of the 1982 national championship team, which won the
title when Jordan hit the big shot and Worthy made the big steal
against Georgetown, sealing the victory. Perkins and Jordan together already had played in twenty-one NCAA tournament games,
before this particular March. The team featured center Brad Daugherty and freshman playmaker Kenny Smith, who had beaten out
Buzz Peterson for the spot early in the season. Four of the five
starters eventually would be drafted in the first round by NBA
teams. Matt Doherty was chosen 119th by Cleveland in the sixth
round; he later became head coach at North Carolina.

But this team was mainly about Jordan and Perkins, two guys
who were as different in temperament as they were in basketball
skill sets. Jordan, a six-foot-six-and-a-half junior, was a social
whirlwind, a force of competitive nature bent on beating you at the
game of your choice. Perkins, a six-foot-ten senior, was a likeable
loner, a quiet, lanky kid who figured things out as he went along.

There was a certain measure of irony that he would receive his degree in communications.

Perkins was a thoughtful quote, but he didn't always seem entirely focused on events that affected him. When an equipment manager asked him what number he wanted on his jersey at North Carolina, Perkins just said, "41," because that happened to be his sleeve size at the time he was measured for a uniform. A year earlier, at the NCAA tournament, Perkins would make a series of honest, undiplomatic mistakes. The Tar Heels were about to play Georgia, and Perkins could not identify the Bulldogs' conference. "Georgia? What league are they in?" he asked. He also said he had never heard of Wayman Tisdale, the University of Oklahoma star. Perkins's ignorance on these matters was somehow considered a terrible insult. Jordan had to explain to players in the Southeastern Conference (SEC) and to Tisdale (who would later become a fast friend of Perkins) that this was just Sam, plain and simple. Georgia wasn't in his immediate world, not like Maryland or Duke. Perkins would fall into things, then diligently work his way out. Jordan, meanwhile, would jump at any of life's experiences, tongue wagging at the next challenge.

The two players had come to this idyllic campus by very different routes, though both paths had been surprisingly color blind. Perkins never lacked for caring supervision but experienced a nomadic childhood. His grandmother, Martha Perkins, raised him as a Jehovah's Witness in Bedford-Stuyvesant, a particularly gritty Brooklyn neighborhood. He was taught that basketball really wasn't a worthwhile endeavor. He also learned through his religion to turn the other cheek when necessary, a respectful attitude that sometimes was mistaken for passivity, even timidity. "Jehovah's Witnesses teach people to be meek and mild, and I think a lot of that rubbed off on me," Perkins told *Sports Illustrated* when he was a senior at North Carolina. "But I can't help it if I look nonchalant. When I play, it may look easy, but it isn't. I sweat."

Perkins had grown tall and athletic as a teenager, and soon the kids at Tilden High School nicknamed him Kareem, after Abdul-Jabbar. He might have been quite the young athlete, but he didn't appear to be very goal-oriented. Nobody bothered to channel Perkins into basketball—at least until his junior year. The direction and geography of his life began to change dramatically in 1975, when Perkins met Herb Crossman, a job placement manager and an AAU coach with the Brooklyn Hoopsters.

"I had a couple guys on the team from Tilden," Crossman said. "I would see Sam going to school every day, coming from Bed Stuy, walking with the girls. I asked the other players if they knew that tall kid—he was about 6–5, with a big Afro. They said, 'That's Kareem. He doesn't play ball.'" Crossman asked his team members to approach Perkins and ask him to play. Perkins agreed, and the coach took a liking to this gentle giant. Crossman set up Perkins with jobs painting windows and facades, climbing ladders. When Crossman got a job near Albany, New York, he checked back with the junior varsity coach at Tilden to see how Sam was faring on his new team. "You know, he's all right," the Tilden coach told Crossman, "but he's not coming to class. Not consistently." Crossman drove down to the school. Classes were in session, but Perkins was hanging around outside. Sam was just wasting away here, Crossman figured. It was high time for a rescue.

Crossman asked Sam if he would be willing to relocate to suburban Albany. The boy, true to form, said sure, he would go with the flow. "It was hard leaving Brooklyn, for sure, coming to a place where you had no idea what was in store for you," Perkins recalled. "I was kind of looking forward to going, though. I knew I wasn't doing well in school, and my routine wasn't consistent as it would be in Albany. I had support there, and I thought I'd get on the right track there. And when I got to Albany, things started falling into place, I started getting good grades." Crossman checked with

Perkins's mother and grandmother. Both said they wouldn't mind, that it would be best for the child. And so in September 1978, Perkins moved to the state capitol area and attended Shaker High School in Latham. He had grown to six-foot-eight by now, in his junior year, and his appearance created quite a stir. "It was shocking for [his classmates]," Crossman said. Here was this big, athletic African-American kid, and he was starting to play real basketball. Crossman noticed this and knew Perkins belonged there. But Crossman's own family was getting too large, so he needed to relocate Perkins to another welcoming base. As it turned out, a family was waiting for him.

Marilyn Elacqua and her husband, John, had three daughters. Susan was a cheerleader at Shaker High and in one of Sam's classes. She invited Sam back to the house for a spaghetti dinner, and he accepted. Marilyn Elacqua answered the door, her eyes staring at his shirt buttons as she met Perkins for the first time. Sam, as always, was a man of few words. "I'm Sam," he said. "I'm here for spaghetti." He ate his spaghetti, and then soon enough Perkins moved in with the Elacquas, who effectively became his third family—after his own grandmother back in Brooklyn and Crossman, who remained nearby.

Sam followed the same rules as the Elacquas' daughters. He made the beds, swept the floor, did the dishes, told the Elacquas when he was going to be late. Perkins called John and Marilyn "Mr. E" and "Mrs. E." "We'd laugh and have a lot of fun together," Marilyn said. He never made trouble. His story became part *Leave It to Beaver*, part *The Fresh Prince of Bel-Air*. Once Sam came home late from a date, and Marilyn waited up for him, raised herself on her toes to scold him for this rare transgression. "I'm only 5–1," she said. "But I told Sam straight up, 'I want you to call me if you're going to be late.' He was never late again. He was great with house rules." From the inside, the arrangement was workable, almost ideal. "We thought he was the best thing since popcorn," Marilyn said. From the outside, it probably appeared a bit strange, a gangly black kid with this white family. "I think there was a subtle concern in both communities, black and white," she remembered. "There was never anything said. But he'd introduce us as, 'My folks,' and maybe people were thinking, 'Why is he living with that white, Italian family?'" At times, Perkins wondered, too. "I didn't know what I was getting into," Perkins said. "The school was predominately white. I didn't see too many blacks there. And I wondered, 'How would I be accepted?' You had your racial tension there, but I didn't come in there with a militant attitude, just to stand my ground, be like everybody else. For the most part, I did that. I made friends, both black and white. And the Elacquas became just like family."

He grew as close to the Elacquas as he had to Crossman. During the summers Sam would work for John, who was in construction. "This isn't going to be my life," Perkins told the Elacquas, and they understood. One thing was certain: Sam's basketball career was benefiting from all these arrangements. He was working out harder, and Crossman would make certain that the boy was seen in all the right places. Perkins had already made a splash at the Rucker Tournament in New York City, the summer of 1978, when he impressed the college scouts. St. John's coaches saw him there and were very interested. Perkins was becoming a pure forward, his rebounding skills improving rapidly. By the end of his junior year at Shaker High, several top universities were monitoring his progress. He averaged 25 points and 16 rebounds during his two years at Shaker. His high school coach wrote a letter to Dean Smith, and Smith wrote back. Syracuse and UCLA were also interested. "Sam was so laid back, even when he was picking colleges," Crossman said. "He didn't know which colleges he'd pick, right up to the end."

John Elacqua and Herb Crossman kept close tabs on Perkins at North Carolina. If they could, they would fly down for games. But sometimes they would wake up at 3 AM, drive the nine hours, sleep briefly, then commute back and go to work the next day. They attended twelve to fifteen games a year, joining James and Deloris Jordan on many trips. Marilyn came, too, sometimes. The two couples bonded and became good friends. There were some fine, funny memories from those trips. The parents got lost in a snowstorm in Syracuse because James Jordan and John Elacqua were too stubborn to ask for directions to the Carrier Dome. After an ACC tournament in Greensboro, the parents wanted to celebrate the championship in their hotel. They ordered pizza for everyone, a dozen pies altogether, and the fathers were scrambling around, scrounging for cash to pay for this modest feast. John Elacqua had only $8. James Jordan had only $11. Walter Daugherty, Brad's father, was emptying his pockets, desperately searching for money. Years later, when the million-dollar contracts were signed and the kids were moneyed celebrities, the parents and guardians would joke about this occasion: "Remember when we could hardly get enough money to buy pizza?"

The 1981–82 season turned into something special, an NCAA title. Everybody was there in New Orleans on March 29 when Michael Jordan hit the seventeen-foot jumper with fifteen seconds left and North Carolina won the championship over Georgetown. The Elacquas were sitting with the Jordans and the Daughertys. A row behind them were James Worthy's parents. Crossman was worried back then, he remembered, that Jordan might be a little too cocky. Perkins had arrived in Chapel Hill one season earlier and already had played in an NCAA championship game against Indiana, a 63–50 defeat. Now this Michael Jordan kid was making these uncanny moves all over the place in practice, his tongue always wagging. "I wondered, 'Is this guy going to fit the program?'" Crossman said, laughing at those misplaced concerns. Crossman even asked Dean Smith that question; Smith told him not to worry. The coach knew Jordan's character. On that championship team James Worthy was the star, and Jordan generally was pleased to take a back seat in order to help the team win.

They won plenty. Perkins and Jordan always got along with each other, and on the court they blended well. Both were hybrid players. Jordan was a guard who still hadn't mastered the outside shot, who preferred to slash toward the basket or create a ten-footer for himself. Perkins had a soft touch for a big man. He had a nice lefty hook shot, but he could move back further, near the foul line, and bury the fifteen-footer with consistency. On defense, both stars were remarkably quick and could guard virtually anyone of any size. Perkins had been assigned at different times to cover shooting guards, and he was also asked to match up against Ralph Sampson, who was seven-foot-four. Perkins had the quickness and the height to do it. And Jordan, of course, was a wonder.

Off the court at North Carolina, Perkins and Jordan led very different lives from the start. Jordan became fast buddies with Jimmy Black, an older teammate. Jordan would play cards with anyone, anytime, into the early morning hours. When Tar Heel players became juniors, they had the option of moving off campus. Perkins jumped at the chance, migrated to his own quiet place with teammate Cecil Exum, a place where he could do his own laundry and cook a bit for himself. Few teammates ever came over to visit. "I thought it was a chance to grow a little bit," Perkins said. "We had the opportunity to do that. Cecil and I lived together in a dorm our freshman and sophomore years. We just wanted to move away. I still had training table with the team, but this was a chance to experience life on my own."

Perkins was well-liked, and he could be helpful to anybody who required some guidance. Kenny Smith was a freshman point guard from New York City when Perkins was a senior, and Perkins took him under his wing. "I was Sam's 'Freshy,'" Kenny Smith said. Perkins would check on Smith, making sure he'd eaten properly and taken a pre-game nap. What Kenny Smith most remembers about Perkins, though, was his unflappable nature. "Sam just sat back, stress free," Smith said.

> One time, Sam says, "Let's go get a haircut before the pre-game meal." So we do, and then there's this unusual, huge traffic jam, costing us maybe 45 minutes, and we're running late, and I'm afraid we're going to miss the game. Then we get to this school bus stopped along the side of the road, and Sam won't go around the school bus, because he says it's illegal. My heart fell to the floor. I'm looking at the clock, stressing out, wondering what Coach Smith will do to us if we're late for the game. And Sam just turns up the music and says, "I don't know, maybe he won't start us." And we get to the game late against Tennessee–Chattanooga, against Gerald Wilkins, and that's what happens. We don't start, but we play [North Carolina won, 85–63]. And Sam just comes up to me and says, "I told you."

As another teammate, Buzz Peterson, would say, "Sam was definitely not in a hurry."

Jordan was different; he was never late for anything. He wanted to be in the middle of it all. He stuck to the sprawling Granville Towers, which were nine-story, red-brick, private student dorms on the northwest corner of campus, where he roomed with Peterson, an old friend. The two of them lived on the first floor of the South Tower, and they were spoiled rotten. Why move out of this place? Meals were prepared by staff, and whenever the room became too messy, which was often, Jordan's younger sister, Roslyn, also enrolled at UNC, would drop by and pitch in. "Everything stayed dirty," Peterson said, "until Roslyn did the laundry."

Peterson, who was white, had practically grown up with Jordan in a basketball sense. Buzz had played his high school ball in Asheville,

North Carolina, and was named the state's Mr. Basketball and Athlete of the Year his senior year, just ahead of Jordan. The two of them had played with and against each other for what seemed to be forever. Jordan knew the Peterson family. When Buzz's mother bought her son Bally loafers before each season, she already knew Jordan would wear them so much he'd stretch them out. The two young men played Monopoly and cards together. And of course Jordan was crazy competitive in all of these games. "I've always said this," Peterson said. "[Although Michael was] the youngest of three boys, Mr. Jordan never said to his kid, 'Larry, don't pick on Michael.' He told Michael, 'Fend for yourself.' And after a while in that situation, you learn to be competitive."

Peterson liked to tell the story of when Jordan was hanging out with the Petersons back in 1980 at a Syracuse hotel and Buzz caught Michael cheating at the card game Crazy Eights by hiding an eight—while playing against Peterson's own mother. "There it was, right under his leg," Peterson said. Outrageous, but that was Michael—or Mike. When Jordan first came to North Carolina, Rick Brewer, the school sports information director, asked Jordan whether he preferred one name over the other. Jordan said he didn't care. Brewer dubbed him "Michael," because it sounded better with Jordan.

When they were freshmen at North Carolina, Jordan beat out Peterson at shooting guard, fair and square. They remained friends, and Peterson switched to starting point guard his sophomore season. Peterson then wrecked his knee, lost a year, and was never the same player. Jordan remained a loyal friend and roommate. And at the Granville Towers they would relax and enjoy the pampering together. Jordan didn't mind the attention from all the other students, not a bit. All those fans could become easy marks when he wanted to beat them at a game of cards or pool.

Decision Time

When the NCAA tournament started in March, Terry Holland, coach of rival Virginia, heaped more pressure on the Tar Heels and Dean Smith. "Carolina has the best team ever assembled in college basketball," Holland said, in a much-quoted sound bite. Jordan had significantly improved his game from his sophomore to his junior season. He put on twelve pounds of muscle with some lifting, and he lowered his time in the forty-yard dash from 4.6 to 4.3 seconds. He worked again on that outside shot, hoping to sharpen it. He displayed the defensive energy of three players. If there were one player in the college ranks who represented "total basketball," it was Jordan. But the Tar Heels had a big problem: their bench was paper-thin. "That was a great team, as long as we weren't in foul trouble," Smith recalled.

The Tar Heels could ill afford injuries, and that's exactly what happened to them. Kenny Smith suffered a broken wrist in late January, when he was fouled hard from behind on a fast break by John Tudor of Louisiana State University. A month later, Daugherty

injured his hand in the ACC tournament. The speedy Smith continued to play with a cast on his left hand, but he clearly was not the
same steady playmaker. "I couldn't dribble with my left hand for
long, so I would fake with my left hand, one or two dribbles with the
left, then switch to the right," he said. "That limited what I could do.
There were a lot of right-handed fast breaks that year, when you
look at the tapes."

So this was now a vulnerable team, not necessarily a juggernaut,
and its weakness was apparent very early on in the tournament. Jordan, Perkins, and Matt Doherty were still a mighty core of stars, but
they were not going to coast to any title. Earlier in March, the Tar
Heels had barely survived a two-overtime victory over Duke to complete the regular ACC season undefeated, and that was before
Daugherty's injury. They lost to the same Duke team in the final of
the ACC tournament. And then in just the second round of the
NCAA Eastern regional, North Carolina struggled against Temple,
a physically smaller and less accomplished opponent.

The game was played at the Charlotte Coliseum, and Temple
coach John Chaney was amused when Dean Smith termed it "a
neutral court." The Tar Heels contracted for several lucrative
home games there and had already won seventeen straight in the
Charlotte arena. But with 10:57 left in the game, the Owls closed
the gap to 48–47 and an extraordinary fleet guard, Terence Stansbury, was giving North Carolina fits. Smith's game plan to attack
Temple's relentless zone defense called for Jordan to stealthily
sneak back door for lob passes, leading to alley-oop slams. And the
plan worked to perfection, except for one thing: the usually inde-
fatigable Jordan was getting worn down in this role and uncharac-
teristically asked to be taken out of the game at different intervals
to catch his breath. With six minutes left in the first half, Jordan
petitioned Smith for a brief respite. "Michael, are you sure you're
tired?" Smith asked.

Stansbury scored 18 points in the first half. Finally, Smith put Doherty, a six-foot-six forward, on Stansbury, with help from Jordan, Perkins, and Steve Hale. "A few times I got free on the baseline," Stansbury said, "and Sam was waiting for me." This seemed to tip the game to North Carolina, for a 77–66 victory. "We were careless and nervous," said Smith, who created a turnover himself when he referred to Stansbury after the game as "Salisbury." Chaney, known to grump on occasion, complained that the referees had given North Carolina too much leeway under the basket. "I don't want to taint a great victory for North Carolina, but I'm really upset," Chaney told reporters. "I just don't have a 7-footer."

Beating Temple in Charlotte was one thing. But in the regional semifinal, the Tar Heels next faced a more formidable opponent, Indiana (21–8), in a slightly more neutral arena, the Omni in Atlanta. Jordan hated the Omni for reasons he could never quite explain. He just didn't play well there. And Indiana owned another psychological advantage or two: Hoosier coach Bob Knight had beaten North Carolina, 63–50, in the 1981 NCAA final and already owned two national championships under his ever-expanding belt. Knight was a palpable factor in any game, a big man with a grand plan. He also had been named the United States Olympic coach for 1984, an honor bestowed on only the most senior and decorated American basketball coaches. Still, North Carolina remained a heavy favorite.

This was not Knight's most intimidating group of Hoosiers. They had a rough trail getting this far. They were unranked in the same Associated Press poll that regarded North Carolina with such esteem. Knight had graduated four of his five starters from his 1983 NCAA team, and Indiana was just 2–3 after its first five games. Another key player, Winston Morgan, was lost to a knee injury. But Knight was as resourceful as he was volatile, and this game would go a long way toward cementing his reputation as one of the top tacticians in the game.

On game days Knight would often chat by phone with a good friend and basketball guru, Pete Newell, who was a former U.S. Olympic coach and well-regarded hoop strategist. Together these two fine minds devised a scheme just hours before the game: Knight would not budge from his man-to-man defensive coverage, while putting little-known junior guard Dan Dakich on Jordan—instead of Todd Meier or Stew Robinson. Dakich had only started five games for Knight all season. He was quick, if nothing else. Being the contrarian that he was, Knight always insisted the move to Dakich was done for offensive purposes, but clearly this was a strategy to contain the Tar Heels' high scorer. Three hours before the game, Dakich was told of his impossible assignment. "I went back to my room and threw up," he said.

There was a method to the madness, though. Jordan was not yet the perfect scoring machine who would dominate the NBA, with unstoppable transition and halfcourt games. His outside shot was still suspect. When his jumper wasn't falling, it was important to take advantage of this flaw by backing off him on defense and eliminating his drives to the basket. That is what Dakich did, offering Jordan far more slack than usual. "I was staying away ten feet until he went up to shoot and then going up on him," Dakich said. This uncustomary strategy unnerved Jordan. To compound the problem, he fell into foul trouble and scored only 4 points in the first half. In the second half, he went scoreless for thirteen minutes, finishing with a small burst for 13 points on 6-of-14 shooting.

Indiana presented problems on the other end of the court, as well. Uwe Blab, a center from West Germany, was enough of an interior threat to keep the Tar Heels from properly monitoring the perimeter. Hoosier freshman guard Steve Alford was red hot from the outside, finishing with 27 points. Alford had become Knight's personal project and sometime whipping boy. The Indiana coach hounded Alford about his efforts in guarding the opposition. When he was asked during the season whether he'd picked up any hobbies since arriving in Bloomington, Alford said, "Yeah—defense." On this night, that end of the bargain was mostly kept by Dakich. Perkins, playing with uncommonly focused energy in his last college game, tried to compensate for Jordan's ineffectiveness, scoring 26 points. Still, the game was slipping away. Indiana led by 12 with four minutes to go. The Tar Heels made one last run, climbing within 2 points with 2:07 left. Then Knight ordered his team to spread the floor and draw some fouls. Alford calmly buried six straight free throws to seal the result. Indiana won 72–68 in one of the greatest upsets in the tournament's history.

The Tar Heels were stunned, most of them into silence. "Sam and Michael, this was their last chance," Kenny Smith said. "I had three more years, so I didn't understand the ramifications of the loss until I was in the locker room afterward, and saw them take it so hard. I felt like I let them down." Dean Smith didn't like to speak much in postgame locker rooms. He felt that emotions were too high then, that he might say something he would regret later. Instead, the coach always walked in, told his players, "Let's get it in," and then gathered them together for a brief prayer in thanks that nobody was hurt or that the athletes had been given this wonderful opportunity. He did the same that day, Kenny Smith remembered, even after the crushing defeat. Then he walked out to the requisite press conference. There, finally, the disappointment was evident. Coach Smith, usually the most cordial and expansive of interviews, ended his postgame press conference abruptly and walked off. He knew well that this team had represented one of his best shots at a national title, and now he would hear the murmurings again about his tournament record shortcomings.

Historians and journalists would forever wonder at the notion that three seasons of Jordan and Perkins at North Carolina failed to create more than a single NCAA championship. But in the deepest reaches of his appreciative basketball soul, Smith respected what Indiana had accomplished against his superior team. He was nothing like Knight, on any level. Smith was relatively even-tempered, a political liberal, a gentleman. Knight could be a flaming idiot, confrontational with the press, likely to do or say anything antagonistic at any moment. And yet the two men were alike in at least a couple of ways. They both adored the game of basketball, and neither of them cheated. It could be argued that Smith and Knight were not such saints, because their virtue was never truly tested. They coached at famous basketball universities with great resources at their disposal. Perhaps they never needed to bend the rules to remain competitive, like the coaches at Cleveland State or University of Nevada, Las Vegas. Nonetheless, there was a tacit understanding between Smith and Knight, that they were among the good guys when it came to this sort of thing. And since they generally recruited in different parts of the country, they would remain friendly, respectful rivals throughout their careers. The handshake they shared at the end of the game in Atlanta was genuine. The top dog had been toppled, in a valiant upset. And after Indiana had beaten North Carolina, Terry Holland was forced to reconsider his earlier proclamation about the Tar Heels' status as the greatest college squad in history. "I guess Indiana is four points better than the best team ever assembled," Holland said.

It was a terrible loss for the Tar Heels. "We should have, could have . . . ," Perkins said. "We had a lot of injuries, but during the NCAA we believed in ourselves. We were really disappointed. We thought we were better than Indiana. They had a lot of role players that played those roles really well. But we were really down. This was my last year." Peterson remembered it as "the toughest loss at North Carolina." He was already frustrated by his own limitations, at how he'd never fully recovered from the knee injury two years earlier. Peterson had started at point guard during a preseason tour-

nament in Greece, then lost the spot to Kenny Smith. "I wasn't anything as capable as Kenny was; he was a much better player," said
Peterson, who would eventually become head coach at Coastal Carolina. "But the thing that kept me going all year was that this team
was very, very good, and we were good enough to win a title." Now
there was no championship—only all this free time, and nobody
wanted to play pickup basketball anymore. "We got done so early.
What do we do now?" Peterson said. "That's when we got hooked
on golf."

Peterson was taking a psychology course with Davis Love III, a
Tar Heel and future pro star who lived by the golf course. "I told
Michael, 'I'm going with Davis to play golf,' and he came," Peterson
recalled. "We'd go with John Inman [who became the golf coach at
North Carolina], hit some range balls, then played nine holes, then
played eighteen on the Finley Course, grabbing hot dogs along the
way to eat. Michael couldn't get enough." Jordan wasn't particularly
successful at this sport. One day on the course, Davis ran inside for
a minute to get something from his room. "I'm bigger than that guy;
I should be able to hit it farther," Jordan told Peterson, referring to
Love. Jordan was obsessed with distance. He grabbed Davis's favorite driver and took a swing with it; the persimmon head cracked
right off. "The head is going forty yards to the right, the ball is fifteen yards in front," Peterson said. Jordan ran to collect the stray
piece, jamming the head back on the shaft. "Davis was not happy
that round," Peterson said.

Life went on for Perkins, for Jordan, for Dean Smith, and soon
some decisions had to be made. The biggest one of all involved Jordan, who needed to decide within the next few weeks whether or not
he would turn professional and give up his final year of eligibility at
North Carolina. He conferred with James Worthy, who advised him
to go for it. Still, Jordan hesitated. Riches awaited him on the other
side, but this was not such a simple decision. Jordan had wanted to

go out a champion, and now if he left that would not be the case. He also clung to familiar surroundings, to rituals. He told Coach Smith he was most concerned about missing his chance to give the traditional senior speech to Tar Heel teammates. That bothered him.

Jordan was still a twenty-one-year-old, a bit clumsy with life's transitions. On campus he enjoyed the dorms and loved to be the center of attention. He played pool nearly every day, enjoyed video games. He juggled girlfriends, never getting too serious with anyone. He maintained a B average in classes and even talked of becoming a college professor some day. Jordan didn't drink much. He was wary of losing restraint. He wished to be in total control of his body and mind at all times, the same way he directed his motions and thoughts on a basketball court. He went to movies or watched them on TV—preferably those that didn't scare him too much. Jordan hated snakes every bit as much as Indiana Jones hated them. He practiced his shot over and over at Carmichael Auditorium or Woollen Gym, home to North Carolina basketball until 1965.

Jordan sought out games of every variety. Competition remained his only great vice. He had treated basketball practices as if they were NCAA tournament games, writing on the blackboard after drills and scrimmages exactly how many times he'd dunked on each of his teammates. "On a basketball court, he'd impose his will on everyone," Kenny Smith said. His tongue would start wagging, and he would argue over rules, fouls, whatever. Jordan really only came alive when he was competing against someone. Then he would rev up the playful trash talk, focusing all his energy on the task at hand. Those teammates closest to him over the years—Jimmy Black, Kenny Smith, his roommate, Buzz Peterson—all saw this side of him, which was endearing until it became tiresome. Nobody had the patience to play these games forever, it seemed, except Jordan.

His latest passion was golf, which seemed to drive him to new heights of insanity. Love would confide to Dean Smith that Jordan could never be very good at this sport, if only because he was too tall. "Too many things can go wrong with a swing from that height," Love said. But that did not stop Jordan. And he often used the golf outings to contemplate his impending decision about turning pro. Jordan would not—could not—admit to friends or teammates or even to his roommate, Peterson, that he was likely to head for the NBA. In Jordan's mind, such an action bordered on betrayal.

To understand Jordan's conflicted feelings about turning professional, you have to understand the depth of his loyalties to family. Michael was the third son of five children born to the Jordans from Wilmington, North Carolina, who had lavished great amounts of attention on all of their children. The kids were each talented in his or her own way, but soon enough it became apparent that Michael would be the chosen one, if only because of his oddly athletic build. Nobody else in the family was over six feet tall, and it actually took some time for Michael to sprout. His athletic career survived an unfortunate accident when he was five; he nearly cut off his big toe with an axe while chopping wood at home. He wasn't wearing shoes at the time. A neighbor poured kerosene on the wound, and it miraculously healed. A legendary career was rescued. He suddenly grew four inches between his sophomore and junior years at Laney High School, where he ran so fast that his nickname was "The Rabbit." His older brother Larry, a teammate at Laney High, was nearly a foot shorter than Michael. Their mom, Deloris, told the boys to sprinkle salt in their shoes if they wanted to grow. It worked with Michael, not with Larry, who never really cracked five-foot-seven. Michael honored his brother by selecting jersey number 23, which was as close to half of Larry's number 45 as Michael could get.

Michael's parents didn't just attend a few Tar Heel games along the way. They attended every game. They would travel as far as Hawaii, if that was required, to see their son firsthand, to revel in his wondrous play. Even after North Carolina was eliminated from the

NCAA tournament by Indiana, the parents went across country to Seattle to see their son receive a couple of Player of the Year awards. And Michael enjoyed their support, and proximity, greatly. If he gave up North Carolina, if he moved to some far-off, strange NBA city, his parents would not be able to come to all his games. That would surely become a geographic impossibility. Jordan also felt considerable loyalty to Dean Smith, who had kept all his vows. Perhaps most important, Jordan had promised his mom he would earn his bachelor's degree in geography, even if he really didn't see any practical reason for such an academic accomplishment. So he put off the decision and told everyone at school he intended to stay—for now. That's what they wanted to hear, and Jordan was accommodating.

Most of his time was spent playing basketball, anyway. While classes were still going on in Chapel Hill, he was summoned to auditions in Bloomington, Indiana, where Knight was holding tryouts for the Olympic team scheduled to compete that summer in Los Angeles. It was a foregone conclusion that Jordan would make the squad, but after surviving two cuts he returned to the campus and held a press conference in Carmichael Auditorium on April 26 to update the local media about his experiences. Classes were just ending on campus. And of course, the only thing that reporters wanted to know was whether he intended to remain at North Carolina for his senior year. The deadline for such an announcement was less than two weeks away—a letter needed to be postmarked by May 5— and still there was no definitive word. This was clearly a very big deal around Chapel Hill. The team's future hinged on his decision.

It was an awkward press conference at Carmichael. Dean Smith started out the proceeding by declaring straight out that nothing important was going to be announced. "He's already said he's staying," Smith said. "I'm still looking into that situation. It's his decision to make, and his parents'. It's still too early. I'm sure you'll know something by May 6th [the morning after the midnight deadline], and that's not too far off." Jordan sat at a table before four microphones, in an open polo shirt, and echoed Smith's words.

I'm planning on staying here and I'm looking forward to my next year here. Coach has always looked out for his players and wants what's best for them. He's looking into all the situations to see if there's any way my life could be better for me. . . . My folks know a lot more than I do. And I'll take their advice into consideration, too. My mother, she's a teacher, and I think I already have an idea what she thinks. But my father's a clown. I really don't know what he's thinking about. I don't know. I don't want to put any pressure on them. I just want to talk to them this weekend and have a family conversation.

Nothing was particularly clear from this press conference except that these reporters knew much less about the upcoming draft than the coach. By this juncture, pending the result of the Houston-Portland coin flip nearly a month away, Smith could pretty much list the top five or six picks. The questions at this no-news conference demonstrated that the media were not nearly as well connected. For some reason, a couple of reporters had Jordan slotted for the 76ers' number-5 pick and asked Jordan about Philadelphia. It was probably a romantic notion, since ex-Tar Heel Billy Cunningham was coaching there. "I don't like the Sixers," Jordan declared. "I like the Lakers." Another reporter asked whether his choice was dependent on Hakeem Olajuwon's decision about entering the NBA draft, which was a fait accompli to those in the know. Olajuwon, a junior, would surely be in the mix. Patrick Ewing, another junior, would eventually elect to stay at Georgetown. "Akeem will do what's best for him," Jordan said. "I don't think in my mind that my decision will rely on anybody else's decision. If [Ewing is] going to go or anything like that. I'm not worried about that. I'm just thinking about myself and coming back." Jordan had no reason to ponder these permutations. Smith already had explained to him he would go no lower than number 3 in the draft, even with Olajuwon joining the pros.

The local papers played these developments cautiously. "Jordan Still Not Sure If He'll Stay at UNC," proclaimed the headline in the *Winston-Salem Journal.* The more perceptive reporters, like Lenox Rawlings of *The Journal*, made note of what happened after this press conference. Jordan went off to play golf, while Coach Smith drove away with Donald Dell, the renowned player agent. This was a clear signal. Smith was already making plans, feeling out the forever-changing landscape in business representation. There was a split going on among the top player agents. Dell, Ray Benton, and David Falk were heading in one direction, while Lee Fentress and Frank Craighill were branching out in another. The way it turned out, Jordan would sign with Dell and Falk, while Perkins would go with Fentress and Craighill. "I liked it ideally that way," Smith said. "I was thinking, 'Let 'em compete, and see who does the best job.'"

Dick Motta and Bobby Weiss from the Dallas Mavericks would soon come to campus to interview Perkins. "They sat down with me just to say hello, and let me know it was between me and Mel Turpin," Perkins recalled. Sam was a senior. Everyone knew he was gone. The locals still held out hope for Jordan, thinking his mom would hold final sway on the matter. But by Saturday, May 5, when the final press conference was set for 11 AM at Fetzer Gymnasium, hope had largely evaporated. On the morning of the event, the *Raleigh News and Observer* accurately warned, "Jordan Likely to Opt for NBA." Still, there was no absolute proof of this decision, mostly just circumstantial evidence. On Friday afternoon, Jordan huddled with Coach Smith again. He played some golf to clear his head. That evening, while Smith was telling people that Jordan had yet to make up his mind, Michael met with his parents and brother Larry. Then he went out that night, later than usual, with Peterson and a couple other friends. Jordan found it hard to admit to such a definitive, life-changing choice. "We went out to a Red Lobster the night before," Buzz Peterson said. "We drove back, still talking about it a little bit. He wanted to talk about it. I asked him, 'What did your mom and dad say?' We got back to our dorm; it was a quiet night. We went to bed pretty quickly. He gets up the next morning for the press conference, he's getting dressed, and he says to me, 'Hey, I still don't know what I'm doing.'"

"You better make up your mind, there are people waiting out there," Peterson told Jordan. "You want to play in the NBA, don't you?"

"I don't know," Jordan responded. "You want to play a lot next year, don't you, Buzz?"

"I want to play, but I'd like to play with you," said Peterson, who had a year of eligibility left.

Peterson was lying on the bed as Jordan walked out the door, still proclaiming his confusion. "My gut feeling was, he was gone," Peterson said. "But it wasn't easy for him. We had a comfort level there. It's like I tell my players at Coastal Carolina, 'You'll miss being part of a family.' Michael would miss it, too. He would miss Kenny Smith coming down to visit, talking late into the night. . . . He'd miss Hardy's cinnamon raison biscuits. . . . He'd miss my tales about the mountains in North Carolina."

Many of his teammates believed Jordan would stay at North Carolina, that he couldn't leave, right to the end.

"I didn't think he was going," Kenny Smith said. "He loved the university, loved being a college student so much, loved everything about it. I didn't even go to the press conference. Why should I go? I figured he was not going to say anything. He was still going to class, worried about finals, not missing anything in class. If I was thinking about the NBA, I wasn't going to be living in a dorm worried about some tests."

By May 5, several things had become clearer. Everybody now knew that Olajuwon and Barkley were turning pro, that Ewing wasn't. The other early college departures were far less impressive: Cory Blackwell of Wisconsin, Yommy Sangodeyi of Sam Houston State, Stuart Gray of UCLA, and Sam Norton of University of Texas at Arlington. Only Wayman Tisdale had stalled on this decision as long as Jordan, and he eventually would decide to return for another season of college basketball. Jordan was also one of twenty players left on the U.S. Olympic roster, which would be cut to twelve soon enough, when Charles Barkley and John Stockton were among those dropped by Knight. The projected order of the draft was now more apparent to those reporters who bothered to make a few phone calls, largely because Stu Inman of Portland was so forthcoming about his need for a big man—either Olajuwon at number 1 or Bowie at number 2. It wasn't just Smith who understood the variables. Jordan would likely go to either Houston or Chicago, depending on the coin flip, and this was becoming public knowledge.

Jordan's decision had to be in the mail by midnight Saturday. That was the rule. He met with Coach Smith yet again, but hope was ebbing in Chapel Hill when Jordan finally appeared at Fetzer Gym. And still the student body, forever optimistic, showed up in droves, wandering the halls outside the room, waiting for news. At last, Smith declared the inevitable, in the oddest of terms: "At this time we are announcing that Michael will denounce his college eligibility." Jordan insisted that this decision was spur of the moment, even though it had required consultation with everyone—from Smith to Worthy to his parents. "To tell you the truth, I really just decided about an hour and a half ago," Jordan said. "I didn't know. It was 50–50. One 50 percent was the enjoyment of school. The other 50 percent was for a better future and a healthy future. I talked with coach this morning. He helped me, and my parents helped me. It was right down to the last minute. I really didn't know. I had to think about it in so many ways."

"Money played a big part," Jordan conceded. "Money's a big part in each one of our lives. Who knows? I may not be around next year, and I've got the opportunity at hand right now. Everything looks bright for me, and I think the future holds the best for me. I felt it would be better for me to start now while I'm young."

Jordan's parents were there, at his side as usual. They had not changed their opinions on the matter. James Jordan was quite pleased at this development. Deloris was disappointed. She wanted her son to earn his degree. That had been the plan all along. In the eleventh hour, Dean Smith had offered an interesting alternative, a compromise plan. He suggested Jordan come out as a junior eligible, get drafted, sign a contract, then sit out the 1984–85 season while attending classes at UNC. That didn't fly. Smith knew it wouldn't. Instead, for Deloris's sake, the coach exacted a promise from Michael about completing his degree—a vow that Jordan would keep.

When James Jordan spoke at the press conference, he kept it light—the way he always did.

> I can be very comfortable with it for several reasons. First of all, I don't have to play. Second, I might add that I've got a pretty good job and I've had the job the whole while he's been in college. Michael knew he didn't have to make the decision predicated on the status of my family. We're doing pretty good. Once he leaves and goes out on his own I'm automatically going to get a raise. I don't have to give him two and three dollars and stuff like that. Michael has turned 21. Once a guy turns 21, he feels like he can make his own decisions.

Deloris appeared more somber. As a young woman, she had given up her own plans for an education by returning home from the Tuskegee Institute in Alabama, homesick for Wilmington and for her boyfriend, James. She always thought that her incomplete education was a terrible error and wished that her own mother had kicked her out, sent her back to Tuskegee on the next train. She had always viewed basketball differently from the way her husband and her son saw the sport. It was a means to an end. And that end, very simply, was a college education, with everything that went with it. Michael was supposed to spend four years on a campus, breathing the academic atmosphere of a fine university. He would graduate with his class, and Deloris would be there to snap the photo as he accepted his diploma.

"When he and Roslyn came to Carolina, that was one of my dreams," Deloris explained. "I said, 'I want both of you to get your degree. I just want to sit there and watch both of you walk down the aisle.' So that was my idea. But then again, that was *my* dream."

It was a mother's fantasy, and it probably wasn't realistic. Phil Ford had decided to stay in school the extra year, but he had been the exception.

"If every Carolina student had the opportunity to make a half million dollars a year and to come back in eight months to get their degree, there might be several . . . there could be . . . that would say, 'No, I'd rather seek knowledge,'" Coach Smith said. "But I think most Carolina students would go."

Jordan went. Perkins was gone, too. Dean Smith had turned his own pockets inside out, dropping his valuables voluntarily into the hands of those robber barons of the NBA.

3

The Achilles Shin

Standing outside his daughter's schoolhouse in Lexington recently and juggling cell phone calls, Sam Bowie was thinking how parents could be wrong sometimes, even when they were right. As a father himself he knew that it was an important lesson. Bowie owned some standardbreds and was plowing headlong into harness racing, sometimes exercising the horses himself in an oversized cart. His primary passion, though, was being the full-time dad of three children. He had constant bits of advice for his oldest daughter, Samantha, who was a six-foot-two center on the Sayre High School basketball team in Lexington. Bowie would drag her to University of Kentucky games just to make fine points about the game as they sat next to each other in the stands. Tubby Smith, the Wildcats' coach, was the godfather of Bowie's son, Marcus, another reason to attend the games. Bowie never enjoyed playing the sport as much as he did watching it now, when his own daughter was out there on defense, standing erect, boxing out, holding hands straight up in the air. He had a constant stream of advice for her, some of it in a loud, shrill voice heard above the high school crowd. But Bowie tried to remember how sometimes the best-intended counsel from parents can go awry.

Back in the spring of 1981, he'd just completed a wonderful sophomore season at the University of Kentucky, averaging 17.4 points and 9.1 assists. Bowie was a coveted seven-foot-one center with the world at his sneakers. Officially, background chatter had to be guarded because of NBA rules on tampering. But Bowie heard some unofficial, second-hand talk that the mighty 52-win Philadelphia 76ers were going to make a deal to move up among the top six picks in the draft and then select him—if only he'd come out of college early. The Sixers had come to the conclusion that they would not win championships with Darryl Dawkins at center. The time was surely perfect, Bowie felt, and so he dialed his mother, Cathy, back in the steel mill town of Lebanon, Pennsylvania, and told her he was thinking of turning pro. "She hung the phone up, she was so disappointed," Bowie said. He couldn't do it; he wouldn't break her heart again.

Less than a year earlier, as his sophomore year at Kentucky was about to start, he had shared another phone conversation with his mother that was more difficult to handle. Cathy Bowie was crying then, dropping the phone, telling him that his father, Ben, had died at the absurdly premature age of forty-five from a burst cyst on his lung. Ben, six-foot-ten, had been quite a player himself not so long ago, performing for six years with the Harlem Magicians. He and Cathy had been divorced for seven years, but they remained in the same town with their two children. Sam had stayed with his mother, then his father, then the other, then with Cathy's mother so as not to drive a wedge between his parents. Sam Bowie always tried to do the right thing. Heading back to Lebanon after he'd heard this bad news about his father, he signed autographs at airports along the way, always being the responsible oldest child, the good role model. Sam made all the funeral arrangements and watched his mother endure the tragedy. So in 1981, after his mother had hung up the phone with disappointment, Bowie knew he would stay at Kentucky, remain in classes, and stick with the Wildcats for his junior year.

Then a few months later in September, it felt like the dumbest, most costly decision of his life. Bowie discovered that he had been walking around on a fractured shin bone in his left leg. He had landed on it the wrong way the previous season, in a game against Vanderbilt, and the problem was misdiagnosed as shin splints. The break was virtually microscopic and hadn't been detected by earlier X-rays. But now, there was no denying something was very wrong. His coach, Joe B. Hall, called it "a small, incomplete fracture." Bowie knew otherwise; he was in considerable chronic pain. He also understood the monetary ramifications: suddenly, he was not such a sure thing, and those millions of NBA dollars were flying out the radiologist's office. What had he been thinking? Why hadn't he ignored his mother and enlisted in the draft when he still had a clean bill of health?

His leg was placed in a cast. From then on, it would all be a struggle for Bowie, a difficult game of catch-up, with moments of true despair. Bowie was cursed, in a way, with the brightness and insight to fully comprehend his dilemma. For forty-four weeks in that cast, he had time to second-guess his decision not to turn pro and to wonder whether he would ever be able to regain his vocational momentum. Everybody liked Bowie, admiring his clear-headed approach to both life and basketball. He lacked the killer instinct, maybe, but he had timing and grace. Top coaches thought enough about Bowie to name him to the U.S. Olympic team after his freshman year, though he never got to Moscow because of the 1980 boycott. Now he had himself a real battle, and the medical world was still divided on the treatment of such athletic injuries.

Doctors gave him options, and he chose the wrong one. Bowie decided to let his leg heal slowly, without surgery, and the strategy appeared to work for a while. The pain lessened, and he renewed workouts in the summer of 1982. The leg swelled almost immediately, though. He was burdened with a new plastic cast in August, and then finally on October 20 he went in for an operation to graft a piece of his own pelvic bone to the left shin. The surgeon, Dr. R. A. Calandruccio, performed the operation at Baptist Memorial Hospital in Memphis, roughening the area to stimulate blood flow and growth, then transplanting the bone from just below the waist. Bowie was now in another recovery phase, another rehab, and he could not help feeling frustrated that he had lost more than a year of his precious basketball life without substantial progress. "I'd be lying to you if I'd say I was always an optimist," Bowie recalled. "Numerous days, you work out, you don't see results, you start questioning yourself." Russell Rice, who was sports information director then at Kentucky, remembered how Bowie would show up for the games, sitting around in street clothes, just "looking lonely."

He kept himself busy and immersed in schoolwork, completing his undergraduate degree in communications in the spring of 1983. He enjoyed the luxury of such an academic focus. When Bowie was playing varsity ball, he would return from a game in Mississippi at three or four o'clock in the morning and then wake up for an eight o'clock class. Coach Joe B. Hall made every class mandatory, and it was difficult. There were other distractions, too. In 1985, Bowie became peripherally involved in a scandal reported in the Lexington *Herald-Leader* involving players from earlier Kentucky teams who accepted illegal payments from boosters while in school. There were twenty-six players involved in the various schemes, and former guard Jay Shidler claimed he made $8,400 selling tickets to an attorney for Hall. Bowie only said that Wildcat players sometimes earned $250 to $500 for speaking engagements, what he termed "easy money."

As the 1983–84 season began, Bowie was that true oddity, enrolled as a graduate student at Kentucky in his third year of NCAA eligibility.

His center of attention shifted back to basketball. There was more time now to concentrate on the sport. He was determined to prove his durability to NBA teams and to Hall.

"We would have been a lot better those two years with Sam," Hall said. "We missed him in so many different ways. He was a press breaker, a good passer, a high post presence. You could lob the ball to him. He could run the floor. You could do a lot of things with Sam you couldn't do with other guys. He wasn't a great shooter, but he had great hands, was an excellent passer, a good free throw shooter."

During Bowie's two-year absence, Hall had moved his other giant, Mel Turpin, into the center position. Now with Bowie back, Turpin would switch to power forward to make room. Turpin was a wider, shorter, slower player who was considered less learned than Bowie in the intricacies of the game. But Turpin could bang, and he was a constant, intimidating force under the basket. "Sam had sat out my freshman year," said Kenny Walker, a sophomore teammate in 1983–1984.

He'd been through such adversity, and then there were some frustrations early, because physically he couldn't do the things he once could. He was a work in progress. Sam was on the national scene before UK, he had early success in high school. Melvin was the local product, a late bloomer. He was a project player, but then he got so good, so fast, he surprised everybody. Melvin was a low-post presence the whole time. Sam had played before with Melvin, but it took adjusting to playing with Sam coming back. Once they got it going, I didn't have to worry about rebounding or blocking shots. I'd flash in the lane, get out on breaks, get a lot of dunks. It was definitely because of the Twin Towers. I have a lot of those games on tape from '84, and I'll pop them in the VCR from time to time. You could see as the year went along, Sam was getting better and better. Early in the season, you could tell in his mind he wanted to do some things, but his body wouldn't allow it. Then he started shooting better from the outside, blocking shots, running, dunking, all those things were coming back. By the middle of his senior year, he hit his stride. Melvin wasn't half the defensive player Sam was.

Turpin had his own NBA aspirations, and Bowie was very conscious that his return had created an awkward coupling of two natural centers, with two divergent personalities. According to one team member, there was some natural tension: "They were completely different, and they tolerated each other." Bowie looked back more nostalgically:

> We were extremely close, no animosity, no jealousy. I always tried to thank Melvin for being my partner. He made my game that much easier, our success that much easier. There was never any favoritism that I could tell. One thing about that team, we did a lot of things together. It was almost corny, looking back, we were such a close team. We were senior oriented, guys like Jim Master, Dicky Beal, we all hung out. When we hit the public eye in Lexington, we were rock stars. You go to the movies, go out to eat, there are autograph seekers everywhere. You try to do normal, average college stuff, but that was part of the fame.

When Bowie and Turpin were both on the court at the same time, they could switch off on men, confuse opponents. Hall had envisioned it this way all along, his two big guys killing opponents under the glass. He loved the double post, with interchangeable big men. He had used this scheme when he was at Regis College in Denver and then at Central Missouri. "I'd have players who fit the competition," Hall said. "They weren't 7–1 and 6–11 like Sam and Melvin. Back then, they were 6–6 and 6–5." Hall always worked with what he had, though that did not necessarily make him flexible.

Joe Beasman Hall was born twenty minutes outside Lexington in Cynthiana, Kentucky. "A shrewd ol' country boy, with a subtle sense of humor," said Russell Rice, who was a former sports editor at the *Lexington Leader*. An explosive scorer in high school and college, Hall had toured a bit with the Harlem Globetrotters in 1951 before returning to finish his education at Kentucky. And there, eventually, Hall was an assistant to the fabled Adolph Rupp. These were the toughest of all shoes to fill back in 1973 when the transition took place, but Hall coached three Kentucky teams to the Final Four and won a national championship in 1978. "It's tough to follow a legend," Rice said. "We had a football coach [Blanton Collier] who tried to be Bear Bryant, and it doesn't work." Like Rupp, Hall always believed that it was not the duty of a head coach to change his coaching philosophy based on the talent or temperament of his players. There was one right way to play this game. Hall would sit on the bench, program rolled in his hand, riding his guys to make certain they were playing that right way. Asked if he ever felt the need to treat Bowie and Turpin at all differently, Hall responded, "I don't even know how to answer that question."

"Coach Hall was a disciplinarian," Bowie said. "He wanted lights out at ten o'clock, all TVs off. He was from the old-school era. He believed if you pounded a kid, that was the way to motivate him. I always got along with him. Some guys can respond to it, but others fold up like a newspaper and quit. First and foremost, I want to be complimentary to Coach Hall. But players are all individuals and sometimes you have to treat them as individuals. You can't treat everyone the same." Hall felt differently; he believed that eventually all his players would come around to his way of thinking. Maybe they resented him now, he figured, but years later they would understand the scoldings were necessary. It was for their own, basketball good. "For order and a society to exist—and a basketball team is a society within itself—it needs discipline," Hall once remarked.

Hall may have handled all his players the same way once they got to the school, but he was smart enough to know that each recruiting chase was a very different hunt. He was arguably the nation's best college recruiter—so good, people often questioned whether his coaching was getting the most of all that talent. "I'm a bad coach because I go out and recruit well," he shot back at reporters during the 1983–84 season. "I could go out and get a bunch of 5-foot–8 kids and go for Coach of the Year award, but I like to win."

So he recruited hard, and smart, and country. Hall would take some kids to his farm, where they'd help him hang up or "house" tobacco leaves to dry. Hall had done this when he played for Rupp. Hall then did it while recruiting players like Kyle Macy and Rick Robey in the late '70s. A few years earlier, he took Kevin Grevey frog-gigging on Stoner Creek and Licking River, teaching his recruit the fine art of spearing these little creatures with three-prong-ended broom handles. Hall immediately declared that he had never met a better left-handed gigger than Grevey, and soon after the kid signed his letter of intent with Kentucky. "There's water all around here, good fishin,' good giggin','" said Hall, taking a break from his sports radio talk show with former Louisville coach Denny Crum. Hall never went gigging with Bowie, though, who was too sophisticated. And he certainly didn't do it with Turpin, whose company Hall did not necessarily enjoy over a long haul. "I don't think he'd take Mel," Rice said, laughing. "He'd have to feed him too much. Joe B. had problems with Mel, with his weight and with his girlfriends."

Turpin was from Lexington, and it was only right and natural for the native son to play at Kentucky. "We'd watched him grow up," Hall said. Bowie was different. He was national player of the year when he was a senior at Lebanon High School, beating out another lanky center, Ralph Sampson. Bowie had a large choice of colleges and didn't need to play for Hall if he desired to go elsewhere. He was good enough and tall enough to become a professional basketball player someday, and so he was looking for a place that would give him national exposure on a regular basis. Kentucky was on television as much as any school, and then on his campus visit to Lexington he was overwhelmed by the sheer fanaticism of the team's following. "All the way from grandparents to young kids, they all knew about Kentucky basketball," Bowie said. "You hear the slogan, 'It's a way of life.' It truly is that way everywhere in the commonwealth." A home visit by the hard-selling Hall sealed the deal.

So Bowie had come to Kentucky, then had lost two years to his leg injury, and now finally was ready to take on the world again. The Wildcats got off to a wonderful start, thumping their first ten opponents. They were gaining national recognition and corresponding expectations. "A lot of people knew about Sam and Melvin, and knew about my potential," Kenny Walker said. "You throw in Jim Master and Dicky Beal, James Blackmon and Winston Bennett, we had a team that was loaded."

On January 22, 1984, Bowie, Turpin, and third-ranked Kentucky faced their first true challenge: the University of Houston and Olajuwon, ranked number 4 in the nation, were at Rupp Arena. The game drew 23,992 fans, plus a large contingent of professional scouts who were salivating at the opportunity to compare three first-round caliber big men in the same game. Unfortunately, the referees intruded on the scene. With Bowie and Turpin both battling him under the boards, Olajuwon fell into characteristic foul trouble and was disqualified after twenty-nine minutes, with 14 points and 12 rebounds. Bowie managed to play thirty-six minutes before fouling out with 8 points and 18 rebounds. Turpin had 19 points, 11 boards. Houston jumped off to an 11–1 lead and then fell behind in a hurry when Olajuwon was neutralized by fouls. Olajuwon complained bitterly after the 74–67 defeat, saying he looked forward to playing Kentucky again on a neutral floor. "Everything I do, [the refs] call me for everything," Olajuwon grumped. "I should be used to it by now, but the Kentucky players, they just jumped into me and the refs called me for the fouls."

"It wasn't really fair," Bowie said graciously. "It was three against one: Mel, Kenny, and myself against Akeem."

Despite his protestations, scouts and reporters left Rupp Arena declaring this had been an impressive, fluid effort by Bowie, his most notable performance since returning from the leg surgery. Then in the Southeast Conference tournament, after beating Georgia and Alabama in the early rounds, Kentucky faced the upstart Charles Barkley from unranked Auburn for the title. It wasn't a pretty victory, 51–49, and Bowie was limited to twenty-six minutes because of foul trouble. But the Wildcats were still ranked number 3 in the country, with a number 1 seed in the Mideast Region of the NCAA tournament. Kentucky had underachieved badly in the postseason during the early '80s, winning only two NCAA games in the last three years. Hall was now shifting into control-freak mode. He assigned his seven student managers eighteen hours of chaperone duty, all waking time, with the 257-pound Turpin. "Dinner Bell" Mel was not to gain another pound or lose his appetite for basketball. The Wildcats had a huge advantage this time: the regional semifinal and final would be played in Rupp Arena, where Kentucky was 106–11 going into the tournament, and where 23,500 fans had a way of intimidating referees.

The Wildcats would require every edge imaginable in a 72–67 win against neighboring Louisville (coached by Hall's future talk-show partner, Crum). "If we were playing anywhere else, we probably would have lost," Walker said. Then things got even dicier against Illinois in a 54–51 thriller for a Final Four spot. Hall had managed to insult the Big 10 team by referring to the school often as "Illi-noise," an apparently innocent twist of the tongue. And then, with just sixteen seconds left, with the score 52–50 for Kentucky, point guard Dicky Beal might have been called for a walk. He was not. "How can we come to Kentucky and have the fouls be 10–2 [in the second half]?" Illinois coach Lou Henson asked afterward. "You can't win under those conditions." Hall's watchdog tactics with Turpin seemed to pay off. The big guy scored the first 8 points for Kentucky, demonstrating that an empty stomach meant a hungry Wildcat. Scouts probably should have noticed that Bowie was not exactly dominating these games—he was just fitting in. Beal was the one making most of the big plays. Like Bowie, Beal had overcome his own medical setbacks, recovering from three arthroscopic surgeries on his right knee. Beal scored 15 points against Louisville, with 9 assists and 6 steals. Bowie had just 11 points, though all in the second half. The worst was yet to come, however, in an NCAA semifinal in Seattle against mighty Georgetown.

Four imposing big men converged at the Final Four. Kentucky owned two of them—Bowie and Turpin, to match up with Ewing of Georgetown and Olajuwon of Houston. In order to win the title, the Wildcats figured they would have to go through both. And for much of the first half of their game against Georgetown, it appeared the Hoyas didn't pose much of a challenge to Kentucky. The Wildcats were up by 12 points, 27–15, with four minutes left until intermission, and Ewing was on the bench with some early foul trouble. That lead dwindled to 7 by the half, but still Kentucky was in control of the tempo and the scoreboard. "Billy Packer was on TV saying Joe B. was playing this just right," Rice recalled. To this day, none of the Kentucky players or coaches can explain what happened next, in that second half. Those twenty minutes will go down as the most statistically bizarre and shattering halves in the history of the school's fabled basketball program. The 'Cats converted only 1 of their first 23 shots, 3 for 33 altogether in the half for a shooting percentage of 9 percent. The five Kentucky starters, including Bowie and Turpin, combined for zero field goals in the second half. Georgetown went on a 30–4 spree that led to a 53–40 humiliation.

"I doubt if any team ever has lost a Final Four game like that," Turpin said. "Everywhere you went there was a hand in your face. We couldn't do anything. It was awful." The Hoyas were quick, they were everywhere with their harassing defense. But still, there was no explanation for this kind of meltdown. "We did everything but seal the deal," Walker said.

> We felt confident. Houston had a very good team, we had beaten one of the best teams in the country. Their style was different from Georgetown, who were the bad boys of the college ranks before the Bad Boys [the Detroit Pistons] came along. They played that style against everybody. Physically, they were more meant for that type of game. But you don't shake off a loss like that. We felt we had the best team. We'd lived up to our preseason billing. Then we go to Seattle, have such a great first half, feel good about ourselves, then go out and shoot 3-for–33. We didn't put our best foot forward.

Hall sat on the bench, watching this inexplicable collapse, throwing his rolled-up program to the floor. Everybody was missing from the field. Bowie clunked his share of shots, missed 6 of them in that second half. When it was over, in a locker room that was leaking water onto the Wildcats from the ceiling, Hall gathered himself together and held his temper. "One of those things," he said. Hall remained mystified for decades, still not believing it happened:

> Nine percent from the field . . . It must have been some strange perspective on that side of the court that second half. I was sitting there thinking we'd start hitting those shots anytime now, that it would have to happen. A lot of it was Georgetown's defense. They were intense, very strong, very athletic. Ewing inside was a big factor. But in the end, it was an absolute mystery to me, something a coach has nightmares about. The shots were not that bad. I can't think it was

all their defense, because Villanova came back and shot like 80 percent against them the next year. I try to ignore that tape of our game, try not to watch it. When I did once, I was really confused.

And that was it at Kentucky for Bowie. His feel for the game was improving, but his stats really didn't blow anybody away. He finished the season with an average of just 10.5 points, down nearly 5 points from his sophomore year, though he pulled down an impressive 9.2 rebounds per game. Turpin averaged 5 points more per game that season, owned the better shooting touch, and demonstrated four years of durability. But Bowie had the reputation of a player who would make teammates better. Looking back, Walker still thought Bowie had the potential to be an early version of Tim Duncan, another soft-spoken, unselfish, mobile, fundamentally sound center who would anchor championship teams later on at San Antonio.

Bowie was ready to be Duncan, before Duncan. It was just that his legs weren't quite as committed.

4

Out of Africa, Into Texas

Guy V. Lewis suffered a stroke on February 26, 2002, and these days his wife, Dena, helps him find the words occasionally when his mind and his tongue are not quite in sync because of the aphasia. They were once teenage sweethearts, though they went to rival high schools in Texas. Guy was from Arp, population 950. Dena was from Troup, nearly twice as large. Dena played snare drum in her school band, and when Troup's football team traveled to Arp she stood behind the goalposts watching the star quarterback for Arp, this cocky boy, Guy Lewis, dominate the game against her own side. On one play, the quarterback scrambled fifty-five yards for a touchdown and laid the ball right at her feet. "Made me so damned mad," Dena Lewis said, "I wouldn't speak to him for two weeks." But it was already a done deal. The two had met at a dance; he'd stepped all over her feet so often that Dena thought his name was, "I'm sorry." Guy told friends, "That's the girl I'm going to marry," and then he did.

And now it was sixty-four years after their wedding, they were both in their mid-eighties, and she was helping him a bit with his speech as he talked basketball history.

Lewis was a living, breathing example of how difficult it was for a college coach to earn the highest respect of his peers if he never collected that one stamp of validation, an NCAA title. He had all the credentials to be a Hall of Famer, surely, yet he was regularly snubbed by the nebulous committees of players, coaches, and media members who voted on this matter. Lewis was once a six-foot-three center for the University of Houston following World War II. He stuck with coaching at the same college for thirty years, leaving with 592 victories and a truly remarkable five appearances in the Final Four. He became a mainstay on the Cougar bench, clutching his red-and-white polka dot towels as if they were a basketball with the clock running down on a one-point game. He had won "The Game of the Century" back in the Astrodome on January 20, 1968, beating Lew Alcindor and John Wooden to end UCLA's forty-seven-game winning streak in front of 52,693 fans and a national TV audience. But that was a regular-season game. If only he had won that championship with Elvin Hayes, or with Hakeem Olajuwon, his path to glory would have been cleared. Instead, Lewis was something of a martyr in Houston, a loyal and worthy coach whose accomplishments had largely been ignored by the basketball aristocracy that anointed coaches as geniuses. Whenever he appeared in public down around his home, he would be serenaded with chants of, "Hall of Fame . . . Hall of Fame . . ." The snub bothered him. It bothered Dena, too. Lewis had been a finalist for Hall election in 2003, before his bid somehow lost momentum. He had heard nothing about it since.

Lewis's memory was as sharp as ever, and he got a kick out of recounting the details of one of the oddest recruiting stories in college basketball: how he happened to find upon his doorstep in Houston, Texas, a superstar center from Nigeria.

"Oh, that story again?" Lewis said, laughing.

The tale really went back to late September 1980, and arguably before that. Hakeem Olajuwon was playing basketball for the Nigerian national team, and one day the team was competing on an outdoor playground against the Central African Republic in a little town about forty miles from Lagos. It was the third time that summer the two nations had played against each other in exhibitions, and it was under the most difficult of circumstances. The court wasn't quite ready. The rims were being painted orange even as the game began. The coach of the Central African Republic, Christopher Pond, found it necessary to scream at a worker to remove the ladder from the court.

Pond, originally from New Jersey, was a contract employee with the U.S. State Department, getting paid to conduct clinics and to coach kids throughout Africa. He had gone there four years earlier as a Peace Corps volunteer, left that service in 1979, and finagled a government stipend plus room and board from his host countries. Pond loved basketball. His brother, Nick, played with North Carolina State. Chris coached at the YMCA level back in the States. He had a mission now to bring basketball to the Third World.

The game against Nigeria on this rickety court began on a Saturday, but it started to rain and was postponed until the next day. Pond was duly impressed with Olajuwon, who owned enormous athletic skills and a good head for a sport that was not indigenous to Nigeria. Hakeem had been a standout at team handball and soccer before he converted to basketball. He was not quite polished at this new game, but his talent was quite evident. "He just came alive," Pond would tell the *Houston Chronicle* years later. On Monday, while the Central Africans were preparing to head back home, Olajuwon sought out Pond and asked the American if he knew a way to get a college scholarship back in the United States. Olajuwon understood that Pond was a man with basketball connections, at least by African standards. Over the years, the coach would obtain scholarships at Houston Baptist University for players Anicet Lavodrama, Fred Goporo, and Bruno Kongawoin.

Pond's immediate concern was Hakeem's age. He knew Olajuwon was living away from his home in Lagos, where his father, Alhaji Salaam Olude Olajuwon, worked in cement contracting and his mother, Alhaja Abike Olajuwon, helped to raise five children in a three-bedroom house. Pond also knew Olajuwon had toured a bit, playing in such places as Luanda, Angola, and Casablanca. Hakeem already had played for Baptist Academy, for Moslem Teachers College, for the national team. A lot of African players desired scholarships in the United States, but they were too old to hold much promise. Olajuwon, however, said he was only seventeen, and that was all Pond needed to hear. He caught a taxi with the teenager crammed into the back of the little Honda, and they headed straight for the U.S. embassy. There it was determined that this boy was, indeed, a valuable commodity. He was measured at six feet ten and a half inches and 190 pounds, and the rest was history, albeit jumbled a bit. Pond recalled it one way, Olajuwon and Lewis slightly differently.

Pond's version was distinctly more dramatic, more ironic. In order to receive a visa, Olajuwon required a written letter from a U.S. college coach that he would be given a scholarship. Pond knew a couple of big-time coaches, Lewis in Houston and Norm Sloan, who had just been replaced by Jim Valvano at North Carolina State. Pond had once unsuccessfully tried to convince Lewis to recruit another player, Carlos Benhamu of Venezuela. Pond said he flipped a coin—yet another coin flip that would greatly impact the landscape of basketball—and it came up heads for Houston. North Carolina State would have to win its 1983 NCAA championship against Olajuwon, not with him. Pond said he called Lewis, kept losing the connection, and finally convinced the coach after twenty minutes or so that Olajuwon was in fact a six-foot-ten-and-a-half wunderkind. Lewis sent off a telex to the embassy indicating some interest, and Hakeem got his visa.

There was a falling out between Pond and Olajuwon years later, reportedly when the coach divulged the real age of another Nigerian player, Yommy Sangodeyi, ruining his chances at a scholarship with the Cougars. Olajuwon loved and idolized Sangodeyi, a true playground legend who was twenty-five years old by the time he came to Lewis in Houston. Hakeem's version of his own story diminished Pond's role just a bit, contending that Olajuwon was handed a list of several American colleges by Pond, and that a wintry visit to New York was enough to convince him he would need to limit his search to Southern schools.

"He asked me, 'Where is the hottest place I can get to?' Lewis said. "I said Houston. He asked me if he could come, and I said, honestly, 'You can come . . . But I doubt whether you can play much. Do you have a ticket?'"

In any case, Olajuwon arrived in Houston, and Lewis said he was not expecting very much. The former coach is still a little embarrassed to admit that when the kid came by airplane, all the way down to Texas, "I didn't even go out there to meet him, 25 miles out there. I called him a cab." The coach kept remembering that Benhamu of Venezuela had not been anything near the size trumpeted by Pond. So he told Olajuwon to wait for the taxi. That cab ride took forever, Olajuwon remembered. "It is still very long, 45 minutes," he remarked when he came back in 1997 to Hofheinz Pavilion with Clyde Drexler to watch their jerseys retired to the rafters. It was an ugly drive, enough to make any immigrant or basketball recruit think twice about his decision to commit to this steamy sprawl of a city. When he arrived on campus, several people were there to greet him, including Lewis, Drexler, assistant coach Harvey Pate, and a few other players. "Kind of a welcoming committee," Drexler recalled.

"Then when he got out of the cab he just kept going, going, going. We had no idea how tall he was."

If he knew then what he knew now, Lewis admitted, he would have been there on the tarmac with bells on. Lewis hardly remembered at the time that he was supposed to be recruiting Olajuwon, and expected nothing from him. "I thought the guy [Pond] told me he was 6–4, 6–5," Lewis said. "He hadn't played organized ball for more than three, four months. Then I saw him and he wasn't 6–4, 6–5, 190. He was 6–10, 6–11, 250."

Olajuwon surely had not gained sixty pounds in a matter of days. This was wishful thinking on the part of the coach. But suddenly, there was great interest in the young man. An earnest effort was begun to acculturate this large African stranger into his new alien surroundings. Olajuwon quickly came to enjoy this land of strip clubs, oil companies, mechanical bulls, and thick slabs of raw beef. Legends grew from early misunderstandings. When he was asked to fill out a questionnaire by the sports information office, for possible use in the media guide, Olajuwon claimed that his parents were nearly as tall as he was (his father was tall, six-foot-three, but not Hakeem-sized) and that he had a seven-foot-five brother, Kaka. These were great exaggerations, though it was always unclear whether they were deliberate errors by Olajuwon. On that same survey, he spelled his own name "Olajuwoa" and made promises he couldn't possibly keep so soon. "I garantee [*sic*] 9 or 8 block shots," he wrote. The sports information director back then, Jay Goldberg, thought Olajuwon was not nearly as clueless as he sometimes appeared. Olajuwon spelled his name right on the most important papers, like immigration documents, and managed a decent 2.5 grade point average in business technology. One misunderstanding remained for years: Hakeem allowed the college to spell his name "Akeem" instead of "Hakeem." The "H" was pronounced softly, anyway, and Olajuwon didn't want to make a fuss at first.

"It is always difficult when you move to a new place, let alone a new country," Olajuwon wrote recently, from his residence in Jordan.

But my home city of Lagos was a very cosmopolitan city, therefore the adjustment was very minimal. I went to boarding school in Nigeria, so living on campus was very familiar to me. This definitely made things easier along with the fact that most students are from out of state and everyone is making an adjustment. My relationship with Coach Lewis was very good and he was a coach who demanded the best from his players. Coach Lewis was very disciplined in his basketball program which taught me a lot about good work ethics and structure. He was a great motivator and very instrumental in shaping my career and my mindset as an athlete.

Hakeem was an eager visitor. He soon found substitutes for the Nigerian fufu stew and the loffel rice. "He won everybody's heart," Dena Lewis remembered. "He'd never seen ice cream or steak, and he never got enough of it. That's how he gained so much weight." He ate fried chicken by himself, often, at a place called Frenchy's. When Dena Lewis hosted dinner parties for the whole team, Hakeem was an eager partaker in all foods, a true consumer. He was bowled over by the stock of size 16 sneakers available for his use. He was grateful for all this, in many ways humble. For a while, about the only thing Olajuwon could or would say to the media, to strangers, even to the coaching staff was, "I don't understand." Whenever he greeted a stranger, Olajuwon would bend from the waist, bow, a polite gesture that wasn't quite understood but was greatly appreciated by most everyone he encountered. In this way, Hakeem was a perfect ambassador. He was curious, polite, endearing.

"I was brought up to honor and respect older people," Olajuwon told Curry Kirkpatrick, in a 1983 interview with *Sports Illustrated*. "I bow to them out of respect. O.K., they laughed at me, so I stopped.

I know some people still think I was living in Nigeria, naked in the jungle and swinging through the trees. I know what they think about Africa. I do not like it. They are stupid. Lagos is a big, vibrant city. Tall buildings. Offices. Civilization. Designer clothes. We have a Copperfield store just like in Houston. We have videos in Nigeria. We have Pat Benatar."

At the same time, Olajuwon was gaining something of a reputation as a wild man in his personal life. There was no trouble with the law. But Olajuwon was the proverbial kid in a candy store and quite literally the big man on campus. He had yet to fully embrace the tenets of Islam. Team officials were concerned that he might get into trouble, if only because he didn't fully comprehend the stakes or the rules. Cultural chasms aside, Olajuwon also had a lot to learn about basketball at the Division I college level. Olajuwon sat out his first year, and during his inaugural 1981–82 season, Lewis was still afraid to give the red shirt freshman giant too many minutes in the biggest games. When Houston advanced to an NCAA semifinal against mighty North Carolina in the spring of 1982, Olajuwon sat out the critical early minutes of the game as the Cougars fell behind, 18–8. In his twenty-minute stint later, Olajuwon grabbed 6 rebounds, but the Tar Heels would win, 68–63. Olajuwon was not thrilled with his lack of playing time. "I am so mad I don't care if we lose," he said then.

Lewis would not budge on the matter of playing time. Olajuwon was out of shape and at a loss for any recognizable rhythm. He suffered back spasms, and he was committing foolish personal fouls that limited his minutes. The coach was tough with Olajuwon, and at times pride got the best of Hakeem. He was honestly hurt by some of the criticism and said as much. Despite Olajuwon's contention now that he and the coach got along famously from the start, Olajuwon and Lewis would battle for years. They often let off steam in the press. Hakeem was quite certain he knew the game back then. Lewis was just as sure he did not.

"The truth was, he wasn't a player at first," Lewis said. "He didn't play much for us, he played four or five minutes and he'd foul out. Everything was a challenge with him. He didn't know the game at all. Didn't even know the rules. He would take too many steps, travel all over the place. Then right after about two years, all of a sudden, I'm turning to my coaches and saying, 'You guys see what I'm seeing?' This guy hasn't missed a shot, he's just dominating everything."

Lewis's Houston teams throughout the decades were usually known for one thing: the dunk. It had been that way since the days of Elvin Hayes in the '60s, when every starter on the Cougars could dunk. The NCAA was so threatened by the sheer spectacle of these athletic feats—and frightened in anticipation of Alcindor's ascendance—that the organization banished the play entirely for nine years, beginning in 1967. This was akin to a parental, visceral reaction to rock and roll or long baggy pants. The dunk surely could not be a good thing for the nation's young people. But Lewis loved the dunk, wanted his teams to run the court. He worked on it with his players, and he would do so tirelessly with Olajuwon. "I coached the big men myself, 30 minutes a day," he said. "It was something I believed in. I'd have all of them, Hakeem too, line up at the free throw line, take one step and dunk it. I told 'em, 'We don't ever put the ball down on the floor.'"

Michael Young, a six-foot-seven senior swingman, was a year ahead of Olajuwon in school, already settled at Houston when the big guy arrived. Young was immediately struck by Hakeem's commitment to a plan—his own plan. In this way, Olajuwon was similar to Charles Barkley. Basketball would be his means to an end, not necessarily his *raison d'être*. But he would have to master this art before assuring himself a lucrative and dynamic future. "He came over with some goals in mind, short and long-term," Young said. "He needed to get to a place where he could actually play. And the guy worked hard every second. He already had great footwork from playing soccer. Then he played a lot of pickup. He was a gym rat." Olajuwon trained with Moses Malone, going one-on-one with the hard-edged Houston Rocket star at Fonde Recreation Center downtown, and had the nerve to reprimand Malone on occasion for calling their game too tight. "Be a man!" Olajuwon would yell, half seriously. Olajuwon amused Malone, so the veteran allowed this young upstart to live and tell about these sessions. Olajuwon began to feel more comfortable in Houston, blending into his odd new environment.

"And then, boom, it seemed to happen overnight," Young recalled. "His first year there we went to the Final Four in New Orleans. He couldn't play. Then he played a lot in the offseason, some more pickup basketball with the football team, and that made him so physical. After that season, there was more pickup ball, and his game just developed. You could see him blocking shots, running the floor with great speed for his size." It was hard work that did it, Young believed, as much as it was that amazing basketball body. Olajuwon would always say this was never work, though, not really. "It was fun," he said. His work was also his play.

Soon enough, the Cougars were ranked number one in the nation, flamboyant and wildly athletic in their skills, known to the world as the Phi Slamma Jammas. The Cougars dunked, often when there was no need for it, and they were headed for an almost certain national championship in 1983. Lewis had everything he needed on that squad, it seemed—including the dominant center and the gliding, explosive Drexler, a do-it-all swingman. Drexler was another under-recruited standout, as much of a find in his own way as Olajuwon, though he had been discovered much nearer to campus. He had been a high school star at Sterling, not far from Hofheinz Pavilion, and dreamed all his life of being a Cougar. The colleges did not exactly fight over Drexler, who always said he could "count the scholarship offers I had on one hand." Together, Mr. Inside and Mr. Outside, Olajuwon and Drexler, ran the floor, blocked shots, played intimidating defense, and put together highlight films that captured the imagination of a nation. While Michael Jordan was playing with studied restraint under Dean Smith in North Carolina, Olajuwon and Drexler were given greater freedom by Lewis in Houston, and they were creating something brand new, "Big Basketball," a fun and spectacular show that was more NBA than NCAA, more alley-oop dunk than four-corner offense.

But college basketball is a strange and heartbreaking thing, and sure enough the Cougars would pay a price for their free-wheeling style. They were beaten on the crazy night of April 3, 1983, in Albuquerque, New Mexico, in the NCAA final, 54–52, by an overachieving North Carolina State team driven into a frenzy by its emotional coach, Jim Valvano. State had only been the third-place team in the Atlantic Coast Conference and was a 7-point underdog against Houston. The Wolfpack was down 8 points in the second half, and still they came back to topple the favorites.

Everything needed to go wrong in order for Houston to lose, and it did. When Drexler got into early foul trouble, Lewis couldn't pull him out of the game fast enough to avoid a fourth personal in the first half. Forward Larry Micheaux and guard Michael Young did not have their best nights that Monday, and so Lewis ordered his Cougars to play against their nature, to slow the tempo and protect a fragile lead. Ultimately, their downfall arrived in most cruel fashion. With the score tied, Dereck Whittenburg of North Carolina State launched an ugly, desperation bomb that fell short of the rim. Olajuwon, positioned for a long rebound, was beaten to the air ball by Lorenzo Charles, who dunked the ball at the buzzer. The world's most famous college dunkers had been dunked upon, decisively, irreversibly. "A face job," Olajuwon would call it. Valvano stormed on to the court, frozen in time, celebrating the impossible victory. "We're on top of the world!" Valvano would scream, and of course nobody stopped to think where, exactly, that would place the Houston Cougars.

They were shattered, and then Drexler decided to come out early into the NBA, another major blow. "I thought it was going to be tough," Lewis said. "People would come up to me, say, 'Get 'em next year, coach.' And I figured, heck that won't happen." The Cougars still had Olajuwon, though, who had proved his great worth in that 1983 NCAA tournament. His performances then were truly amazing, right down to the final, miserable defeat. He'd managed 21 points, 6 rebounds, and 2 blocks against Memphis State; 20 points, 13 rebounds, and 8 blocks against Villanova; 21 points, 22 rebounds, and 8 blocks against Louisville; then, finally, triple doubles against North Carolina State, with 20 points, 18 rebounds, and 11 blocks. Olajuwon was so intimidating, such a force, he was elected Most Valuable Player in the tournament, even though his team had lost. That was the first time in seventeen years such a thing had happened.

Olajuwon was now, clearly, a fully operational superstar. He had amassed 175 blocked shots in that single season of 1982–83. His explosive first step toward the shooter allowed him to challenge jumpers all around the key, not just under the glass. On offense, not only could he run and see the floor better than players four inches shorter, he also had developed through great practice and patience a soft touch on a mid-range jumper, plus an unstoppable low-post game. His trademark drop step was in its nascent stages, yet it was an offensive weapon comparable in its own way to Kareem Abdul-Jabbar's patented sky hook.

So even after that crushing loss to Valvano, Houston still was ranked in the top five at the start of the 1983–84 campaign. Where there was a dominant center, there was hope. Then the season began with the Hall of Fame game in Springfield, Massachusetts, the Tip-

Off Classic against now-unranked North Carolina State, after another big buildup. And again, Houston lost to the Wolfpack, 76–64. This time it wasn't even close. NC State's center, Cozell McQueen, bottled up Olajuwon and got him into early foul trouble. Little Spud Webb, just five-foot-six, ran circles around the Cougar defense. Webb was a junior college transfer from Midland College in Texas who would have preferred to play at Houston, but there had been no space for him on the roster. At the time, Lewis merely said he was "disturbed" by the result of that game and wondered, "How in the world could we come up here to play in a game like this and not play with any enthusiasm or hustle?" More than two decades later, he confessed to an even greater sense of hopelessness. "I didn't think we'd win a game after that, the whole season," Lewis said. "But we won 32. We got it straightened out."

Young, by then a senior on the Cougars team, said he didn't worry nearly as much as Lewis about this team's potential. He figured Olajuwon was just too good to let the season get away from him—and the others. "We already knew where Hakeem was going to stand," Young said. "He was just an animal. And we had Greg Anderson, Ricky Winslow, they always stood their ground." Sure enough, Houston recovered its mojo and started beating some top teams. There was a regular-season setback in Kentucky, where the Wildcats were deep and big. Sam Bowie and Mel Turpin neutralized Olajuwon, and Houston stumbled briefly. But then the NCAA tournament began, and the Cougars were finding their stride. Nobody could argue with their chances as long as Olajuwon was at center. This time, it seemed, Houston was taking things more seriously than it had in 1983. The Cougars were 29–4 heading into the Midwest Regional semifinal against Memphis State, which had two giants of its own: a freshman, seven-foot William Bedford, and a six-foot-ten junior, Keith Lee. "There is a different attitude with our team this year," said Reid Gettys, a starting guard. "I don't think there is much evidence of us being uptight, but we're more serious. We're not new to this any more."

It was up to Gettys to talk, because Olajuwon had announced through a spokesman he would not speak to the media until the NCAA tournament was done. He was sick of fielding questions about whether he would turn pro by May. His 76 dunks on the season were enough talking. On Lewis's sixty-second birthday, the Cougars responded with a 78–71 victory over Memphis State. Next up in the regional final was Wake Forest (23–8), and Olajuwon was truly overwhelming. In a 68–63 victory over Wake, Olajuwon hit 14 of 16 field goal attempts for 29 points, 12 rebounds, 3 blocks, and 2 steals. He ran the floor tirelessly. His teammates were now relying on him far too heavily: Michael Young was battling through a 12-for-40 shooting slump in the regional ("I'd never missed so many shots before," he said), and nobody else on the Cougars seemed ready to share the offensive load. "No matter where you are," said Kenny Green, a forward on Wake Forest, "you are thinking about Hakeem."

The regional final had been too close for comfort. Wake Forest trailed by only 2 points with seven minutes remaining, and Olajuwon wasn't getting enough help on offense from teammates, who combined for a total of only 39 points. But the Cougars were going to their third straight Final Four. And there in Seattle, Olajuwon forgot his vow of silence and began to speak confidently again. He couldn't help himself, really. He was a cooperative guy with a great deal of pride. The only problem was the reporters wanted to talk about 1983 again, relive the face job, and Olajuwon wanted no part of that. "'Last year's over," Olajuwon told the press. "Now we take them one at a time, but I think we're going to be all right."

While Patrick Ewing battled it out with Sam Bowie in one semi-final, Houston appeared to have an easier path to the championship against lightly regarded Virginia. The Cavaliers had been what is known in college hoops vernacular as "a bubble team," a marginal at-large selection by the tournament selection committee after finishing the season at 17–11, 6–8 in the Atlantic Coast Conference. The Cavs no longer had Ralph Sampson, already playing for the Houston Rockets, and were expected to go out in the first or second round of the tourney. The Cougars already had defeated Virginia, 74–65, at Hofheinz Pavilion less than two months earlier, when Olajuwon deliberately elbowed Olden Polynice in the throat, knocking him out of the game, as the two of them ran downcourt. Polynice had frustrated Olajuwon, pushing him off his usual post position with shoves from the rear. Olajuwon basically got away with it.

In Seattle, as the two teams prepared to face off in one of the most important college games of the season, "The Elbow" became a primary topic of conversation. To his credit, Olajuwon owned up to the misdeed and basically apologized—even if that apology was directed more toward himself than Polynice. "I remember about the elbow," Olajuwon said. "I was very disappointed in myself. But I was frustrated the way he was fouling me around, pushing me on the back. I just couldn't take it anymore. There will be none of that in this game." Polynice said simply, "I try not to think about it because it would only make me mad."

The Cougars found themselves in another dogfight with Virginia, another potential upset humiliation. Thoughts of North Carolina State ran through Lewis's head as he watched his team bodied off its usual game, unable to get the ball to Olajuwon in any decent attacking position. The Cavaliers had all sorts of trouble shooting, but they kept themselves in the game by slowing the pace to a crawl while holding Hakeem to just 5 shots and 12 points on the night. Houston zoomed to an early 14–4 lead when Young buried 5 of his first 8 shots, at which point Virginia coach Terry Holland abandoned his standard 1–2–2 zone for something more fanciful, a diamond-and-one. "They made up their minds that Hakeem wouldn't beat them," Lewis said. Twice, Cleveland had its chances to pull this thing off. With twenty-nine seconds left in regulation, the Cavs' Othell Wilson stripped Alvin Franklin, dribbled downcourt, and hit the breakaway layup to tie the score, 43–43. Olajuwon then traveled, which spelled potential disaster. He made up for it, though, by stepping out toward the right baseline on defense, intimidating Wilson into an errant pass and a turnover leading to overtime.

This was an extra period the Cougars never thought would be necessary. "It was the first one we'd played in more than two years," Lewis said. "I could see at the end of regulation that our players were a little dejected." With Houston leading 47–45, Olajuwon missed a short shot over three defenders, leaving teammate Rickie Winslow alone to follow the miss with a dunk. Houston held on from there for a 49–47 victory, though there was a further bit of melodrama after the game was done. A couple of officials from the university's athletic department told Young that his brother, James Earl Young, had suffered superficial gunshot wounds to the head back in Houston. Young was reassured his brother would be fine, though, and soon enough the tournament hype was refocused on that dream showdown in the pivot, Ewing versus Olajuwon, for an NCAA championship. Olajuwon had never played against Ewing, a fellow junior who was also debating whether to come out of Georgetown early and turn pro. Just in case they both went pro, this game was supposed to go a long way in determining which impact center went number 1 and which one went number 2.

There was great excitement, and many photos taken, when Olajuwon and Ewing leaped for the ball at tip-off on Monday night, April 2. It turned out this was just a tease. Both players fell into early foul trouble. Ewing picked up his second personal with more than seven minutes left in the first half, while Olajuwon was charged with his fourth just twenty-three seconds into the second half. Olajuwon was particularly annoyed with one referee, Booker Turner. Hakeem felt the official had targeted him. Lewis tended to keep his key players in games despite foul trouble. He had taken some heat in 1983 about his deployment of Drexler. This time, he really had no choice. There was no doubt that Georgetown without Ewing was a better team than Houston without Olajuwon. He needed Olajuwon on the floor, for as many minutes as possible.

Houston grabbed an early 8-point lead, hitting its first 7 shots. But eventually Reggie Williams, Michael Graham, and Fred Brown took apart the Cougars, 84–75. Olajuwon finished with 15 points, while Ewing scored 10. Both grabbed 9 rebounds. There had been little support for Hakeem. The Hoya bench outscored the Houston reserves, 33–13. This wasn't the kind of heartbreaking loss that had occurred in 1983 against North Carolina State, when the Cougars were quite certain they were the better team. Defeat hurt, nonetheless. Houston became only the second team in history to drop successive NCAA finals, following the forlorn footsteps of Ohio State in 1961–62.

"It was a tough loss, to lose another NCAA championship game, a tough one," Young said. "But the one we lost the year before, it doesn't get any tougher than that. I was a senior in 1984, so this was it for me. But in that locker room afterward, we were still a team, and we'd played a good game. You can just imagine how quiet the atmosphere was. Coach came in, said we had a good season. 'You played hard. You don't get this far without playing hard.' And that was about it."

That was enough said for Lewis, but not for Olajuwon, who had refused to read the writing on the wall all season. If the ending to 1983 was shocking, then this bad finish to 1984 should have been more expected. The roster was thin, and any college team can slow any given player with the right defense. In this game, his own foul troubles made it impossible for teammates to rely on him. Olajuwon did not see it that way. Still steaming about the defeat, he reacted in typical fashion: from his gut, not his head. "We lost the game because we didn't play as a team," he told reporters after the game. "[Georgetown] passed the ball to the open man, like a team. We were selfish. I ask my teammates to get me the ball, they say, 'Next time, next time.' They wanted me to be wide open, but that can never be against a team like Georgetown because they play good defense. I told them, 'Just pass me the ball, I'll take care of it.' I told Coach Lewis about it, and he said, 'Just cool down, we'll get you the ball.' But they didn't try hard enough."

Olajuwon was fed up, and it appeared his supporting cast was not going to get any better after Young graduated. Still, Lewis did not like to think in terms of Hakeem leaving Houston for the pros, because the player still had so much to learn. Olajuwon hedged, trying to please everybody. On April 1 in Seattle, he had told reporters he would stay with the Cougars for his senior year. But after the defeat, Olajuwon was waffling again. He said he wouldn't make up his mind until May 2, then changed the date to May 5, which was the final deadline for undergraduates to declare for the draft. There was now a lot of pressure on Olajuwon to come out, if only for economic reasons. The salary cap, set at $3.6 million beginning in 1984, was going to get tighter as team payrolls increased. Agents were advising potential clients through the media to go pro now, perhaps sign for only one year, then become free agents when all twenty-three franchises could bid on them. "If I were an Olajuwon and had the chance to sign a contract that would mean a year from now I could have the entire league bidding on me, that would be ideal," Larry Fleisher told the *Washington Post* at the time. Fleisher was not only head of the NBA Players' Association, he was also one of the biggest agents around. "It's unfortunate, but the cap might affect certain players if their agents are afraid of losing them and want them to sign long-term contracts right away. Otherwise, it should not affect a player's decision on whether or not to turn pro."

David Falk from ProServ, who would become Jordan's agent, also argued at that time on behalf of the one-year contract scenario. "Don't forget that Kareem [Abdul-Jabbar] may retire after next season," Falk said. "Even if Olajuwon didn't have a great rookie year, he would get an awful lot of money because he's a premium resource. Power forwards can make a lot of money, but not like a true center can."

With all this business advice spinning through his mind, Olajuwon didn't wait until May 5, after all. On April 27, a Friday, Olajuwon held a news conference in Houston to announce he was turning pro. The *New York Post* had already reported that he'd come to some kind of tentative agreement with the Portland Trail Blazers for $1.2 million, if they won the coin toss in May or if Patrick Ewing came out and was chosen first by the Rockets. Olajuwon said this was not true, there was no deal in place, but he had discussed things with his parents and with Lewis. "This is very hard to do," Olajuwon explained. "I was thinking I was going to stay in school, but this is my decision. I'm going to have to live with it." Olajuwon was being practical, above all else. He figured that both Portland and Houston were well under the NBA's new salary cap and both would be able to pay him decent money. Both franchises also were relatively attractive options. If he were chosen by Houston, he would remain in his second home and join Ralph Sampson on a team with unlimited potential. If Portland picked him, then he would be reunited with Clyde Drexler on a club that already was above .500 and in need only of the right pivot man to complete its well-rounded roster.

"As you know I played my college career in Houston and really wanted to remain there if I could," he wrote recently. "When I saw that the Rockets had an opportunity to get the first pick in the draft I thought it was the best time to declare myself eligible. My parents were very supportive of me and when they agreed with my decision, I felt comfortable to leave college."

There would be no such guarantees if he stayed with the Cougars another season. He might then be drafted by some capped team, or some terrible team, in some cold-weather city. Olajuwon would leave campus and throw his lot into the draft. Not before he completed final exams, though. He had promised his parents that much.

5

The Well-Rounded Recruit

Charles Barkley and Auburn's head basketball coach, Sonny Smith, had a deal—several deals, in fact, depending on which of these two unique and boisterous characters you cared to believe. Barkley came to Auburn out of Leeds High School, a small, working-class town of eight thousand outside of Birmingham, Alabama. At Leeds, Barkley would hang out shooting pool at the Fuzzy Mule Lounge or put on a few more pounds at Old Smokey Bar B-Q. He was largely ignored by college scouts until the day he humbled Bobby Lee Hurt, a vaunted six-foot-nine center, in a holiday tournament game. Barkley, a senior, scored 24 points and grabbed 20 rebounds in the game, and that single performance changed everything. By the time he was eighteen Charles knew he was great, but until that game against Hurt nobody else seemed to believe him. Suddenly, the kid who had been a chubby, five-foot-ten sophomore was a six-foot-four whirling dervish deciding between several different colleges. Auburn might have passed on him, if it were up to Smith. The coach saw Barkley play a couple times and just thought of him as an obese kid without a jumper. But Smith's assistant, Herbert Greene, who would become coach at Virginia Commonwealth, lobbied tirelessly on behalf of this special talent. Barkley was a relentless rebounder, with a knack for passing and for seeing the court.

Barkley wanted to stay near home. Despite all his bluster, he was basically a mama's and grandmama's boy. When Charles was just a baby, his father, Frank, left the family to go to Los Angeles, where Frank would remain largely out of contact except for some brief visits from Charles over the years. The two men never grew close. Barkley's grandmother, Johnnie Edwards, was always the family mainstay, a strong-minded meatpacking worker with big plans for her three grandsons. Barkley's mom, Charcey Mae Glenn, was a maid in middle-class white homes around Leeds—a town largely segregated by neighborhood and attitude, but with integrated schools. Charcey had been twenty-one when Barkley was born, and her mom was just fifteen years older. Charcey was cautious by nature, though to make ends meet the family would occasionally sell bootleg alcohol. Such work was rarely discussed around the house, but it became apparent to Charles that hard, consistent labor was very much a part of life. Nobody called in sick. Everybody pitched in. Charles was in charge of his two brothers around town. Both mother and grandmother would come to each and every one of his high school and college games. Later, when he was an NBA star, they would watch all his games on satellite television, on the dish Barkley had installed in their backyard, outside their refurbished five-bedroom house.

Barkley probably would have gone to the University of Alabama back in 1981, but the coaching staff went after Hurt instead. A Crimson Tide assistant, Benny Dees, didn't listen to his wife, a women's basketball coach. She had told Dees to go out and recruit this kid she had seen who was even fatter than her husband. That did not seem like enough of an endorsement to Dees, who would take considerable ribbing from his wife for ignoring her. So Barkley enrolled in nearby Auburn, at a traditional football school that was to be ruled by the truly Big Man on Campus, Bo Jackson. There was another reason for the decision, Sonny Smith said, though Barkley had no memory of this. Barkley supposedly expressed to Smith up front the desire to spend no more than three years in college before turning pro. Back then, this was a bit of a revolutionary advance plan, but it was fine with Smith, who was desperately trying to reverse the program's fortunes. "We had to have somebody to jumpstart it," Smith said. Smith thought Barkley was lazy in high school but reasoned that maybe he could change that. The Tigers had just finished a fourth straight sub-.500 season, going 11–16 and 4–14 in the Southeast Conference. If this kid Charles Barkley gave him three good years, then that was better than more of the same thing.

Smith and Barkley immediately understood this was an opportunity to change everything about the basketball program. But in order to accomplish the goal, they needed to drum up some support. "It was very frustrating," Barkley recalled. "You get like 100,000 fans to the football games, 5,000 to the basketball games. We had 22,000 students. If just the students showed up, we'd have sold out every game. But we had a hard time recruiting against schools like Kentucky and Alabama." The Tigers required some national attention. Sonny and Charles were just the vaudeville act to get it done. Almost immediately, they began to promote Barkley as something of a freak show, a man who could eat his weight in basketballs. "We were trying to market me as a fat kid who could jump," Barkley said.

The nicknames and the weight estimates flew fat and furious. Barkley was Lard of the Rings, Leaning Tower of Pizza, Love Boat, Crisco Kid, Bread Truck, Boy Gorge, Pillsbury Doughboy, and, most frequently, the Round Mound of Rebound. Smith fed the publicity flames. He had little else going for him or the program. "We promoted the fat thing, because it got publicity for us," Smith admitted. "We searched for nicknames. I told him one time I did a disservice by promoting it. But he was into stunts. He marketed himself, and he was marketing his teammates along with him. When the pizza man (actually a rival fan dressed as a Domino's delivery guy) took his order at the Tennessee game, that sort of clinched it. Whenever Charles would come on the court, the guys would all ask me, 'Did you order any snacks?'"

Barkley was about six-foot-five and 270 pounds while playing for Smith, but his actual weight fluctuated nearly as much as the estimates in the national newspapers. When he didn't play or practice much over the summer, he would balloon to 290, 295. Barkley weighed in once at 259, but then his back muscles flared up, his workouts decreased, and the blubber returned. Barkley insisted his playing weight should never have been an issue, that it was simply "whatever weight I was playing at." He dispensed many pearls of wisdom in college, and he quickly became known among the national media as a go-to guy when a bit of anarchy was required. "My goal in life is to become President," Barkley said, without much provocation, "then lock up everybody over 12 and let the kids rule the world." He was in danger of becoming something of a joke, actually hurting his own future worth, except for a couple things: Barkley was a tremendous, explosive player with an uncanny rebounding ability. And he cared deeply about winning and losing, despite the outward, cynical marketing ploys. "We'd lost a total of maybe six or seven games in all my years in high school," Barkley said. "Then I got to Auburn, and we were losing a lot, and at first I would cry about it in the locker room. People would say to me, 'You can't be crying after every game. You don't understand. You're going to be losing a lot here.' We were playing .500 basketball, and people were going nuts, they were so happy."

Barkley played center against much bigger and more experienced players, holding his own. Auburn was 14–14 during Barkley's freshman season, then 15–13 his sophomore year, then 20–11 his junior year, when the Tigers received their first NCAA tournament invitation ever. All the while, Barkley was a rebounding wonder, averaging 9.6 boards per game over his college career. He was not nearly as tall as Sam Bowie, yet he was able to out-rebound him over the course of their college careers in the SEC. "What I realized early on, I realized I was a great rebounder," Barkley said. "I honestly couldn't understand why anybody can't average 10 points, 10 rebounds. I never knew I could score, but I knew after my freshman year, I just loved the rebounding. Suddenly, I'm leading the league in rebounding, once I figured out how to work hard."

That was a real issue, the work ethic, a sticky point of contention between Barkley and Sonny Smith. Nobody denied the kid could play, in a truly crazy way. Curry Kirkpatrick from *Sports Illustrated* once famously described Barkley's style as "Porky Pig gone berserk on a trampoline." The coach would ride his prize recruit mercilessly. Smith's other star, six-foot-eight forward Chuck Person, was a sleek, streak-shooting scoring machine and one of the team's hardest workers. Person presented this living, sweating contrast to Barkley, and that didn't help Barkley's image a bit with Smith. If Chuck was willing to work this hard, then why not Charles? According to Smith:

Person, you would practice three hours, he'd want to stay another hour. He'd work like a dog. He knew he had limitations, that had nothing to do with his shooting—like balance, off-the-dribble moves. Barkley never had those limitations. He'd get the rebound, head downcourt, dribble through his legs, behind the back, dunk it on the other end. Barkley was a great athlete, who could have been a super tight end in football. His first-step quickness was really good, he had unbelievable hands. He didn't jump that high, but he just had amazing timing. And he could take a blow against anybody. He had great strength in his hips and upper body.

Smith expected more from Barkley, always more and more, and did not necessarily employ the gentlest tactics while trying to coax it out of the player. Smith also wasn't thrilled when Barkley, who was playing either at power forward or center, would start acting as if he were a point guard. Although few people knew this at the time, Smith and Barkley grew miserable together those first two seasons. Smith was annoyed that Barkley showed great enthusiasm for the game only on a sporadic basis, mostly against the toughest competition. The coach tried everything. He used motivational films, pep talks, even what Smith called "puke sessions," which were workouts so tough they were intended to induce vomiting. Smith actually struck Barkley one time, smacking him in the chest after the coach warned the freshman he would hit him if Barkley once again knocked down a teammate, forward Alvin Mumphord, in the lane during practice. Mumphord tried to slice toward the basket, Barkley bumped him down yet again, and Smith shoved Barkley. Barkley told Smith right then, "Never do that again," and Smith never did.

But there were other intimidation attempts. Sometimes, Smith would take out a directory of colleges and ask his player to pick a school, any school, and Smith would help him transfer. Despite all the lighthearted public antics and all the good will produced for the Auburn basketball team, Barkley finally had enough. He decided to transfer to Alabama after his sophomore year—even if it meant he lost a year of eligibility. At the very least, the threat of such a transfer was a hefty bargaining tool. Barkley left school for three days, started looking into the transfer paperwork before he forced another sit-down with Smith to straighten things out.

"I told him, 'Here I am 18 years old [actually twenty, by then], leading the league in rebounding, and all you're saying is how fat and lazy I am," Barkley said. "I must be doing something right, because I'm All-SEC." Smith knew a crisis when he saw one. He had managed to recruit two standouts to Auburn—Barkley and Person—

and was expecting to contend for a conference championship in 1983–84. Smith had to do something fast. So he agreed to ease up on Barkley and treat him with the respect worthy of a college star. "We weren't on good terms until Charles was a junior, when he was working for a pro contract," Smith remembered. "Then we were fine. He couldn't practice half the time his junior year because he had a bad back. So he had to ride a bicycle. There were times he'd rather sit on a stationary bike, just work on a few plays for timing. But he got along very well with teammates, and though there was mention of jealousy with Chuck Person, I never saw it. Just a lot of joking in the locker room."

Barkley returned to Auburn his junior year, after all. His mother and grandmother still came to the games. Barkley became pals with Bo Jackson ("He took a lot of heat off me down there," Barkley said). And suddenly the Tigers were very much a force in the SEC. They went 12–6 in the conference and won a couple of close SEC tourney games against Vanderbilt and Tennessee. Gerald White hit 2 free throws with twenty-eight seconds left to beat Vanderbilt, 59–58, and then Barkley took over late in the game against Tennessee in a 60–58 win.

On March 10, 1984, Auburn found itself in the SEC final against Kentucky in Nashville. Barkley and Person were smack up against Sam Bowie and Mel Turpin, another one of those scouting smorgasbords for NBA teams. Each school had routed the other once during the regular season. This time, the game seesawed until the very end, when Kenny Walker's fifteen-foot jumper climbed over the front of the rim at the buzzer for a 51–49 Kentucky victory. Walker had been left wide open on a switch. At first, when it seemed Walker's shot was a clanger, Barkley went into a premature, mini-celebration. When the ball dropped, Barkley fell to his knees, head held in his hands, in a rare show of public disappointment. "It was the most helpless feeling I've ever had in my life," he said. "It was over and there was nothing I could do." Barkley was named both the tournament MVP and the league MVP. Auburn, 20–12, received an at-large bid to the NCAA tournament, its first in history. The Tigers had won the SEC championship in 1960 but weren't allowed into the tourney that year because of NCAA probationary terms imposed on their entire athletic program as a result of football violations. This time there was no scandal to interfere with March Madness.

The tournament did not go well, though the pain passed quickly. The first-round opponent was Richmond, which had lost to little William and Mary by 18 points less than two weeks earlier. The Spiders had to play their way into the tournament in a preliminary game against Rider and were not expected to provide much of a challenge for Barkley and Person in the first round. But the nineteenth-ranked Tigers were brand new to the NCAA tournament, and Smith felt his team was a nervous wreck going into the game. Auburn was caught cold, flatfooted, a step behind. These Spiders didn't crawl; they flew. Johnny Newman, a future pro and a renowned streak shooter, scored 14 points in the first half, when Richmond shot 64.3 percent from the field. The Spiders outscored Auburn, 18–2, over seven minutes for a 22–8 lead, then pushed the advantage to 48–28 six minutes into the second half.

It was then that Barkley came alive to lead a valiant but ultimately futile comeback. In the final eight minutes of the game, Barkley scored 17 points and led a charge that cut the lead dramatically. His bucket with five seconds left brought Auburn to within a point. Auburn had no timeouts left, however, and Smith couldn't gain the attention of his players to foul Richmond on the inbounds pass. Barkley finished with 23 points, 17 rebounds, and 4 assists. "Richmond just kicked our behinds," Barkley commented. "We just waited too late to start coming back."

His season was done, and now Barkley knew what he wanted to do. He wanted to hire an agent and turn pro. Sonny Smith was aware of the deal from the start. Barkley would be leaving after his junior year. Now the coach found himself arguing against the move; he also didn't want Barkley to hire agent Lance Jay Luchnick, but he failed in both these arguments. "I knew I was ready after my junior year," Barkley said. "You have to make that decision yourself. A lot of guys, they listen to an agent or a coach or to a freeloading family. I didn't do that." Barkley would leave Auburn, as planned, and with Luchnick, a relationship which turned into something of a disaster down the road. Barkley brought Luchnick back home to Leeds, where the attorney sat down with the family to go over the agent's contract. Barkley, at this stage still uninterested in such specific financial affairs, quickly fell asleep on the couch. His mother went to bed, too, leaving Barkley's grandmother, Edwards, to hammer out details with Luchnick. She had little notion of the troubles to come.

After he left for the draft, Barkley was named SEC Player of the Decade, and Auburn remained a basketball contender through 1988. The school enjoyed another revival a decade later under coach Cliff Ellis. Barkley did not always do his old alma mater great favors in the image department, however. He was more a storyteller than a journalist, and so his tales about college would vary wildly. Sometimes he waxed nostalgically and spoke about the wonderful opportunities afforded him at the school. "A great school, it was cool," he said. Sometimes he declared—joked?—that he was not required to do much academic work as long as he scored points, and that agents were paying him money while he was still in college. In a 2003 interview with *Stuff* magazine, Barkley was quoted as saying, "When I was recruited at Auburn, they took me to a strip joint," Barkley said. "When I saw those titties on Buffy, I knew that Auburn met my academic requirements. . . . All I know is, as long as I led the Southeastern Conference in scoring, my grades would be fine." He told the *Philadelphia Daily News* in 1988 that agents were basically bribing and enticing him at Auburn. Barkley also insisted that school officials never knew about it and that he deserved every penny: "I made a lot of money for Auburn when I was there. My junior year, we were on TV a lot. People wanted to see the little fat boy run up and dunk on people." Still, after all that, his jersey was retired in a halftime ceremony at Auburn during 2001, and Barkley donated $1 million to the school in 1999. Barkley always had a soft spot for children, too. When he was a player at Auburn, he would stop his car, climb out, and play hoops with the local kids. He also donated $1 million to Leeds High and another $1 million to the Cornerstone School in Birmingham.

That kind of big money would come later. Back in the spring of 1984, Barkley was fighting for a fat contract by way of the draft and the scales.

Spokane Man

It is now Jack and Dan's Bar and Grill, not just a mere tavern, and it has been remodeled, expanded, fancified, and even added to the Spokane Register of Historic Places, as of February 27, 2006. The vote was unanimous by the City Council, which ignored the bar's citation and $300 fine imposed less than a year earlier from the Washington State Liquor Control Board for furnishing alcohol to a minor (hey, these things happen, and the bar also is host to Gonzaga's Theology on Tap program events, "where faith and suds are shared over an evening"). The place at 1226 North Hamilton Street is famous, and not just because it has served beer, and more recently hard liquor, since Prohibition expired in 1933. The building was erected in 1909 as the two-story brick home of Gonzaga's Pioneer Education Society, a block from the main campus of the Catholic university. It was once home to druggists, butchers, and a couple other bars named Joey's Tavern and Snappie Beer Parlor. "Joey" was Joey August, who was Gonzaga's boxing coach and who first turned the establishment into a jock hangout. Tommy Lasorda, among others, would come to Joey's when he was pitching for the minor-league Spokane Indians. There must be some kind of karma in the old bricks, because Jack Stockton opened his place in 1961, and a year later his wife gave birth to a rather extraordinary athlete named John.

If you walk into Jack and Dan's, you see no photos of John Stockton, no trophies, no video clips. There is a stained glass ornament with the word "Jazz" and a big rug with a team logo, but that is about it. "We've got a saying around here," Jack Stockton said. "I've been working here for 45 years, and there are no pictures of me. John never put in a shift. Why the hell would we have his stuff up on the wall?" He acts gruff enough, but of course Jack will tell you everything about his son if you ask him, and relate it proudly. Jack Stockton grew up in the very same neighborhood as his bar. "I've moved about four blocks in 78 years," he said. He was a Navy vet who got together with a friend to open a business and put the kids through school. Jack Stockton was never worried about his son growing up around the bar, because Jack had done so himself and because John was never the kind of child to get in real trouble. John was "a prankster" around the dinner table, Jack said, but he was very quiet in public. He only let loose around his family and later around teammates, his surrogate family.

The father really didn't expect much from John when it came to basketball. "He was just too small," Jack Stockton said. "I thought, 'If he just gets a letter in high school, that would be great.' But he kept getting better and better." Here was this potential college recruit from Spokane, growing worthier of a scholarship by the day, but he was still small, and he was still in many ways below the radar. Playing for Gonzaga Preparatory School as a senior in 1980, John was a gem, but his team-oriented skills weren't so easily recognized.

Dan Fitzgerald was the head coach at Gonzaga University at the time and had turned things around since arriving there in 1978. Jay Hillock was an assistant who was about to become head coach after another year, when Fitzgerald dedicated himself to the role of athletic director. The two debated intensely at the time about whether to chase after this local kid. Fitzgerald had watched Stockton outwork another city high school team, Shadle Park, in a game at the old Spokane Coliseum, and he came back determined to recruit him. Hillock was more skeptical. "The last thing we need is another white guy out of Gonzaga Prep," he told Fitzgerald. Hillock was also concerned, frankly, with the notion of signing a kid whose father owned the local bar.

Hillock was no puritan; he occasionally would go on his own "paper route"—Gonzaga slang for an all-nighter of Rainier beer and basketball arguments, right up until the delivery boy arrived with the morning newspaper. Hillock worried, though, about all the distractions for a very visible athlete on campus. "A lot of coaches don't like recruiting in their back yard," he said. The coaches kept scouting Stockton in high school. This was a low-budget recruiting trip they could afford to make. They saw him repeatedly grab the rebound, run all the way downcourt, drive to the basket for a layup or dish off for an assist. They made the decision to go after John, who was still no sure thing.

Stockton did not attract scholarship offers from an A-list of basketball schools. But the University of Idaho, the University of Montana, Seattle Pacific, Washington State, and Gonzaga showed interest. In the end, only Idaho, Montana, and Gonzaga came through with scholarship offers. Gonzaga then was not the Gonzaga of today in terms of basketball prestige. The team played in Martin Centre, where the official capacity was 2,800 (4,700 could squeeze in, very uncomfortably) and where the upper bleachers were often shut down for games because of general apathy. "The biggest difference now is the attention," explained Ken Anderson, a former Gonzaga teammate who worked at the school as an athletic faculty representative. "I could walk through Spokane as a player, and nobody would know who I was. The media wasn't crazy about us, like it is now. The new arena seats over 6,000 and it looks like a big-time place, just a bit smaller. You look at Martin Centre now over on the East End of campus, they're playing volleyball there. It has bleachers on both sides and walls under the baskets, there have to be a thousand high school gyms that are more impressive."

The new McCarthey Athletic Center was built in 467 days and opened in the fall of 2004, after there had been some talk of simply knocking down the east wall at Martin and adding another side of bleachers. But by then, the Gonzaga basketball team was a big deal, and enough corporate boosters lined up to foot much of the $25 million bill. The McCarthey brothers, Gonzaga alums, and media tycoons from Salt Lake City, were the biggest donors. The seats all had backs now, and season tickets would go for anywhere from $400 to $3,700. The new arena boasted two oversized video screens, cushy offices for coaches, hardwood lockers for the players, and a wide concourse featuring giant murals of past Zag greats like Dan Dickau, Blake Stepp, and, of course, John Stockton.

Back in 1980, Gonzaga didn't have the facilities or recruiting money of other local colleges, like Washington State or Portland. Martin Centre, completed in 1965, when it was first called Kennedy Pavilion, became known as The Kennel. The place had a history, not all of it good. Even before its doors officially opened, the school's star center, Gary Lechman, suffered a broken arm slamming into a wall during wind sprints. The lighting was so bad early on, nobody could see the upper rows of the arena, even though the building wasn't very big at all. There were great moments here, though. In Stockton's freshman and senior seasons, average attendance grew greater than three thousand for the first time. The place would get a $4.5 million renovation two years later, in part because of Stockton's winning legacy.

The athletics budget was modest, any way you looked at it. Hillock could not afford to make any recruiting trips down to Los Angeles. The University of Washington in Seattle might have stolen Stockton but never mustered even a minimal effort. Gonzaga had its charms, even then, and had shown some promise. The previous two seasons, Gonzaga finished 16–10 and 16–11. "We were known to have a solid program," Hillock said. "We played hard and smart basketball. Every year we would step up and spank somebody, a high profile team, then finish third in the conference, behind Pepperdine, which was very good, and somebody else."

Jack Stockton watched over the recruiting visits very carefully, making certain that each coach who came for a home visit would sit at the same spot at the same kitchen table. There would be no advantages for anybody, even with all of Jack's business connections with Spokane and the local college. Nonetheless, John was just as anchored to the community as his father. He'd gone to grade school in the neighborhood, St. Aloysius. He'd gone to high school right there, too. And he had no desire, really, to leave the place. There was no wanderlust when it came to the Stockton males. Finally, John Stockton called Fitzgerald on Easter Sunday to give the coach some news. "I'm going to Montana . . . ," he began. And it was at this moment that the staff at Gonzaga first learned about Stockton's impish humor, because Stockton wasn't quite finished with his sentence: ". . . when you play over there next year." This was good news at Gonzaga, and about to become much better news.

Jack's kid could play basketball, it turned out; he could raise his game to the next level and then some. His freshman year, he started out as a backup to a point guard named Don Baldwin. Then he was a starter his sophomore year and a flat-out star by the time he was a junior. Gonzaga's fortunes changed accordingly. The Bulldogs were 19–8 during Stockton's freshman year, 64–45 during the four years he played at the Martin Centre, which was suddenly packed for every home game. "He was very popular with his teammates, our leader," said Hillock, who would later become director of pro personnel with the Chicago Bulls. "He started to talk a lot more then, he was almost chirpy. He'd exchange barbs, digs."

Stockton didn't experience the same kind of big-college glory or major tournament showcases as Jordan, Perkins, Bowie, or even Barkley. Instead, his career at Gonzaga could be viewed only in private snapshots, in the headlines stored in scrapbooks that were hidden in drawers:

February 28, 1981, his freshman season: Gonzaga pulls off a 79–67 upset at The Kennel against the nationally ranked University of San Francisco, which features two future NBA players. Though Stockton plays only a marginal role, this is arguably the biggest victory he will experience in his college career.

December 20, 1981, his sophomore season: Stockton scores 8 points and has 4 steals during a 21–4 rally in the second half, as Gonzaga comes back from 7 points down to beat Boise State on the road, 59–58.

December 10, 1982, his junior year: Stockton scores 18 points to beat Boise State again, this time in Spokane.

December 2, 1983, his senior year: Stockton scores 23 points in a wonderful 65–63 overtime win against Idaho State in Pocatello. Down 58–56 in regulation, Stockton drives the lane and hits the tying layup to send the game into overtime. Then he buries 2 free throws with six seconds left in overtime for the victory.

December 12, 1983: Stockton is named West Coast Athletic Conference (WCAC) player of the week for scoring 41 points in 2 games and quarterbacking Gonzaga to a 5–1 start.

December 29, 1983: Stockton scores 17 points to lead Gonzaga to a 73–57 victory over Robert Morris in the first round of the Far West Classic.

February 13, 1984: Stockton shares WCAC player of the week honors after becoming the first Gonzaga player in history to score more than 1,000 career points and hand out 500 career assists—while beating both Whitworth and Portland.

March 10, 1984: Stockton is named the WCAC's most valuable player, heading an All-WCAC team that includes Forrest McKenzie and Keith Smith of Loyola, Victor Anger of Pepperdine, Mike Whitmarsh and Anthony Reuss of San Diego, David Boone and Paul Pickett of St. Mary's, and Nick Vanos and Harold Keeling of Santa Clara.

Stockton became the only pro basketball success story in that entire WCAC bunch. McKenzie ended up playing 42 minutes during
six games with San Antonio. Smith played 42 games with Milwaukee. Nick Vanos managed a total of 68 games over two seasons with
Phoenix. Harold Keeling played 20 games with Dallas. Frankly, that
was the general expectation level for players coming out of the
WCAC. The time had not yet arrived when an Adam Morrison out
of Gonzaga would be touted among the very top draft picks, or when
the Zags would get a number 3 seed in an NCAA tournament region, as they did in March 2006. Morrison's campus press conference on April 19, 2006, underscored the difference in status now
enjoyed by the Gonzaga basketball team.

Morrison, like Stockton twenty-two years earlier, was WCAC
player of the year. He led the nation in scoring with a 28.1 point average and was Gonzaga's second first-team All American (the first
was not Stockton but Dan Dickau in 2002). By comparison, Stockton had averaged 20.9 points his senior year and led the conference
in assists and steals. At his news conference, Morrison officially declared he was turning pro early and had signed with super agent
Mark Bartelstein. Because he had diabetes, the floppy-haired forward said that he couldn't be certain how long he might be able to
play and that he had to accelerate his basketball career. His announcement garnered considerable national attention. Morrison became the second Gonzaga player to leave the school early for the
NBA, after Paul Rogers, who came out prematurely in 1997 and
never made a dent in the league.

It was always very different with Stockton, a pioneer from the
mid-majors. He was never quite certain if he fit into any NBA picture, and neither were his coaches or teammates. "We knew he would
be a good college player," Anderson said. "He didn't start as a freshman. He played, though, which was very unusual for our program at
the time. For the coaching staff, that was a big deal. Freshmen didn't

play. But if you'd asked me at the end of '81, would he be in the top 50 players of all time, I'd have to say, 'No.'" Anderson graduated after Stockton's freshman season, but he caught up with his former teammate in Santa Clara, California, as Stockton was closing in on his own diploma during a successful senior year. "He was talking about going to Europe," Anderson recalled. "And at the time, I walked away from that conversation thinking he didn't have a whole lot of other options. He probably felt he'd get drafted, but this was January or February, and he didn't think he would go in the first round. The talent was there, but his legend around Gonzaga wasn't what it would become later after the coaches' All-Star games, the Olympic trials. . . ." Hillock wasn't sure himself. "Absolutely not," Hillock said.

> He didn't shave as a senior in college, and he looked sixteen years old instead of twenty-two. He had ungodly speed, not quite to the extent that he did in the NBA, but he was always a pass-first guard. I got on him to shoot the ball at least ten times a game, but many times he didn't. You have to remember the point guards out there in the NBA at the time were big guys, Robert Reid (six-foot-eight), Magic Johnson (six-foot-nine), Michael Cooper (six-foot-seven). This guy looked around five-eleven-and-a-half. I didn't think of him as NBA material for most of his career at Gonzaga. But then he was MVP of the Far West Classic, with eight teams competing, and I started to think it was possible.

That Far West tournament, the senior All-Star showcases, and the Olympic trials woke up many people. As the 1984 draft approached, Stockton was summoned for interviews in Seattle and Portland—the two NBA depots where he most wanted to play. They were both within commuting distance of Spokane, after all, just a few bounce passes from Jack and Dan's Bar and Grill.

Trial by Knight

Coach Knight was still Bobby from Indiana in 1984—not Bob from Texas Tech. He was rough-hewn, full of fire, fresh off his upset victory over Michael Jordan and the Tar Heels in the NCAA tournament. In many ways, Knight was the most provocative choice possible by USA Basketball to coach the Olympic team, a diplomatic slap at the rest of the world. Knight had captured two NCAA titles, which was portfolio enough, but he was more than a bit of a cowboy. Back in 1979, Knight had been convicted in absentia of aggravated assault, after he'd tangled with a policeman at the Pan Am Games in San Juan, Puerto Rico. The cop had foolishly stood between the coach and an available practice gym. Knight was sentenced to six months in prison and fined $500. He left for the sanctuary of the U.S. mainland, and the territory of Puerto Rico never sought his extradition. It took only a slight stretch of semantics to call Knight an international fugitive from justice. Then in 1981, Knight got into a little brawl with an LSU booster after an argument at a cocktail lounge in Cherry Hill, New Jersey.

Trouble shadowed Knight. Over his long, often intemperate career, he would become famous for hurling a chair across the court, choking one of his players, making light of rape, and using a bullwhip as a demonstration to his team of his toughness. But back in 1984, U.S. Olympic officials also knew that Knight would be the perfect fit for selecting and molding a national team in quick order. He took this job very seriously. He would scout players for a couple years and assemble a staff of twenty-two assistants—including one of Knight's mentors, Pete Newell, who had been tremendously successful in Rome at the 1960 Olympic Games. Knight had a knack for creating chemistry, and his scowling presence alone demanded both discipline and respect.

The Americans were still the undisputed world champions of basketball in 1984, even if there were already signs of slippage. The U.S. amateurs had lost a famous, controversial Olympic final to the Soviets at Munich in 1972, and then a Soviet team toured the States in 1982, going 7–1 against top college opponents. After the Americans boycotted the Moscow Olympics in 1980, the Russians were threatening to retaliate with a similar absence at Los Angeles in 1984. And in the end, there would be no Cold War showdown, though that was not clear when Knight began organizing his team. The Soviets were still out there, somewhere, Knight figured. Yugoslavia, a rogue communist nation, would be competing in L.A., and was considered a bigger threat at the time than Spain, West Germany, or Italy. Many countries would soon become major land mines for the United States in international play. In Los Angeles, however, they were not quite ready to compete with the more athletic, polished Americans. There was still no need and little talk about bringing an NBA "dream team" to the Summer Games, which would have required negotiations on several fronts. The collegiate stars were just fine, selected by a committee of eighteen coaches and officials, headed by Knight. He picked his staff and aides carefully.

His most active assistants on the courts were Don Donoher of Dayton, George Raveling of Iowa, and C. M. Newton of Vanderbilt. They were college basketball coaches he trusted to watch his back and share his evaluations.

"We're going to choose our players as to their ability and how they relate to the way we want to play," Knight told the *New York Times*, as he began the recruiting process and prepared to meet with his committee. "I don't know if I'll have the last word, but I've got to have a word. It could be the first or the last or the middle." This process was nothing like the one that followed years later in 2002, when many of the top players avoided Athens at all costs. In 1984 there was little ambiguity among the invited players, who still wanted very much to be part of the Olympic experience.

Sam Bowie and Kenny Smith were arguably the only top-level collegians to beg out of the trials, and their decisions were fully understandable. Bowie had been on the 1980 national team that was cheated of its Olympics because of the boycott. Now he was just recovered from his series of leg problems. Bowie could not afford to take a chance with the NBA draft right around the corner. He also figured to play behind Patrick Ewing, even if he made the team. Bowie was concerned, a bit, that his decision to pass would be considered un-American. But he did what he had to do, avoiding potential injury and embarrassment. "I just didn't have the desire and motivation that I felt I needed to make the team," Bowie explained. Kenny Smith had even less of a choice. Surgery was performed on his left wrist soon after the NCAA tournament, and a pin was inserted to assist the recovery.

The original plan was to invite anywhere from forty-eight to sixty-four top college players to the Olympic trials on the Indiana campus in Bloomington and to have them play scrimmages from April 16 to April 22. The team would be cut to sixteen, tour against NBA All-Star teams, and then be whittled to twelve players in time for the July 15 roster deadline. Knight's goal was to go to L.A. with two centers, three guards, and seven frontcourt swingmen. Most of the players would be missing some classes back at their campuses, and most of them didn't really care. When it came time to send out invitations, officials found they could not stop at sixty-four, adding another ten to the list.

Seventy-two of the seventy-four players accepted the challenge. Four of them—Ewing, Jordan, Perkins, and Tisdale—were college All Americans and locks for the final roster, which meant there were really only eight remaining slots for all these candidates. They showed up, anyway, representing quite a mixed bag of talent and experience. There were well-known stars like Chris Mullin of St. John's, Mel Turpin of Kentucky, Keith Lee of Memphis State, and Leon Wood of California State University–Fullerton. There were oddities, like teenager Danny Manning and Walter Berry, who had gone to San Jacinto Junior College after being declared academically ineligible at St. John's. Four Kentucky players, the most from any college, were invited to Bloomington—though Bowie soon RSVP'd in the negative. North Carolina had three players, if you counted Kenny Smith. Louisville had three, including Lancaster Gordon. Barkley and Person were both invited from Auburn. Half the future Dream Team that would perform at the 1992 Olympics was already in this camp.

The first six days were a mix of fourteen sessions filled with drills and scrimmages, open at different times to the public, to the media, and to NBA scouts, drawing occasional crowds of more than seventeen thousand fans to Assembly Hall at basketball-crazy Indiana University. Knight watched from above, on a makeshift platform, like a detached general or football coach. "We were like cattle below," Sam Perkins remembered. The press was informed that it was limited to covering practices on Wednesday only and would have little or no interview time with Knight or the players. If reporters dared to converse with players, even offer casual greetings, their credentials might be pulled. The writers were still thrilled to be there, able to watch all this amazing basketball talent assembled in one location. "I felt like a kid in a candy store," said Charlie Pierce, then with the *Boston Herald*. Whenever Knight deigned to speak with the media, the press conference often turned into sparring sessions, like when Knight would insist his defense was not a zone, as Mike Bruton of the *Philadelphia Inquirer* contended, but a "help man" scheme.

NBA general managers like Rod Thorn of the Chicago Bulls were afforded much freer access, and so Thorn strolled about the gym while getting a very good look at potential draftees. "There were several courts, you could walk around and view the guys," Thorn said. "Then they'd play a feature game on one main court. One time I remember Michael Jordan, Charles Barkley, Patrick Ewing, and Joe Dumars were all on the same team at the end of practice, and they absolutely blitzed the other team. Barkley was something else. He was possessed. You just didn't see people other than Dr. J get a rebound at one end, go downcourt by himself, dunk the ball to finish the play."

In the morning, the coaches would work with players by position—guards at one end of the court, big men at the other. At night, the games began in earnest. Most everybody agreed that the best two players on the courts were Michael Jordan and Charles Barkley—not necessarily in that order. Jordan had been expected to do wonders, and he did, but Barkley's exploits arrived without such fanfare. He was running the court, slamming people all over the place, thoroughly infuriating his fellow candidates. In one noteworthy scrimmage against Ewing's team, Barkley proved unstoppable around the basket, often out-jostling and out-rebounding Ewing, an All-Everything center who was more than a half foot taller.

"The first week, we had three-a-days," recalled Leon Wood, later an NBA referee.

We'd play early morning, midday, early evening. The top players around were all there—Pearl Washington, the Kentucky guys, Antoine Carr was there early on. This was quite interesting, people going at it. And Charles Barkley just completely dominated the first week. He wanted to prove himself, let everybody know he belonged in the top five. But I don't think he wanted to spend another two or three months playing under the tutelage of Bobby Knight. When he made the first cut after the first week, he was told to drop a few pounds. Instead, he gained weight. But that first week, he would get a rebound, go coast to coast, dunk it. He would dunk it to get the crowd going. He was going to do his thing, play his game, but Knight was going to win that battle. You could read that was going to be the way it was going to be.

Until such a comeuppance, Barkley did his thing. Reporters watched in awe during one scrimmage as Barkley tore down a defensive rebound, dribbled behind his back downcourt, and crashed into Mark Alarie, all of six feet, eight inches. Barkley tumbled to the floor. Alarie flew right off the court. Unperturbed, Barkley simply stood back up and nailed the eighteen-foot jumper on his way to a game-high 19 points. After another outlandish collision on a blindside pick, feisty little John Stockton, an unknown then, got up and cocked a fist in Barkley's direction, though nothing came of it. Barkley bashed the high school invitee, Danny Manning. The kid's father, Ed, was philosophical. "He has to learn sometime," Ed Manning told reporters. Barkley was treating everyone this way, literally throwing his weight around. "He threw me down with his left hand and dunked with his right," Mark Halsel of Northeastern told *Sports Illustrated*. "I figured he didn't want to be interrupted. And that we should become friends."

Barkley has since said repeatedly that he really didn't care much if he made the team. That was not his mission in Bloomington. He had grander plans, already lining up endorsements, looking to improve his draft position. He told people as much, and at first they thought he was just trying to shock them. But it was at least partly true, and in his autobiography, *I May Be Wrong, But I Doubt It*, Barkley was emphatic in this regard. "Number one, I didn't like Bobby Knight," he wrote. "And number two, I was leaving Auburn to turn pro. I didn't want to dedicate my entire summer just to playing basketball. My primary goal was to move up in the draft, which meant working out, getting mentally and physically prepared to play professional basketball. I wanted to go to the Olympic trials, kick a little butt, and move up in the draft." Barkley really did have a completely different agenda from that of everybody else there, just as he had a different goal at Auburn. He wished to have some fun and to make some money down the road. But he needed Knight to let him play hard that first week, impress people. And that wasn't a given. Barkley worried Knight might exclude him from the trials based on his weight alone. Barkley was in the 280s, and Knight wanted him at 215 pounds, an impossible fantasy. Asked if he had ever dealt with an overweight player before, Knight answered, "Not for long." In uncharacteristic fashion, Barkley panicked and went on a crash diet before the trials that weakened him badly. He learned a hard lesson, swearing he would never betray his appetite again. Boy Gorge was reborn.

Barkley's roommate at the trials was Steve Alford from Indiana, who was viewed as the buffer between Knight and the Olympic candidates. Alford, just nineteen years old at the time, shook his head in disbelief every time Barkley did something crazy, or when Barkley went on a tangent about becoming a spokesman for some company.

"Coach Knight and I loved him," Alford said. "He knew how to run offenses. Had it been based on talent and ability, he would have made it. He was undersized, but had quickness and a jumper. Charles was a terrific person. I just don't know if the Olympics at that time was as important to him as getting endorsements. He got a big head start on everybody. At the time, we thought he was crazy. But it was brilliant on his part. And he got the Right Guard endorsement and others, even before Michael."

Alford's reading on this matter differed a bit from most players in Bloomington, who saw instead of a great love affair a far less positive relationship between Barkley and Knight. Barkley was not Sam Perkins. He did not simply allow a coach to rant and lay down rules without a challenge. When Knight showed up late for a practice, Barkley let him know about the double standard in place. Barkley wanted to become one of the game's great characters. He had both the personality and the game for it. And as the trials progressed, as Barkley grew more confident and less afraid that Knight might sabotage his grand scheme, he grew bolder in his public statements. He played the fat card to the hilt, telling the *Washington Post*, "I really don't eat that much. I just, more or less, tend to eat all the time. If I could go into a room and peel some of this stuff off of me, I'd come out looking like Hercules." He loved doing outrageous things in front of this new audience, his peers, the best college players in basketball. So they thought he was fat? He would show them why. Each evening, two pizzas were delivered to each dorm room, one per player. Barkley made a public show of hogging the goods. "I was lucky if I got one piece," Alford said.

The first cuts were made April 21, after five days of workouts. Seventy-two players were culled to thirty-two, as Dave Gavitt, chairman of the selection committee, rattled off the names of qualifiers in alphabetical order. "Not one player who made the list did so by virtue of reputation or press clippings," Gavitt said. Terry Porter, the six-foot-two guard from little Wisconsin–Stevens Point, missed the last two days of the trials with chicken pox but made the cut anyway. Porter had been the only non–Division I college player invited, not counting Walter Berry. "I kinda' bleed for him," Knight said of

Porter, "and so does our doctor." Knight still needed thirty-two players for scrimmages over the weekend, so he reinstated Dell Curry of Virginia Tech, who had been dismissed. Larry Krystowiak, a six-foot-eight forward from the University of Montana, also caught chicken pox. Four natural centers survived to the next round: Ewing, Jon Koncak of Southern Methodist University (SMU), Tim McCormick of Michigan, and Joe Kleine of Arkansas. At least two players were unknown to most outsiders: Maurice Martin, a six-foot-five sophomore from St. Joseph's, and the six-foot-one guard from Gonzaga University named John Stockton. Karl Malone also made this first cut, along with Barkley and Person. Other famous players were not so fortunate. Gone were Pearl Washington of Syracuse, Michael Cage of San Diego State, Ed Pinckney of Villanova, and Mark Price of Georgia Tech.

It was during this time, Stockton once told Steve Luhm of the *Salt Lake Tribune*, that the Gonzaga senior got to know this guy Malone—two long shots from little colleges, sitting together and enjoying lunch. "It's not real common at those things to be folksy," Stockton said. "I'm not saying you're sizing each other up or just glaring at each other. But there's a lot of quiet. And here we are, sitting at a table being folksy." Stockton, like many other athletes there, understood that the tryouts represented a chance to move up in the draft, not only to make an Olympic team. The players were constantly trying to read Knight's mind, to figure out exactly how to become what Arkansas coach Eddie Sutton would term "Bobby types." Whenever cuts were about to be made, Knight would give a short speech, which was supposed to ease the pain for those whose names were among the missing. "Not making this team does not affect your future," Knight said. "You affect your future." Nobody bought that. The players understood that surviving to the round of thirty-two was a very good way of becoming a first-round draft pick. "When they got to the R's, my heart stopped," Stockton said. "Then when I heard my name, it got going so fast it made up for the time it had been stopped."

By April 22, the squad was down to twenty: Ewing, Koncak, Kleine, and McCormick at center; Perkins, Barkley, Person, Tisdale, and Jeff Turner at forward; Jordan and Mullin swinging from guard to forward; Alford, Gordon, Martin, Porter, Wood, Stockton, Johnny Dawkins, Vern Fleming, and Alvin Robertson at guard. Knight said there were too many good guard, that he couldn't make up his mind and needed to watch them a bit longer. Gone were Karl Malone and Antoine Carr, who was earning about $200,000 at the time playing for Milan in the Italian league yet was still considered an amateur by Olympic standards. The roll call of the fallen made the remaining players appreciate their own accomplishment. Malone faced a sad and complicated trip back to his home in Louisiana. He would have to connect from Bloomington to Charlotte, to Nashville, to New Orleans, to Shreveport. Pierce spotted him at the airport that day. "I don't understand what I had to do to make the team," Malone told him.

Many of the players who were released felt the same sense of randomness about the selection process. They tried their best, nonetheless. "When you get this many great players—the cream of the crop—playing this hard, you better play as hard as you can," Ewing told the *Washington Post*, still just a few weeks past winning the national championship. "I think I played pretty consistently through the Trials. I did my best. It was a long, hard week. Your body gets run down. This surface is like playing on concrete."

The twenty remaining players returned to Indiana on May 10, for five scheduled days of boot camp under Knight and his assistants, in preparation for more cuts and exhibitions against the NBA All-Star teams. About seventeen other coaches were conferring, making decisions. Clearly, though, it was Knight's call from here on, and the head coach wanted his team to have a neat balance of stars and role players. The practices were still tough, still draining. The players hardly had time to socialize. When they did, they tended to group by position, guards with guards, big men with big men. Jordan hung with Fleming and Robertson, usually playing cards or showing off with a pool cue. Perkins had made a fast friend in Tisdale. And once in a while, the players wondered aloud where they would be drafted—and where they wanted to be drafted. "I was trying to figure out who was going to take me," Leon Wood said. "I wanted it to be the Clippers, because they could use some help in the backcourt. Philly was already loaded with Andrew Toney and Maurice Cheeks."

The waltz with Knight was becoming clumsy at times. "I got along with him fine," Perkins said.

> But I tried to do everything fine, fundamentally sound. You had to mind his system, his personality. Some guys didn't like it. He got on guys he probably wanted to develop more. Coach was yelling at us for a reason. Wayman Tisdale had become my good friend, and he was in Coach's doghouse the whole time. He didn't know why Coach was on him. But he took it in stride, picked up his game, and after a while he adjusted. There were similarities in the way Coach Knight and Coach Smith wanted things done. It's just how they achieved it that was different.

Barkley, for one, appeared to be losing interest in the whole process. He had proven his point and was ready for the draft. He had moved up, in his own estimation, from a mid first round pick to a top five. Others were browbeaten or rebellious, and they were not quite sure what it was that Knight wanted from them. The coach did not tend to counsel any player on specifics. And so the players found support groups within the roster. They tried to buffer themselves from the onslaught. Wood hung with Chris

Mullin and Jon Koncak, and they would all discuss Knight, trying to read him. The players often guessed at what he wanted from them and usually guessed wrong.

On one occasion, Wood recalled, Knight chased the players from the gym during a practice, telling them to get out because he didn't like what he saw. Jordan, as unofficial leader of the players, convinced teammates to go back into the gym and start practicing again on their own. Knight grew even more furious and threw them out again. He didn't want his players to leave the building, however. He wanted them to hang out, exhibit remorse, and wait for him to summon them back for practice. This was a delicate balancing act, and it was a good thing that Alford was around to help interpret. It still was not always enough. Jordan was trying to please. He was getting frustrated, though. Knight shared Dean Smith's no-star-is-too-big attitude, but he didn't have Smith's consistent temperament. Smith had learned to filter his rawest thoughts, to wait until emotions ebbed before telling players what he thought. Knight was pure, undiluted id. He said whatever he felt, whenever he had the itch. For somebody like Jordan, who was accustomed to gentler, kinder words, this kind of treatment was abrasive and often hurtful. "Coach Smith is the master of the four-corner offense and Coach Knight is master of the four-letter word," Jordan would say.

On May 13, after just two days of this second-round camp, the next cuts came down. They would be startling moves when considered years later, from a historical standpoint. With one fell swoop, Knight axed Barkley, Stockton, and Terry Porter—three future NBA stars—along with Maurice Martin, the lesser-known six-foot-six sophomore from St. Joseph's. Of the four, Barkley's departure made the biggest news, inside and outside camp. "Him being cut clearly had nothing to do with his play," Wood said. Perkins figured that if Barkley was cut, then he would surely be next. Knight had used

Barkley to send out a warning to everyone that talent was not enough. Hard-working but limited Jeff Turner, clearly a lesser light, had been retained on the roster, presumably for reasons of chemistry, perhaps because of his Vanderbilt connections with C. M. Newton.

"I saw nothing that whole time that demonstrated why Jeff Turner, Jon Koncak, and Joe Kleine should all make the team," said Charlie Pierce, who labeled these players in the *Boston Herald* as "the great white fleet." To this day, Sonny Smith, Barkley's coach at Auburn, believes the only reason that Knight cut Barkley was because of global events, because of the latest development in deteriorating relations between East and West. The Soviets had just announced officially on May 8 they were boycotting the Olympics. Although they did not mention the U.S. boycott of the 1980 Games in Moscow, the connection was clear. The Soviets charged that U.S. authorities held a "cavalier attitude" toward the Olympic charter and were aware that a private American group calling itself the Ban the Soviets Coalition was planning to aid Soviet athletes who wished to defect during the Games. The boycott was not the decision of Russian coach Alexander Gomelsky, who badly wanted a piece of Knight. This was a Kremlin job, and it cut the heart out of the Olympic basketball competition.

"Extremist organizations and groupings of all sorts, openly aiming to create unbearable conditions for the stay of the Soviet delegation and performance by Soviet athletes, have sharply stepped up their activity with direct connivance of the American authorities," the Soviet National Olympic Committee announced. And at that moment, Sonny Smith became quite certain that Knight was afforded the luxury of replacing Barkley, the superior athlete, with Turner, the cooperative bench sitter. "When the Soviets dropped out, Knight didn't need Charles to win the gold medal anymore," Sonny Smith said. "I've always thought if the Soviets were playing, then Charles would have been on that team."

Barkley did not think the boycott was such an important development, even though he had repeatedly expressed his opinion during the trials: "I hate the Russians." Barkley would still like to know what happened, why he was dropped. Looking back, despite his frequent contention that he didn't really care, Barkley sounded a bit hurt and puzzled by Knight's decision. "I'm not sure why I didn't make the team," Barkley said. "I don't think he tried to embarrass me. I have no idea." Barkley insisted he had not suddenly lost his verve or commitment after that first week. "We were only there for a week, then we went home for a month," Barkley said. "I didn't start stinking up the joint in a month." More important, Barkley had proven something to himself. He now was quite certain he could play with anybody on the planet, except maybe Michael Jordan. "That Olympic Trials let me know I could play at a higher level," Barkley said. "Those guys you see on TV, they're the same as you. You don't know that until you get there and start playing against them."

Barkley remembered riding away from camp with Stockton and Porter, and how Stockton said he would love one chance for the players in the van to challenge the players who made the team. Barkley thought the situation was ridiculous, that Knight was keeping the athletes he could control. A lot of players remaining in camp believed that theory, too. How else could you explain the absence of such dominant stars as Antoine Carr, Karl Malone, and Joe Dumars? They did not fit Knight's vision. The remaining group would be with the U.S. team through the pro draft. The series of games against NBA All-Stars would begin on June 28 in Providence, and the U.S. team would then barnstorm around the country for more exhibitions in Minneapolis, Iowa City, Indianapolis, Greensboro, North Carolina, Milwaukee, and San Diego. The game at the Hoosier Dome on July 9 in Indianapolis was played as a doubleheader that included the U.S. women's Olympic team and had already sold sixty-two thousand tickets, nearly two months in advance.

First there was a fund-raiser in the Hoosier Dome, and three thousand fans showed up to pay $100 a plate and hobnob with the players. Jordan spoke briefly, acknowledging the pro-Indiana crowd. "The only players we heard of when we played IU were Alford and Blab, but we learned they had a lot more than just those two," Jordan told the audience, to cackles. "My coach, Dean Smith, and Coach Knight are about the same, except for the language." Several former Olympians, like Oscar Robertson and Walt Bellamy, were introduced. The public love-fest continued with Knight. "I've never seen a group of guys work any harder," the coach said. "They're not getting paid. They're just going out and doing this for themselves and their country."

Knight was now growing more intense. He invited the remaining players to his house for dinner, another way of keeping an eye on everybody, continuing the evaluation process. He brought the players down into his basement and showed them his memorabilia collection. But if anybody thought this was a new policy of informality, that the coach was softening, Knight soon proved him wrong. Practices only became more rigorous, his tantrums more frequent. "I had a tough time, because his system was totally different than what I was used to," Wood said. "He kicked me out of a shootaround, made me run up and down the bleachers in 104-degree heat. Quinn Buckner came out and asked me, 'What did you do wrong?' and I had to say, 'Nothing.' Knight was nervous, as we were getting close. But I kept asking myself, 'Why me?'"

Knight wasn't all that pleased with his group's play. After the first exhibition in Providence, Knight trimmed his roster to twelve, to the final group. He cut Gordon, McCormick, Person, and Dawkins. On July 1 in Minneapolis, each and every remaining player was allotted between fourteen and eighteen minutes in a game against some NBA All-Stars and came away with a 94–90 victory on national television. Knight would stop being such an egalitarian soon enough, leaning more on starters like Jordan and Ewing. He required both inside and outside scoring threats to counter and penetrate the famously sticky European zone defenses. Easier said than done. "We didn't have our zone offense in there," Knight complained. He didn't like what he saw when the NBA stars went to an unfamiliar 3–2 zone in the second half and when his Olympic team shot only 31 percent, blowing a 12-point lead. The pros played hard, showing some pride. "They weren't going against a bunch of cupcakes," Kevin McHale said. "I think if we had a week together, we could beat them."

Knight's theories about his team changed several times in the remaining weeks. For an exhibition in Iowa City he went to a smaller lineup, featuring Jordan, Chris Mullin, and Alvin Robertson. "We just didn't play particularly well inside today," Knight said. Try as he might to disguise his intent, it was a no-brainer that Knight would eventually settle on a lineup that most often featured Jordan, Perkins, and Ewing. And by the time the Olympics arrived, Jordan had become quite the national celebrity from all his broadcast time and all his remarkable choreography. For the first time, fans crowded around the buses and the hotels hoping to get an autograph or a glimpse of this rising star who had flashed such brilliance against NBA All-Stars.

Jordan didn't disappoint at the Olympics, either. The United States coasted to a gold medal, one rout at a time. The Americans whupped China, 97–49, then thumped Canada, 89–68, then ripped Uruguay, 104–68, then took apart France, 120–62, then embarrassed Spain, 101–68. Jordan looked spectacular whenever he got playing minutes, though he averaged only 17 points per game. Knight had the luxury of juggling his lineups, giving nearly everybody on his roster substantial time.

There was one notable speed bump, a game against West Germany in which the Americans allowed a 22-point lead to dissipate somewhat before winning, 78–67. Jordan had a rare mediocre performance, shooting 4-for–14 with 6 turnovers. Knight went berserk on the bench, and afterward he ordered Jordan to apologize to his teammates for the way he'd played. This was a particular affront not only to Jordan but to his peers, who understood the depth of Jordan's pride and commitment to competition. Jordan's eyes teared up as he stood in defiance, not quite knowing what to say to Knight. "Michael was more talented than everybody else, his talent was far above the rest," Perkins said.

> Coach Knight had to put him in his place. He yelled at people he didn't like, and at guys who didn't give a hundred percent. We understood that. But then he yelled at Michael, 'You should be embarrassed the way you played!' I'm not surprised Michael didn't say anything back. He kind of cried. It was the first time Coach did that to him. And everybody was patting him on the back, saying, 'Don't worry about it.' We didn't think Michael played that bad, really. But that was us. Coach Knight knew what was in store. And it propelled Michael.

Wood, Perkins, and the others went to Jordan and told him to forget it, and the moment passed. Team USA had no other games that rankled Knight. He toppled a few paper cups, nothing more. Before the final against Spain, Knight found a note taped to the blackboard in the dressing room, and he would show it to friends for years to come: "Coach, after all the shit we've been through, there's no way we lose tonight," it said. The note was from Jordan. The Americans beat Spain again by 31 points for the gold medal.

Jordan and Perkins had survived Knight, each in his own way. Perkins was the good soldier. Jordan was the respected lieutenant who questioned orders from the general, then got the job done anyway. If this had been the NBA, years later, Jordan would have had Knight fired long before the Summer Games. But that was one of the reasons Knight wouldn't work with the pros. He always said he didn't want to coach players who earned more money than he did, who enjoyed the entitlements that came with the salary. Knight would never coach a player of Jordan's talents again. Then again, not many coaches would.

Embracing Defeat

They would deny it all to this day and then the day after that. The officials from the 1984 Houston Rockets will tell you that they were not dumping games at the end of that season, they were not obsessed with getting a top draft pick, and everybody else was just a conspiracy nut. "No coach of any integrity, which Bill Fitch was, would go ahead, monkey around, do something like that and last," said Ray Patterson, who was president and general manager of the Rockets in 1984. "The players would know he wasn't playing his best team, the press would know, the public would know. That whole thing got carried away."

Whether it was mythology, manipulation, or simple logic, the tanking theory became accepted as fact by practically everyone who closely watched the Rockets play a horrid and often unintentionally humorous version of professional basketball that March and April. Houston wasn't just losing games down the stretch; it was falling apart at the seams. The Rockets dropped 14 of their last 17 games, 9 of their last 10, and their final 5. And all the while, Fitch was distributing playing minutes in almost random fashion, like a broken lawn sprinkler. The players out there on the court were trying, certainly, and would gripe about the lineups together in the hotel bars at night. The beat writers simply laughed at the perceived shenanigans. And whenever people talked about the situation, the name Elvin Hayes inevitably entered the conversation at about the same moment that all eyebrows were raised skyward.

Hayes was once a wonderful player, a college star at the University of Houston who stopped Lew Alcindor's winning streak in the most famous college basketball game of all time, before 52,693 at the Astrodome on January 20, 1968. He had a lengthy NBA career, missed only 5 games in sixteen seasons, won a championship with the Bullets in 1978, and was now winding down his career at age thirty-eight. The Rockets had erred badly when they gave up on him back in 1972, trading him to Baltimore for Jack Marin and future considerations. By 1984, however, Hayes was a shadow of his old self, shooting around 40 percent from the field, galumphing up and down the court with a gait only vaguely reminiscent of his erstwhile acrobatic steps. Yet Fitch chose to use Hayes suddenly as if he were Larry Bird at his peak in Game 7 of the Finals. On April 13, the eighty-first game of the season against San Antonio, Hayes played all fifty-three minutes of a 129–128 overtime defeat in a game that Houston might have won—ruining everything—if Terry Teagle had buried a late jumper. Nobody played fifty-three minutes, ever. Hayes now had all the spring and fluidity of a bench, his usual resting place during regular season games. "Baseball's got Lou Gehrig and football has Jim Brown," Fitch declared at the time. "Elvin's got to be the iron man of basketball."

The box score went out across the country, further infuriating the likes of Dick Motta in Dallas and Pat Williams in Philadelphia, whose own draft positions were very much at stake. "Weird things were happening," recalled Williams, then general manager of the Philadelphia 76ers, who owned the rights to the Clippers' pick. "A lot of funny stuff going on, leaving a dark mark on the integrity of the game." Jack Ramsay, the coach of Portland, was sitting on a top pick from Indiana and felt the same way. "There was a lot of reason for concern, for suspicion," he said.

This controversy might have been avoided, if only the Rockets had performed as expected at the start of the season. Back in November 1983, they were not supposed to be vying for Olajuwon or Jordan but rather striving for greatness. They had won the pre-draft coin flip the previous spring, affording them the privilege of drafting Ralph Sampson, a sure-fire franchise maker. Sampson was seven feet, four inches, and could dribble the floor like a point guard, around the back and through the legs if necessary. He had been that way since his high school days in Harrisonburg, Virginia, a playmaker in a center's body. Sampson was expected to revolutionize his position, the way Magic Johnson had changed the scope and imagination of the point guard spot. Teamed in Houston with a pair of versatile six-foot-eight swingmen, Rodney McCray and Robert Reid, Sampson figured to restore the Rockets to contender status—a position they enjoyed until burly center Moses Malone was sent on September 15, 1982, to Philadelphia for Caldwell Jones and a draft pick originally belonging to the Cleveland Cavaliers, which was obtained by the Sixers in 1977.

The Malone affair had been an epic deal and one that completely remade a team already reinvented several times. Malone signed an offer sheet on September 2, 1982, with the Sixers for what amounted to anywhere from $11.2 to $13 million, depending on incentives, and the Rockets had fifteen days under league rules to match the offer. After talking with Malone, Houston ownership became convinced the star center preferred to play in Philadelphia. That was the company line, anyway. The cost of the contract was also intimidating. So Malone was traded to Philadelphia, where he immediately won the league's Most Valuable Player award and an NBA championship the next season. This did not go down well in Houston, where the Rockets suffered badly without a top center in 1982–83, finishing at 14–68, the worst record in the league by far. There was consolation, however. The

Rockets now owned their own first pick plus Cleveland's first pick, which translated into the first and third overall choices in the draft. This was an enviable and historically important situation. They chose Sampson and McCray with those two picks and were fully expected to make giant strides, perhaps even the playoffs, in 1983–84.

The best-laid plans fell apart, however. Sampson was not a bona fide center, not a leader. He was merely a very promising rookie, trying to find his place on the court. The Rockets struggled badly, and when the team fell to an 18–26 mark going into the All-Star break, it appeared that the franchise consciously shifted priorities, that officials decided they would stop trying so hard to win games and start focusing on re-building around the 1984 draft. Fran Blinebury, the *Houston Chronicle* beat writer at the time, believed this evaluation was made among the Rockets brass after the team lost by 29 points to the Lakers in Los Angeles, the final, depressing game before the All-Star break. "They got to Los Angeles, and that's where the plotting took place," Blinebury said. "Patterson, Fitch, and [chairman of the board] Charlie Thomas had a meeting, and what they said was, 'This isn't coming together.'"

Judging by the box scores and lineups, it certainly appeared the Rockets had a new set of aims. "The lineups they were trotting out after that, they were ridiculous," Blinebury said. "Elvin with 53 minutes? He looked like he needed an IV stuck in his arm out there."

Fitch insisted that this was nonsense and that his feelings were injured when his old rival, Motta, suggested the Rockets were manipulating games. "We were playing so bad, I think we lost two intra-squad games that year," said Fitch, retired and living in Texas. "But Dick Motta was a crybaby. He apologized to me later a bit for saying those things, though not much. I don't know what got into him. I think it was that I played Elvin Hayes a lot of minutes one night. Elvin had played for Dick [in Washington, from 1976–1980], and Dick just didn't like him a bit. But Elvin had the best year he'd ever had for me." Patterson, too, argued, "That was just sour grapes on Motta's part."

Fitch was on a crusade of sorts, he would say. He wanted to help Hayes reach the 50,000-minute mark in his NBA career, before Hayes officially retired at the end of the season. According to official records, he played a total of exactly 50,000 minutes in 1303 games. He played the first thirty-five minutes of the Rockets' final game in 1984 in order to reach the mark. But there was little reason for such devotion on Fitch's part, no obvious motive other than draft position. For one thing, 50,000 minutes was never considered a particularly notable achievement. The figure did not represent numerical immortality. Hayes was the first to reach 50,000, though Kareem Abdul-Jabbar (57,446) would soon surpass him. And when Abdul-Jabbar topped 50,000, the Lakers weren't immediately aware of it. After scanning old box scores, the team issued an announcement on February 21, 1986, that the event had already occurred, unnoticed. This was an obscure record in a sport that had never worshipped career-amassed numbers in the fashion of baseball. Basketball was more about the moment, the 100-point game, the championship trophy. And Fitch showed no interest in the 50,000 mark earlier in the season, when Hayes sat dolefully behind at least eight other players in the Rockets' rotation.

It was also tough to buy the notion of Fitch's benevolence in this matter, if only because he was unlikely to do Hayes any special favors. It was not just Motta who didn't particularly enjoy Hayes's company. The player had fashioned a second career—with the Rockets, the Bullets, and then the Rockets again—of alienating coaches and teammates alike. Hayes was a gunner by nature, which served him well on the court and not so well in the hearts and minds of peers. "One of the things that makes great athletes go is ego," Hayes once said. He warred with the likes of Wes Unseld, the rock of the Washington Bullets' championship team. "Fitch was no different than anybody else, they all hated him," Blinebury remarked. Hayes seemed to think he was an excellent role model and tutor for Sampson, and he often said as much. But back in 1983 Fitch privately admitted to pulling Sampson aside early on in training camp with some important words of advice: "You stay away from that no-good, fucking prick," Fitch said.

The final word on this whole controversy belonged to Frank Layden, the former Utah coach, who reported that a team official once admitted to him that there was, in fact, a scheme of sorts. "They were losing on purpose. That was told to me by one of their executives, that it was a business decision," said Layden, who would not identify the snitch. "And that's why we went to the lottery system. It's still going on a little bit today, anyway. People are saying, 'If I'm going to come in 28th, I might as well come in 30th and get more balls in the lottery.' Me, I never worried about draft position. I always figured if I had the first pick, I'd probably just take Joe Barry Carroll." Carroll was one of the most famous NBA flops, a center drafted with the first pick overall in 1980 by the Golden State Warriors, acquired when general manager Scotty Stirling traded both Robert Parish and the right to draft Kevin McHale to Boston. The Rockets had no intention of making such a stupid deal, however, in 1984. They had Olajuwon or Jordan squarely in their sights.

The NBA's image suffered a severe blow that spring from all the suspicious losing. It was difficult for anybody to comprehend how the Rockets could have such a terrible record. After all, they owned the unanimous Rookie of the Year selection at center, Sampson, who averaged 21 points, 11.1 rebounds, and about 2.4 blocks per game. They also had several other promising young players. The league was so concerned about the perceived chicanery that its board of governors instituted a lottery system weeks after the 1984 draft to assure such nonsense would never happen again. The reformed system offered the seven non-playoff teams an equal chance at the top pick, regardless of their records, in the form of a televised lottery. Ewing would be the first prize in 1985, and no amount of losing by the Golden State Warriors could help their cause. But that would be 1985, a different playing field.

In May 1984, the Rockets went into the coin flip knowing they'd take Olajuwon at number 1 if they won and Jordan at number 2 if they lost. This should not have been such an easy decision. Since the Rockets already had a young, standout center in Sampson, it made considerable sense to draft Jordan as a complement, even at the number 1 spot. But this was ultimately Fitch's call, and he was completely committed to the notion of a Twin Towers setup, which was a concept that intrigued him. It would be a challenge, surely. But Fitch had successfully devised a somewhat similar scheme in Boston, with giants Kevin McHale and Robert Parish. This was a time when the prevailing assumption held that the road to a title was constructed only by way of giant bodies. Red Auerbach, the renowned Celtic architect, was among those unable to envision a future of Michael Jordan and Scottie Pippen. He endorsed the notion of pairing Sampson and Olajuwon. "The days when you're going to win with ten Oscar Robertsons or Jerry Wests are over," he told the *New York Times*. "Oh, you'll win a few games. But you'll always win with ten Bill Russells. Plus, you need more than one big man. A guy can go down. Or over the course of the season and the playoffs, he'll get tired." Fitch, who worked under Auerbach for four seasons in Boston, echoed that sentiment. "You can't pass up a great player at the big position for a great player at another position," he declared. "History bears that out."

There were other reasons why Fitch leaned in the Olajuwon direction, away from Jordan. As much as he liked Jordan and trusted Dean Smith's judgment about the guard, Fitch was never the greatest believer in Sampson. Fitch was an old-school guy from Cedar Rapids, Iowa, who liked his players tough and mean. In the parlance of the game, Sampson was "soft," less likely to intimidate opponents with a scowl and a sneer, not about to elbow someone in the face or slam somebody to the floor in the lane to make a statement. Sampson wasn't Moses Malone or Parish. When Sampson finally lost his temper and struck somebody in a famous on-court incident, he threw an unfortunate punch at little Jerry Sichting, fifteen inches shorter, during Game 5 of the 1986 NBA finals against the Boston Celtics. In Olajuwon, Fitch saw a more conventional center and a tougher player. The coach figured he would ask Sampson to move to power forward, where the player might use his quickness better and grow more comfortable.

There was also the parochial factor in selecting Olajuwon, a matter of making things right by the local fan base. "There was never a doubt we'd take Hakeem," Patterson said. "He was the hometown guy." A year earlier, Fitch had selected McCray behind Sampson with the Rockets' second, first-round pick in the draft, number 3 overall. He ignored Clyde Drexler, the talented and popular shooting guard from the University of Houston. Fitch had turned his back once already on a big part of Phi Slamma Jamma. "After that, if we didn't take Olajuwon, the people of Houston would have burned down my house," Fitch said. One of the few voices in opposition to the Olajuwon selection was Hayes, the very same man who had helped the Rockets attain that first pick. Hayes was retiring, so this wasn't a self-serving opinion. If it were up to him, Hayes said, he would choose Jordan, "as fast as I could get the words out of my mouth."

The Rockets still had another, more imaginative option—a trade of Sampson for Jordan, straight up—leaving the Rockets with Olajuwon at center, and Jordan at shooting guard, in a more conventional lineup. But the deal was dismissed as soon as it was brought up among Houston executives. It never was discussed seriously, because trading Sampson was a responsibility not even Fitch dared assume. Sampson had been too good his rookie season, and he was just too tall to exchange for a guard. So the Rockets went ahead and took Olajuwon, while Fitch rolled up his sleeves and prepared for the challenge of fitting two giant bodies into one lane. If he succeeded, Fitch knew, this could be a brand new kind of championship team.

9

Finishing the Picasso

The NBA family was still a cozy one back in 1984, sometimes a bit too snug, chock full of incestuous friendships and conflicts of interest at the executive level. The New Jersey Nets, for example, were owned by a group of businessmen with close ties to Alan Cohen, who was previously a Madison Square Garden executive and later became co-owner of the Boston Celtics. Even after he had left for Boston, Cohen would occasionally suggest a hire. According to one former New Jersey coach, Dave Wohl, the Nets would leap through hoops to heed Cohen's advice. But even by those standards, it is now hard in retrospect to comprehend the convoluted scandal that struck the Portland Trail Blazers in 1984, leading up to the NBA draft coin flip in May.

Alan Rothenberg, then president of the San Diego Clippers, was somehow enlisted by Portland to put out feelers to Hakeem Olajuwon and Patrick Ewing, two superstar juniors debating whether to come out early. Rothenberg, an attorney, was to explain the salary cap so that these players could make more reasoned decisions. That was the theory, anyway. Rothenberg met with Michael McKenzie, Olajuwon's agent, and Pat Ellis, Olajuwon's attorney, on April 17. Soon after, Rothenberg met with John Thompson, Ewing's coach at Georgetown, during the U.S. Olympic trials in Bloomington. Originally, the Blazers used Rothenberg's nonaffiliation with Portland as something of a cover for their misdeeds. Larry Weinberg, owner of the team, released a disingenuous statement on May 7: "No member of the Portland Trail Blazers has made an offer to, or been in touch with, Akeem Olajuwon or Patrick Ewing or their agents, if they have any."

The Oregonian in Portland was the first media outlet to report the meetings and to quote Blazer vice president Harry Glickman admitting that Rothenberg represented Portland at the sessions. "He was working for the Trail Blazers," Glickman said. "[McKenzie and Ellis] wanted to talk to the two teams that were going to draft Olajuwon. They wanted to advise Olajuwon about coming out and they wanted to know what the implications of the cap were."

The New York Post reported the Blazers had come to a tentative agreement with Olajuwon, offering him a conditional $1.2 million per year if they drafted him. Clearly, it would greatly benefit the Blazers if both seven-foot All Americans, Olajuwon and Ewing, came out of college for the draft. In that way, the team would be guaranteed the opportunity to draft either Olajuwon or Ewing as the number 2 pick, in case the Blazers lost the coin flip. The league also investigated reports that the Houston Rockets had done more or less the same thing. It was found, however, that Rockets' officials had called off a meeting with Olajuwon's advisers once they discovered those representatives were not prepared to provide a letter stating that Olajuwon officially had renounced his NCAA eligibility.

There was considerable concern in Portland during the probe by NBA security chief Jack Joyce. A tough precedent had been set back in 1975, when then-commissioner Lawrence O'Brien stripped the New York Knicks of a first-round draft pick as penalty for tampering with and illegally signing forward George McGinnis—whose NBA rights belonged to the Philadelphia 76ers. The Blazers this time appeared to violate an NBA bylaw, Rule 6.05, that stated, "Prior to 45 days before the annual draft meeting, members may not, directly or indirectly, have or engage in, or attempt to have or engage in, any discussions, communications or contacts whatsoever with any player who has remaining basketball eligibility or is otherwise ineligible to be selected in such annual draft."

Harry Glickman, vice president of the Blazers, told the *Oregonian* that the Blazers had informed the NBA about Rothenberg's meeting. "Nobody negotiated any contract with them," he said. "According to our interpretation of Rule 6.05, we didn't do anything wrong."

David Stern was curiously uncurious about Rothenberg's double-dealings on behalf of another franchise. "People could function as lawyers for others," he said. But when it came to tampering with the college ranks, the commissioner clearly wanted to protect his golden goose. Stern sent a strong message to the ranks by fining the Trail Blazers $250,000, a gigantic sum in those times. The investigation had shown, Stern said in a brief statement, that Portland "did not conduct any contract negotiations and engaged only in general discussions of NBA procedures." But the commissioner added that "this penalty should serve as notice to all NBA teams that any future violations of this rule will not be tolerated."

McKenzie insisted that this was all nonsense, that Rothenberg had not enticed Olajuwon to come out at all. The whole mess was terribly embarrassing to Trail Blazer ownership, which was soon to lose the coin toss on top of everything else. But at least they still owned that precious first-round pick, the one the Blazers received in an opportunistic 1981 trade with Indiana for Tom Owens—a clunky center who would average just 10.5 points and 5 rebounds in 74 games for the Pacers before he was traded again to Detroit. In order to put a happy face on the affair, Glickman announced that the franchise had been absolved of the worst charges and that it was now only looking ahead to the flip.

"The real difference between our position and that of the commissioner is one of semantics," Glickman said. "We never once thought we were doing something wrong. As far as I'm concerned, we've been exonerated of the charge that was made, and I think that's what the commissioner found. We have been sidetracked long enough. We are excited about the coin flip. Win or lose, Portland will draft a player who should substantially improve our team."

This had all been a difficult and distasteful affair for Stern, who was a close friend of Weinberg until this decision. The investigation and fine drove a wedge between the two. "It put a whole lot of pressure on that friendship," Stern admitted. "But if we were going to have rules, then I was going to be commissioner. What happened in my view was not acceptable. I thought he should have known what was allowed and not allowed. We had to make certain the rewards [of such an intervention] was not worth the risk."

The tempest and probe had been enough to postpone that coin flip from May 10 to May 22. Stu Inman, the team's director of personnel, was standing nervously down the hallway from David Stern's office when the Blazers lost that flip. "What good would I have done in there?" he said. When the coin came up heads, Inman understood there would be no simple choice, no Olajuwon. It would be up to Inman to make certain this precious number 2 pick in the draft was used to cement the team's future. And it was over the next few weeks when one of the most respected talent evaluators in the league made arguably the greatest blunder in NBA history.

Two decades later, now in his eighties, Inman knew all too well that his remarkable executive career had been tainted by one draft pick in 1984 and its destructive impact on a franchise. Inman was a basketball man from the start, a kid who grew up in San Francisco admiring future Hall of Famer Jim Pollard. As a young teen, Inman would go see the star player at Oakland Technical High School in the late 1930s. Long before Billy Cunningham ever came around, Pollard was the original "Kangaroo Kid." He moved with great velocity about the court and possessed a remarkable jumper from the corner. Pollard went on to lead Stanford to a national championship in 1942, though he missed the final game against Dartmouth due to the flu. He went off to war, returned to San Francisco State, and eventually became a Minneapolis Laker. Inman followed Pollard's every career move before he made any of his own. Inman played forward for San Jose State from 1946–1950, and he played some serious AAU ball with the likes of another all-time great, George Yardley.

Inman coached at San Jose State and eventually took over from Rolland Todd in 1972 as interim coach of the Blazers, 56 games into that franchise's second season. The season ended in a dismal 18–64 mark. Portland had a decent inaugural year in 1970–71 as an expansion team, the best of the three clubs that came into the league at the same time. The Blazers finished 29–53, while Buffalo was 22–60 and Cleveland finished 15–67. There were embarrassing moments in Portland, like a 52-point loss to Baltimore. But the team ended the schedule with a 6–6 run, and there was little doubt that the community was embracing its only big-time pro franchise. The next season, though, the defeats grew tiresome. Inman still remembers his one great moment as coach, when Red Holzman brought his wonderful team into Portland for the Knicks' fifth game in seven nights. "We clobbered them," Inman said. And afterward, Inman joked to Holzman, 'If you treat me right, I'll teach you my secrets.'"

In the course of his long career Inman would work as a general manager or personnel director for the Milwaukee Bucks and Miami Heat. In 1984 he was very much in charge of the Blazers' scouting and drafting operations, with assistant Bucky Buckwalter and coach Jack Ramsay. Glickman trusted Inman, giving him plenty of space. "A great guy to work for," Inman said of Glickman. Inman had authority, and he was considered, arguably, the best personnel man in the league. He was so good, so respected, that other clubs would track his scouting missions and listen very carefully to rumors about which players might interest him. "Stu, in the subculture of basketball gurus, was near the apex," said Norm Sonju, president of the Mavericks. "He was considered a genius. And this was his defining moment on the wrong side of the ledger. What I've learned in basketball is there are no geniuses, and that it's very hard to know the heart of a person being drafted."

With all this leeway, all this authority and respect from peers, Inman went about his job of deciding that Sam Bowie was the better pick than Michael Jordan. Before one condemns the decision as utter folly, it is important to appreciate the Blazers' situation that spring of 1984 and to understand the distorted glimpses Inman had of Jordan.

Portland was a proud and healthy franchise at this time, already NBA champion in 1977, selling out its building for the 300th consecutive game on March 3, 1984, near the end of the regular season. The Blazers had a strong year, their best in seven seasons, finishing at 48–34, and were certainly among the most fun teams to watch now that they had added the smooth shooting guard, Clyde Drexler, from Houston with the fourteenth pick in the 1983 draft. The Rockets had been under great pressure to pick Drexler in that draft, but Fitch was adamant that he wanted a bigger player, Rodney McCray, with the third overall choice. Drexler fell to Portland, and so Fitch's decision directly led Inman to pass on Jordan in the next draft for fear of overlapping talents.

The Blazers at this time were a team with successful chemistry but without much star power. They played up-tempo and had a potent offense, averaging 108.1 points per game. Back in November, they had beaten the Denver Nuggets, 156–116, in one of those crazy Western Conference games that made East Coast fans shrug with incomprehension. The Blazers were led by Jim Paxson, a somewhat stagnant shooting guard with a tremendous shooting touch (51.4 percent from the field) and a 21.3-point scoring average. Paxson had just enough of a first step to create his own shot, and then he usually sank it. Darnell Valentine and Fat Lever shared the playmaking load. Mychal Thompson, Calvin Natt, Kenny Carr, and Wayne Cooper took care of the interior work, outworking and out-rebounding opponents. Clyde Drexler was still a hopeful project, Paxson's understudy, after a promising rookie year. This was a delicate balance and one that worked to a degree. But Portland was not in love with Thompson, who was viewed as more of a backup despite starter numbers. He'd had a satisfying all-around season, averaging 15.7 points, 8.7 rebounds, and 3.9 assists. He was still young enough at twenty-nine. He wasn't a giant, though, at six feet, ten inches. Inman and team officials were quite certain that a lack of size contributed to their first-round, five-game playoff defeat to the Phoenix Suns. The Blazers had captured that championship back in 1977 on the back of Bill Walton, and they did not think they would ever repeat such a run without a big horse in the middle.

"I have no excuse in that area," Inman said, though he had a couple of explanations for his obsession with largeness, his blind spot to the magnificent Jordan. Inman, like most everyone else, didn't know how good Jordan could be and didn't know what to do with him. "He had played at North Carolina with Dean Smith, and his talent was hidden there," Inman said.

Inman had other chances to recognize Jordan's magic. Bobby Knight asked him to speak with the players who were at the Olympic trials in Bloomington, to give them a talk about the NBA. So Inman came, and he watched Jordan play for ten days in a row. Ten days of practices, scrimmages, fast breaks, and dunks. Jordan was clearly a great talent, but Jordan was still trying to fit into a system, and Inman could not be sure that he would be a breakout NBA talent. Knight, like Smith, did not countenance superstars.

"Even on that team, he was hidden," Inman said. "You never questioned the guy was very good. But I wondered, 'Where's he going to play?'"

Inman laughed at his own comments now, which he knew sounded ridiculous. "I really did great with that one, didn't I?" he said. "I'll tell all the jokes on myself, because I know them. I made Rod Thorn's career." Back in 1984, Inman said, there was a different mentality, and he was trapped inside it. The Celtics were winning with that big frontcourt of Kevin McHale, Larry Bird, and Robert Parish. The Lakers had Kareem Abdul-Jabbar. Before them, there had been the Russell-Chamberlain era. Everyone thought a franchise center was requisite for a title team, and the Blazers didn't have one. How could they waste their pick on a shooting guard, no matter how good? Jordan would change that philosophy soon enough. He would force personnel directors and general managers to think more like the fans, who instinctively understood that passion and sheer, hot talent always trumped convenience. The best available athlete was the best available pick. Not in Inman's heyday, though.

"You start watching Magic Johnson, he has that high bounce on his dribble, he's not a guard or a power forward and you wonder, 'Where do you play him?'" Inman said. "You get lured into that silly mentality. Then you realize a player like Magic has as much or more inside him than physical prowess. Magic and Larry Bird, they were all physically gifted, but so much more. Bill Russell, what do you like about him? He had a bad body, 6–9, too small for the NBA, can't shoot the ball, can't pass. All he does is kill you. We did a pretty good job with scouting, but we never measured what the inside of a champion looks like."

Inman knew where he would play Sam Bowie. He looked at films and scouted him directly. Inman typically watched a player early in the season, then away from home in conference games, then in some NCAA tournament games to form an idea of how the player had matured over the season and performed under pressure. Inman was satisfied on all these accounts. He just needed to make certain that Bowie's legs would hold together. The Blazers talked with team doctors in Lexington, with doctors down in Memphis, where Bowie had his most recent operation. They performed their own examination, as well. "We did everything we could on his background," Inman said. Even then, in the spring of 1984, Inman knew this decision was no slam dunk. "We do our investigation as thoroughly as anyone," he said then, "and yet we are fully aware that the evaluation process is a difficult one, this year particularly, because Sam played on the perimeter and not in the middle. He is a very quick kid. He has enormous defensive potential, an intimidator, as such. He's a good scorer and an excellent passer. I wouldn't rate him as an exceptional shooter. He's very upbeat, a kid who will play more harmoniously in structure than away from structure and Jack Ramsay runs a structured system."

It was Inman's call. He would gather his scouts, his coaches, ask their opinions, and keep them up to date. "All of our scouts, every one, would have been involved in scouting at games and practice," Inman said. "I was young enough then to travel around, I was a similar age to coaches in the college ranks, and you were welcome then to come to practice, have coffee, get game films." Everybody agreed on this pick—Ramsay, Buckwalter, Glickman. Everybody was excited to apply that final brushstroke to the canvas, to complete the Picasso. "There was no dissent whatsoever, but the coaches would not have known enough because they weren't scouting," Inman said. From what the others saw, this all made sense. Proof came in the biggest showdown. Bowie had more than held his own against Olajuwon back in January at Lexington, when the Kentucky center grabbed 18 rebounds and held Olajuwon to 14 points in an easy Wildcat victory. "It was a difficult decision, but we had to do what was best for the franchise," Buckwalter said. "We all loved Michael. But no one could have predicted how good he was going to be. I don't think Michael thought he would be as good as he turned out."

Bowie came to Portland on May 24 for a physical exam, days after the Blazers lost the coin flip. Doctors scoured the bone graft he received to treat the shin fracture that forced him to miss two seasons.

Even before officials knew the results of the exam, they were fairly set on Bowie, very hopeful. Portland owner Larry Weinberg was the only one hedging, hinting that Michael Jordan was still under consideration. His staff was dead set on Bowie, however. They were now even saying Bowie might be a better choice than Olajuwon.

"Olajuwon is going to need a lot of work," Ramsay said, in an Associated Press interview. "Bowie needs less of that. Bowie is the more complete ballplayer. Olajuwon is more spectacular and his skills around the basket are excellent, but Bowie's all-around game is probably better than Akeem's all-around game."

Joe B. Hall, the coach at Kentucky, stubbornly but honestly enough, wouldn't attest to the health of Bowie's leg. He was no doctor, he said. Hall gave Bowie a strong recommendation in all other matters. "Ability to play I can discuss," Hall said. "He has the completeness to play. The intelligent play Ramsay requires is the style Sam gave us. He learns well. He fits into an intricate patterned system." Hall was complimenting himself, of course, as much as he was complimenting Bowie.

There was another reason for the Blazers to draft Bowie, a matter of sheer convenience. Personnel matters were getting complicated because of the new salary cap, and Larry Fleisher represented both Bowie and Paxson, who had become a free agent. This could become sort of a one-stop shop. Portland could quickly sign Bowie, then match another team's offer for Paxson, while dealing with the same cooperative representative. In retrospect, Ramsay, the Portland coach who became a respected TV analyst, knew later that the Blazers should have drafted Jordan, then signed and traded Paxson and Clyde Drexler for a center. "Oh, sure, you can second-guess yourself forever," Ramsay said. "Those things change your life, but there's nothing you can do about it. You look ahead, not back. Nobody thought Michael would be Michael. It's hard to evaluate players when they're playing with their peers in college. We needed a center, and we were only interested in three guys: There was Olajuwon. There was Bowie. And at the time, there was a lot of thinking that Patrick Ewing might come out a year early from Georgetown. All our talks centered around those three guys."

Ewing, fresh off an NCAA championship and a tangential part of this story, stuck it out another season at Georgetown for his mother and for his coach, John Thompson. The Portland players had mixed feelings about the Bowie pick, largely dependent on their own selfish interests. Mychal Thompson, Portland's talented but stopgap center, thought Bowie was a lousy pick and that the Blazers should take Jordan. "We don't need another big man," he said at the time. Drexler, a shooting guard like Jordan, thought Bowie was the right move.

None of this mattered. Inman had decided on Bowie. And if Bowie was going to be the center of the future for the Blazers, then the rest of the team would be molded accordingly. Bowie would bring an interior presence on defense and take care of much of the rebounding load. So a week before the draft, Inman dealt his bulldog of a forward, Calvin Natt, plus a backup center, Joe Cooper, and a backup guard, Lafayette Lever, to Denver for Kiki Vandeweghe, considered a soft player with a gorgeous jumper. Vandeweghe and Clyde Drexler would now take care of the scoring. Bowie, with an assist from Mychal Thompson, would do the dirty work inside where Natt had excelled. Darnell Valentine would take over most playmaking duties.

The Blazers had other important picks in this draft, and these days Inman understandably prefers to speak about those. They offered a bit of redemption, a clue to the personnel director's overall successes. For one thing, Inman was one of the very few to show a real interest in John Stockton. Stockton was practically a local kid, and Inman had watched him closely. Inman even brought him into Portland for a second look. "It was easy to fall in love with John," Inman said. "There was something about the spirit of this kid." Inman thought there was a "quickness" to him. He rated Stockton above average as a player. Some scouts were warning Inman that Stockton couldn't really shoot and that his foot speed, in a straight-out sprint, was questionable. But that did not trouble Inman. "It's the same things they were saying about Larry Bird: 'He can't jump. He labors changing ends of the court,'" Inman said. He used to tell his scouts, "There's something wrong with everybody." He wanted instead to hear about the positive things.

Inman saw the big upside in Stockton. But the Blazers were picking nineteenth, and Utah was at number 16. The Jazz plucked Stockton before Inman could draft him. Inman would call Frank Layden from Utah minutes after the draft.

"What in the world are you going to do with Stockton?" Inman asked.

"Well, we're going to keep him," Layden responded.

"I thought he was trying to bamboozle us," Inman said. Layden wouldn't let go of the pick, and so the Blazers finally took a six-foot-six swingman, Bernard Thompson from California State–Fresno.

The draft droned on, and this was where Inman would catch his peers asleep at the switch. While the pool of available talent was arguably the best in history, it was never considered particularly deep. Somehow, Inman paid enough attention to grab Jerome Kersey from little Longwood University in Farmville, Virginia, with the forty-sixth pick overall, the Blazers' fifth pick in the draft. Kersey was a six-foot-seven small forward with a pro's body, but only Inman, NBA super scout Marty Blake, and a few others knew much about him. Kersey would play eleven years with Portland, seventeen years and 1,153 games altogether in the NBA. He would score nearly 12,000 points and pull down more than 6,000 rebounds. At his peak in 1987–88, this late second-round draft pick would average 19.2 points and 8.3 rebounds per game.

Kersey was a real find, a gem. Bowie would prove to be something else.

(10)

Liking Mike

Rod Thorn was blessed with an unlimited capacity to laugh both loudly and painfully at his own gaffes. It was his relatively humble West Virginia beginnings that inspired such self-deprecation, along with one season of college basketball practices he had spent chasing around a teammate, Jerry West.

Thorn grew up a lanky, athletic kid, an only child driven by a no-nonsense father, Joe, who practically ran the town of Princeton, West Virginia, back in the '50s. Princeton was the Mercer County seat but had precious few demographics in common with its affluent New Jersey namesake. The town's official census of 2,243 was first taken in 1840, when the place was named in honor of General Hugh Mercer of Fredericksburg, who died during the Revolutionary War at the Battle of Princeton, New Jersey. Confederate troops burned the settlement down to the ground during the Civil War to keep Union soldiers from pilfering supplies. It was little more than a ghost town until 1908, when the Virginia railroad reached its borders and brought with it plenty of new jobs. The town bustled and expanded with this business, then stalled. Princeton's population has shrunk in recent years to its current level of about 6,300. One-third of the mostly blue-collar town has not graduated from high school, and only 12 percent earned a bachelor's degree from college. Its average household income is about $22,000. The town has a tourist center, a courthouse, a Vietnam Memorial, and a shopping mall.

The Devil Rays of the Appalachian League, a minor league baseball franchise, also make their home in Princeton. And more than sixty years ago, Joe Thorn played on a different team in the St. Louis Cardinals' farm system, before his career was cut short in an unexpected and violent manner. When World War II broke out, Joe was shipped to the Pacific and then was shot in the finger at Iwo Jima. He lay wounded on the beach for a day before somebody found him. He could no longer play baseball, so he returned home and became chief of police back in Princeton, where his farming family owned considerable land. He married Jackie, a third-grade teacher at Thorn School (no coincidence—this was Thorn property, too).

Their son, Rod, demonstrated a natural bent for sports, and his father supervised the kid's evolution. Joe had never played basketball, but he coached the town's travel team. Rod was a star from the moment he started playing at age six. He made varsity his freshman year at Princeton High School. He was All-State his sophomore, junior, and senior years. Colleges in the South—colleges everywhere—took notice.

"I could have gone almost anywhere I wanted," Thorn remembered. His final decision came down to Duke and West Virginia. Thorn chose to stay closer to home, to remain the local hero. But there was another star on that West Virginia team who was even better. Thorn was a talented freshman with the Mountaineers when Jerry West already was an other-worldly senior. West would take him to school in that Morgantown gym, run Thorn ragged with an intermediate-range game that Thorn would try to emulate himself, then desperately try to rediscover in one of his players as an NBA executive. Thorn never found anybody like West, though—not until 1984.

Thorn would tell these tales on himself, with his West Virginia twang, about how West made him look just plain silly in front of all their teammates. "JEH-Ree-West" sounded like the name of a single, three-syllable god coming from Thorn, like a deity in the fashion of Jehovah. At the mere mention of this Supreme Basketball Being, Thorn would drop his jaw all over again in amazement. Even his laugh had a twang, and it was entirely infectious. It was this ability to accept his own limitations that had kept Thorn relatively sane in the face of some stunning, disheartening setbacks during his seven seasons as general manager with the sad-sack Chicago Bulls.

During the 1983–84 season, another in a long series of bad spells, the Bulls were losing a ton of games and drawing flies, averaging fewer than seven thousand fans. The Bulls didn't have much of a profile in Chicago. They were a low-rise, low-rent flat on the skyline. And Thorn was all too aware that his high draft picks from previous college drafts were doing nothing to alleviate the problem.

To some degree, these failures were understandable. At the time the draft was more of a crapshoot than it is now, because there were fewer scouts and almost no game films available. Pat Williams, general manager for Philadelphia, had this theory that they should let players into the NBA for a couple of years, then hold the draft after everybody knew how good they really were. "Not a single GM would get fired, ever," Williams said. Without such an edge, Thorn's selections had ranged from mediocre to disastrous, and his luck was even worse. He'd lost the coin flip to the Lakers in 1979, when Magic Johnson was the first pick. Thorn had traveled with great hopes to New York City that day, with the eyes of Chicago upon him, and called "tails" in the NBA commissioner's office. Traditionally, optimists called "heads." But Thorn was a contrarian by nature. He had been lucky all his life with tails, and of course it came back to bite him badly. If Magic had gone to Chicago, the league's entire history would have been rewritten, great rivalries redrawn. As it turned out, the Lakers won five championships in the '80s and the Bulls got stuck with that great disappointment, David Greenwood.

What could he do? Nothing. That was just rotten fortune, Thorn figured. But the pick that really irked him, the one that kept him up nights and caused substantial self-flagellation, was the 1982 selection of shooting guard Quintin Dailey from the University of San Francisco. Dailey was a supremely talented guard, and in a basketball sense he was a logical choice as the sixth overall pick, even ahead of the next choice, solid forward Clark Kellogg. But Thorn ignored a bunch of red flags and off-court problems that made Dailey a dangerous selection. By the time the Bulls tabbed him on draft day, Dailey had been charged with attacking a student nurse in a dorm room on the San Francisco campus. Eventually, Dailey would negotiate an out-of-court settlement with the woman, but some public contrition was demanded if this rookie were to gain acceptance in Chicago. Instead, Dailey demonstrated something best described not as defiance but as indifference. A sincere statement of apology or remorse might have gone a long way. It was not forthcoming. When Chicago sportswriters asked Dailey on draft day if he regretted some of his actions, Dailey responded, "No. I am just going to put that whole thing behind me and concentrate on playing basketball for the Bulls and having a long, successful career."

By the time he played his first game with the Bulls in the fall, women's groups were picketing outside Chicago Stadium, and Thorn was hunkered down in his office, already ruing his decision. Dailey would go on to have drug and weight problems in a long but largely wasted career, while Thorn would be terribly embarrassed by the whole episode. "If I'd only known some of those things . . . ," he would say, as much to himself as to anybody listening. In the process of making this and other ill-conceived picks, Thorn had missed out on Sidney Moncrief in 1979, Kiki Vandeweghe in 1980, both Tom Chambers and Rolando Blackman in 1981, and then Clyde Drexler in 1983. His roster might have been considerably stronger, though not quite championship caliber.

As he evaluated this promising but murky draft arriving in June 1984, Thorn felt the weight of past misjudgments on his shoulders. He had fired a coach, Jerry Sloan, who was one of the best teachers in the business. There was the Dailey fiasco to overcome, along with several other draft selections that had not quite turned out as planned. Thorn chose Sidney Green as his first pick in 1983, and the burly Green had hardly torn up the league his rookie season. He'd also used the fourth overall pick in 1980 for Kelvin Ransey, then immediately traded Ransey to Portland for an Iowa guard named Ronnie Lester. Lester was already a physical mess when he got to Chicago, and he never overcame injury problems. That was yet another lesson Thorn brought with him to the 1984 draft: no more injury-prone players like Lester, and no more problem players, like Dailey. Thorn had a decent relationship with the owners in Chicago, but he was at the end of his rope. He sensed that his job was very much on the line with this decision.

The Olajuwon Draft had been hyped and viewed with great anticipation for nearly a year. Most people did not yet realize that the pool of eligible juniors and seniors included other franchise makers, as well. Everybody, including the Bulls, wanted the number 1 pick, envisioning an instant change in fortune. And like the Rockets, the Bulls lost big down the stretch that spring. They dropped 14 of their final 15 games, including their last 5. Thorn insisted all along that he and his coach, Kevin Loughery, were doing nothing fishy, that they just stunk.

"I'm superstitious enough to believe that if you don't try your best, something bad is going to happen to you," Thorn said. But near the end of the season, Chicago was definitely snatching key defeats from potentially disastrous victories. The Bulls were on a six-game losing streak when they visited New York to begin an early April home-and-home set, in a virtual tie with Cleveland in that race to finish lower and get a higher pick. Madison Square Garden was practically empty. Orlando Woolridge, one of the team's top players and arguably the only reason to watch the Bulls, was sitting out with an injury, raising more eyebrows around the league. The Knicks were having a solid season (they finished at 47–35) and were jockeying for playoff position. This figured to be a blowout for the home team, a game that most New York fans decided was eminently missable. Somehow, a hard-fought contest broke out. Dailey was ridiculously hot, scoring 44 points on 17-of-26 shooting. Here was a potential upset that might gravely wound Chicago's draft position.

In the final seconds, however, the Bulls' Steve Johnson was called for goaltending on a Marvin Webster shot. Webster's shots rarely went in of their own accord, rendering this goaltending violation particularly noteworthy. It would be a great stretch, however, to claim conspiracy. Johnson was not nearly coordinated enough to plan and carry out such a violation at a moment's notice. The Knicks won by that basket, 115–113. The Bulls then went back home and rolled over in the rematch, 113–96. Chicago would finish at 27–55, one game behind the Cavaliers, sneaking into that number 3 draft spot ahead of the Mavericks, who owned Cleveland's pick. The Bulls would not get Olajuwon. There was no sense in scouting him. Instead, Thorn faced a dilemma: Should he pick the best available athlete, Michael Jordan, or should he instead follow conventional wisdom at the time and choose the best big man?

For many years, Thorn had preached the big-man philosophy to everyone, including the ownership of the Bulls. But now, as he looked over the landscape of this draft, Thorn no longer believed that big was the best way to go—not if Chicago couldn't draft Olajuwon. Thorn carefully considered the four big men who might be available: Bowie from Kentucky, a wonderful passing center in the mold of Bill Walton but whose leg already had been shattered once; Perkins, a solid, unspectacular six-foot-nine frontcourt star from North Carolina; Barkley, who was only big (six-foot-five, 260 pounds) around the waist; and Mel "Dinner Bell" Turpin, a talented six-foot-eleven player from Kentucky whose nickname more or less told you about his own projected weight problems.

Since the players didn't visit franchises as they do today, Thorn occasionally went on his own cross-country informational treks. He had gone a few years back with Jerry Sloan to see Magic Johnson and his coach at Michigan State, Jud Heathcote. He had traveled to see Tom Chambers in Utah, to San Francisco to visit with Bill Cartwright, to Oregon State to see Steve Johnson. This time, he went to Lexington and chatted with Bowie and Turpin. "Bowie was very sharp," Thorn said. "Turpin was not quite as sharp." Whatever small interest Thorn had in the pudgy player was diminished further by Joe B. Hall, who told tales out of school about how Turpin had sneaked pizzas up to his dorm room, by way of a rope out the window, when he had been placed on a strict diet.

Past experience, and a sudden surge of caution, greatly benefited Thorn. Despite the fine impression that Bowie had made, Thorn wanted no part of him because of what happened to the injury-prone Lester. Nobody knew what to make of Barkley, a six-foot-five post player. In Thorn's mind, the choice was really between Jordan and Perkins, and Thorn just wasn't all that impressed with Perkins. After watching North Carolina game films to scout Jordan, Thorn came to believe that Perkins was not truly an explosive power forward. He would not turn around a franchise that required a gigantic burst of energy.

Jordan was another matter. Thorn had followed the player's very public successes for some time, since he had played in a high school all-star game in Washington called the Capital Classic. Jordan didn't have a very good game that night, but Bob Ferry, the Bullets general manager, watched some of the practices and told Thorn that this kid was clearly the best player on the team, performing impossible tricks at practice. Thorn tucked that deep inside his brain. Then when Thorn traveled down to Chapel Hill on scouting missions, Dean Smith handed him the tapes of all the Atlantic Coast Conference games to watch on those new-fangled VCR gizmos. This was no small deal, because there was a real paucity of such game films in this pre-ESPN era. And Smith talked up Jordan like crazy.

Thorn did not think Jordan was quite as spectacular as Smith trumpeted—"I wish I could claim to be that prescient," he said—but the game films that Thorn watched highlighted an intensely competitive, athletic talent. Jordan's jumper wasn't very good yet. "Nothing broken, but nothing special," Thorn remarked. What Thorn saw, though, were a few moves that were unrecognizable, brand new. The Bulls' GM had experienced this sort of phenomenon before. As an assistant coach with the New York Nets of the American Basketball Association, he had watched Julius Erving patent his own gymnastics. Kevin Loughery, coach of the Bulls, had been the head coach of those Nets. Together, Thorn and Loughery had marveled at the uniqueness of such a natural talent. "Four or five times a game, you'd look at Julius and you'd shake your head and say, 'How did he do that?'" Thorn said. Like Jordan in his early years, Erving didn't have a great jumper, either. He never needed one. Although Jordan didn't look quite as special as Erving on these tapes that Thorn reviewed, the player provided some extraordinary moments, glints of a blinding future. It was decided, then: Jordan would be Thorn's pick.

Again, this was a different era, at least a decade removed from the cynical time when a general manager had to worry about whether an athlete would be willing to play for his team if drafted. Years later, Kobe Bryant would enter the pros out of high school and warn the New Jersey Nets that they had better not draft him, because he would sit out or travel to Europe rather than perform in East Rutherford. Today, draft prospects travel around the country to audition for team officials, and during these visits athletes give off positive or negative vibes, sending meta- or mega-messages about whether they will play hard for certain franchises. That was not the case with Jordan. He never traveled to Chicago, and Thorn never really interviewed him about his feelings on the Bulls. Jordan would likely be happy enough with Chicago. The place was a large, untapped basketball market, a fresh alternative to the established dynasties of Boston on the East Coast and Los Angeles on the West. The Bulls had plenty of money, too. Their owners ranged from William Wirtz, who owned Chicago Stadium and the Chicago Blackhawks, to a minority partner named George Steinbrenner. Jordan and his growing number of handlers, including agent David Falk and his sponsor Nike, preferred Chicago to the alternatives, Portland or Dallas. Here was a super-sized city lacking in superstars. The loyal citizens here were still busy idolizing long-retired Ernie Banks of the Cubbies, in the absence of another sports hero.

For Thorn, then, it was just a matter of waiting, of figuring out whether Jordan would fall to the Bulls. When Ewing decided to stay at Georgetown, rather than enter the draft, Thorn had his doubts that the Bulls would get their shot at Jordan. Portland owned the number 2 pick. The Blazers could pick Bowie. They could pick Jordan. They could make a deal.

Rumors have always flown around the NBA as they do in no other sport, and soon word was out that the Blazers' director of player personnel, Stu Inman, was leaning toward Bowie. Portland already had a fine backcourt in Clyde Drexler and Jim Paxson. Inman was trying to complete his masterpiece, finish the picture with the versatile big man in the middle who had been missing since Bill Walton was crippled with injuries. But would Inman trust Bowie's legs? Thorn figured he would go to the source. With about a month left before the draft, he asked Inman, a straight shooter, whether the Blazers would pick Bowie. There was really no reason for Inman to lie, unless the Portland GM thought he could extract some material from the Bulls for a switch in picks or a promise to pass over Jordan. Inman didn't like those mind games, and he told Thorn straight out that the Blazers would choose Bowie if he passed their physical.

Weeks passed, and Thorn had not heard anything new from the West Coast. No news was good news, he figured. The next time he ran into Inman, Thorn asked if Bowie had passed his physical. Without definitively confirming Portland would draft Bowie, Inman said that, yes, the Kentucky center had passed his physical. Again, Thorn knew Inman well enough to believe he would not be deceptive on this matter. It seemed almost certain that Jordan would be available, and it was time for Thorn to do a selling job inside the offices of his own franchise.

The Bulls' general manager called a meeting in a conference room to break the news of his decision to Loughery, to assistant coaches Bill Blair and Fred Carter, and to chief operating officer Jonathan Kovler. Loughery loved the pick. He, like Thorn, had pipe dreams of Dr. J running through his head. The whole group eventually approved, although Thorn had to rationalize his own inconsistencies a couple of times. Hadn't he always argued that the franchise required a big man to win, Kovler wanted to know? Hadn't he already drafted a shooting guard in Dailey? "They probably heard me say a hundred times, you know, 'Size is what wins for you,'" Thorn recalled. "So they're thinking, 'Now all of a sudden you want to take this guy? If you don't think Bowie will last, why aren't you taking Perkins? Why aren't you taking Dinner Bell?'" Thorn said that Jordan could be a very good player, that he could help the Bulls win immediately. He said Perkins and the others gave him pause. Really, he was preaching to the choir. Everyone wanted an electrifying player like Jordan rather than a big-bodied project. The rule of thumb was that big men required about three years to find their stride in the NBA. Most of the people in the room figured they wouldn't be around the franchise for that long, if the Bulls didn't improve immediately. The meeting broke up with the idea that the Bulls would draft Jordan, unless a unique opportunity presented itself in the last few weeks leading up to the draft.

It nearly did. Several people were high on Jordan, even higher on him than Thorn. Billy Cunningham, coaching the Philadelphia 76ers, was a particularly astute judge of talent. He was also stubbornly loyal to Smith and his alma mater, North Carolina. Cunningham wanted Jordan and pressed Pat Williams, his general manager, to do something about it. Andrew Toney, a dead-eye shooter and perennial All Star with foot problems, would be the bait. Thorn came to understand he could get Toney and possibly Philadelphia's number 5 pick in return for that number 3 pick, Jordan. Thorn could then select Barkley or perhaps Turpin with that fifth draft pick, gaining impact players at two different positions. "God knows, we have needs," Thorn would say. The Philadelphia offer was a tempting one.

Then there were Dick Motta and Rick Sund, the coach and general manager at Dallas, still bristling over the late-season collapses of Chicago and Houston that had pushed their own pick down to number 4. Sund dangled Mark Aguirre, a physical forward in the Barkley mode. Aguirre had finished second in the NBA scoring race during 1983–84 with a 29.5 point average, leading the Mavericks to their best season ever. He was a proven commodity. Even better, he was from Chicago. Aguirre would have been a homecoming present to the fans, a magnet to fill those empty seats.

"Rod said, 'That's more than a fair offer, but I got a special feeling on Michael Jordan,'" Sund said. "Twenty-some years later, I credit Rod Thorn with foresight, insight. . . . I thought we made a helluva offer. Aguirre packed them in at DePaul, he had that great second year with us, and he would have been very popular in Chicago. But Rod didn't even waver. He knew."

Thorn appreciated the compliment but said he was more desperate than prescient. "We were shell-shocked, not doing well. My feeling and the prevailing feeling was that Michael would be a very good player, but I never envisioned he'd be that great. We wanted Olajuwon. That's who we wanted."

Still, Thorn thought Jordan was worth more than Aguirre, and all the interest in Jordan around the league just confirmed that belief. There was one potential deal that tickled Thorn's fancy, though. It took the form of a newspaper rumor out of Texas, and it was a proposition that might have changed everything. A reporter wrote that Bill Fitch, the coach there, was angling to trade Ralph Sampson to the Bulls for the number 3 pick, a move that would have made perfect sense all around. The Rockets were about to draft Olajuwon, who figured to be one of the top centers in the league for years to come. Sampson had not helped the Rockets win, even with his solid rookie season. Why not deal Sampson for Jordan, creating a more-balanced nucleus of Olajuwon and Jordan for years to come?

In hindsight, such a move might have created one of the league's greatest all-time dynasties for Houston. (Dean Smith may be the only one to humbug the idea: "I'm never one to believe in stars," he said, "even though they were *very* big stars.") The great experiment never took place. The report was exaggerated. The Rockets did, in fact, discuss the matter briefly. Nothing came of it, however. Fitch had talked at length with Smith in Carolina about Jordan, and then Fitch praised Jordan generously to the press. Maybe that was the source of the rumor. "You talk and then somebody says something to somebody," Fitch said.

Thorn waited for this intriguing deal, keeping his ears open. If Houston had offered Sampson, that graceful giant, Thorn would have made the deal. How could he not? He had no idea that Jordan was that special. Nobody did. He also had no hint that Sampson's knee would degenerate so quickly, sapping the big man's point-guard athleticism.

The calls were not made in either direction. And on June 19, 1984, Thorn was holed up in a secret location at a Chicago hotel, the Bulls' war room, tethered to a telephone. He smiled with relief when Portland picked Bowie at number 2. He had been right, thankfully. The Bulls had no Plan B, not really. If Portland had chosen Jordan at number 2, Thorn would have been deeply embarrassed by all his speeches and assurances to Bulls' brass. He might have been forced to resign within days.

Instead, at Thorn's long-distance orders, a club representative in New York told the new commissioner, David Stern, that the Bulls would use their third pick to select Jordan. His primary mission accomplished, Thorn had some fun with the rest of the draft. He picked Carl Lewis, the transcendent track star, with his tenth pick. Lewis never bounced a ball for the Bulls, but the selection created a wonderful trivia riddle for future generations of draftniks: Chicago selected two of the greatest athletes of all time in the 1984 draft. Name them. "It was a publicity stunt," Thorn said. Years later, at a chance meeting in New York City, Thorn introduced himself to Lewis as the guy who drafted the sprinter. "You never followed up!" Lewis exclaimed. "And I can play ball. . . ."

Thorn had no idea what a watershed mark this draft would become in the city's previously lackluster basketball history, dating back to 1961, which included not a single NBA championship with the Packers, Zephyrs, or Bulls. Chicago Stadium, an arena that could rock with the loudest of them, never housed much inspiration on the basketball front. Who had been the Bulls' greatest player until this moment? Who knew? The 1984–85 NBA Register listed fifty-six men among the league's greatest players. Only six of them ever played for the Bulls, and they were merely passing through: Walt Bellamy, Andy Phillip, Guy Rodgers, Nate Thurmond, Chet Walker, and Max Zaslofsky. None of these players spent more than four seasons in Chicago. Not one of them was truly associated with the franchise. This was an unimpressive lineage in search of a founding father.

The Safe Pick

More than two decades later, Norm Sonju still believes the Dallas Mavericks were cheated on several occasions out of Michael Jordan—though his theories require considerable explanation. The former Mavs president was a Chicago businessman, the nephew of a University of Wisconsin–Madison crew coach by the same name and a fellow with sports management in his blood. At different times, the nephew helped found two NBA franchises and was part-owner of a third, the Boston Celtics. While working years later as chairman and CEO of a Christian family resort in upstate New York, Sonju still drew a pension from both the Mavericks and the Celtics. Back in the '70s and '80s, he was not so much a basketball man as a master salesman. While Sonju was moving the Buffalo Braves to San Diego in the 1970s, he did enough research on available markets to understand that the two most hospitable vacancies remained in Orange County and Dallas. After Sonju was done fiddling with the Clippers, he focused on starting an expansion franchise in Texas. The Mavs were his studied brainchild from the start.

He would do this right, from sales department to basketball personnel. He was in no hurry, and that helped enormously.

"I realized as an expansion team we wouldn't be very good for a while," Sonju said. "Whether we win 15 or 27 games that first season, it doesn't make a difference. We planned and thought about it." He hired Rick Sund, a first-time GM, and made him his right-hand man. Then the Mavs traded the present for the future, over and over. They became the model for every expansion franchise to come, plucking draft picks from the Cleveland Cavaliers as if they were fat navel oranges in an orchard. During the course of just one season, 1980–81, the Mavs traded away Mike Bratz, Richard Washington, Geoff Huston, Jerome Whitehead, and unsigned number 1 draft pick Kiki Vandeweghe. In return, they got five first-round draft choices, from 1984 through 1986, including all three of the Cavaliers' first picks in those drafts. In '84 and '85, Dallas would have five first-round and four second-round choices. Dallas had plenty of picks, plenty of space under the salary cap. And Cleveland was just terrible enough to make this whole plan work to perfection.

But it turned out the Mavericks were too smart for their own good. Sonju was at the Hilton Airport in Chicago for a board of governors meeting in May 1983, when David Stern and his deputy commissioner, Russ Granik, ambushed Sonju in the hallway and led him into a room for a two-on-one arm-twisting session. "I was thinking, 'What in the world are you talking about?'" Sonju said. "Why this big push for Norm Sonju?" He found out soon enough. Stern and Granik were urging Sonju to think macro, not micro, to be more than the Dallas Maverick president and more like an NBA caretaker. And they wanted Sonju to help rescue the Cleveland Cavaliers.

The Cleveland franchise was a mess, the league's great disgrace. Stern was desperate to get rid of Ted Stepien, the outspoken, self-destructive owner who had stated for the record that it was easier to market white players than black players. And the only way to dump

Stepien, Stern insisted, was to give back the Cavs some first-round picks so they could become an attractive franchise for prospective buyers, Gordon and George Gund, who also owned the Coliseum in Richfield, Ohio. On April 7, 1983, the Gund brothers received an option from Stepien to purchase the team. The NBA was worried the Gunds would back out if they weren't offered further incentives.

"The league was hellbent on getting Ted Stepien out, and they were willing to do whatever it took to get him out," Sonju said. "I thought differently, that Gordon Gund already owned the Coliseum, and that there was no way he could afford not to buy the team. He has got to have the building with people in it. It's not going to do well otherwise. But I lost. They bullied us."

It suited Sonju's purposes to keep Stepien in place for a few more seasons, to ensure chaos in Cleveland at least through 1986. The Mavericks owned the rights to nearly all the regular Cleveland picks, and the value of those picks was inversely linked to the Cavs' improvement. Dallas was the team that would be hurt most by any Cavs' climb in the standings. The NBA board of governors nonetheless voted to allocate special picks to the Cavaliers, and soon enough the deed to the franchise was wrested from Stepien's clumsy hands. Gund, the new owner, was awarded the twenty-fourth pick in 1983. The league gave him more replacement picks in 1984, 1985, and 1986. Cleveland chose Stewart Granger of Villanova, a junior eligible, with that pick in 1983, and Granger did not turn pro with the Cavs until 1984. But with the sale to Gund, the Cleveland franchise was stabilized just enough to begin a slow turnaround. Surely the new ownership was worth one game in the standings, and that was all that it took to sabotage Dallas, because Cleveland ended up with 28 victories while Chicago won 27. Instead of picking third in the 1984 draft, the Mavs picked fourth.

"That draft was not just significant, it was beyond significant," Sonju said. "I can't talk about the 1984 draft without me crying a little bit. Perkins was a fine player, but he wasn't Jordan of course." Sonju would lose Jordan to Thorn and then later to a good friend and fellow Chicagoan, Jerry Krause, the next Bulls' GM. The two of them, Sonju and Krause, would have many conversations over the years about fate and destiny.

In 1984, thanks to the organization's uncommon planning and patience, the Mavericks were clearly on their way to something very good. They had won just 15 games in their inaugural season, 1980–81, when the NBA realigned itself to make room for its twenty-third team. They won 28 the next season, 38 the season after that, and then went 43–39 in 1983–84. Dallas finished second to Utah in the Midwest Division, earning its first playoff spot in its brief history. The season had been hopeful all around, beginning with an eight-game winning streak and a 10–3 record for November. Mark Aguirre was named to the All-Star Game while averaging 29.5 points, 5.9 rebounds, and 4.5 assists. He trailed only Adrian Dantley in scoring. Rolando Blackman averaged 22.4 points, with a 54.6 percent shooting average. The playmaker, Brad Davis, was tenth in assists. There was plenty of pop in the lineup. The Mavs were averaging nearly 110 points per game. And under the controlling reign of coach Dick Motta, the Mavs committed the fewest turnovers in the league, at 15.9 per game. Dallas went on to knock out Seattle in a first-round playoff series before losing to the Lakers in five games, no disgrace. So these were heady times, with all these victories and draft picks, plus a great deal of civic support. Here was a franchise pointed in the right direction, its arrow aiming straight up.

The Mavericks were ruled by a delicately balanced triumvirate that had produced solid success by increments, through a process that was viewed alternately as creative consensus or paralysis by committee. The three men in charge of the ship were very different. Sonju was the team president, a polished, well-dressed businessman and committed Christian. A suspenders-and-tie kind of guy. He was a bit formal, but nobody could deny he was the guiding force behind founding the Mavericks and setting up a sophisticated economic base that was still missing from most teams in the league. Executives from other franchises, like Indiana and Utah, would occasionally visit the Mavs and talk with Sonju just to see how he had laid it all out. Sonju delegated responsibility, and he was good at it. "I was the founder, president, GM, but I had basketball people," Sonju said. "I sat and heard conversations, didn't tell them to take this person or that one."

Motta was the rough-hewn coach, an outdoorsman and a natural outsider who made few friends around the league. Motta, no diplomat, spoke his mind and wanted to make his own decisions. After he finally retired in 1997 with 935 victories (and, yes, 1,017 defeats), Motta was not elected into the Basketball Hall of Fame, even though he had been NBA Coach of the Year in 1971 and won his title in 1978. This is a slight his family believes is the result of an often combative relationship with voters—the press and other basketball officials.

The buffer between Motta and these two vastly different, occasional antagonists was Rick Sund, a top personnel guy who was hired at age twenty-eight after learning at the knee of a renowned innovator, Don Nelson, in Milwaukee. Nelson never accepted conventional wisdom and was always auditioning bizarre isolation plays, sometimes with his biggest men stationed outside the three-point arc. Like Nelson, Sund also thought outside the box, and his personnel decisions were generally as successful as they were unexpected.

Within the Dallas organization, he was the go-to guy with problems, a steady presence beloved by the staff. Sund had a great eye for talent, as he would demonstrate time and again by drafting players like Blackman, Aguirre, Jay Vincent, and Detlef Schrempf, a West German star and among the first international picks in 1985. Sund's one arguable flaw was a tendency to defer to Motta on basketball decisions. Of the three guys, Sund had the best eye for talent. Those closest to the team came to believe Motta too often was swayed by the public opinions of other league executives or coaches. Theoretically, the draft was supposed to be Sund's baby. But Sund always felt there was not much point in drafting a player who was unwanted by the head coach. If Sund did that, Motta would simply not play him. Despite the occasional chafing, however, this was becoming a home-grown team and a very good one.

Since the Mavericks owned Cleveland's first-round pick, Motta was hopeful for a while that the Cavs might fall far enough in the standings so that Dallas would become one of two parties in the coin flip. All his life, most recently in Washington and Dallas, Motta had wanted to work with a great big man like Olajuwon. But then the Rockets went into a terrible tailspin, finishing behind Cleveland, and Motta fumed that it was a fix. Each time he saw the replays on television of Ralph Sampson riding the bench, giggling, Motta went ballistic. Motta believed with every bone in his body that Bill Fitch and the Rockets were playing for last place or second-to-last place. The rest of Dallas management, and much of the NBA, shared his opinion. And in this way, the Mavericks felt they were cheated of Jordan twice: once by Stern, who displaced Stepien, and once by Fitch, who played an aging Elvin Hayes for suspiciously too many minutes.

Memories were fickle, and so two men who had nothing but the highest regard for each other did not agree on one important detail regarding this class of incoming rookies. Sonju said there was never any doubt that Dallas would choose Sam Perkins, that it was a gimme from the start and that not a single sweat bead was shed on draft day. But Kevin Sullivan, who was media director for those same Mavs, remembers that he was ready with alternate plans just in case Perkins was taken among the top three picks and if the team were forced to go in another direction. There was talk, Motta would confirm, of a failed package deal to bring Mel Turpin to Dallas to fill the void at center. And what if Portland had selected Jordan, and Chicago then took Perkins? Sullivan says the team printed little black and white cards, the size of envelopes, with Turpin as the featured alternative. "We did the same thing another year with Penny Hardaway," said Sullivan, who went on to work in the U.S. Department of Education under the George W. Bush administration. "If somebody took Perkins in the top three, we'd have taken whoever fell."

Sonju said Sullivan is dead wrong on that because the Mavs only printed those cards for the Jamal Mashburn and Hardaway crisis in 1993. Dallas, picking number 4 in that draft, wanted Hardaway that year, who was grabbed just ahead by Golden State at the number 3 pick. Despite what Motta and Sullivan said, Sund also did not remember any interest in Turpin. Sund just recalled his futile attempts to steal Jordan from the Bulls, with his offer of Mark Aguirre plus a first-round draft pick.

Another intriguing choice was available, if Dallas had the stomach for it. Barkley was out there, but the Mavs already had a Barkley. They had Aguirre, a talented, high-maintenance small forward with a renowned mouth who also had weight problems. Motta and Aguirre were forever resentful of one another, locked in a feud that would eventually end with Motta's departure. The Mavs also had Jay Vincent, a natural scorer who had finished even higher in the Rookie of the Year balloting than Aguirre when they both came out of college. And they had Blackman, a reliable shooter. Besides, Barkley did not quite fit the civic-minded image that Mavs' ownership was hoping to create at Reunion Arena. "Barkley was interesting, an incredible rebounder," Sonju said. But there was a particularly negative report from John McClendon, a Hall of Fame coach at Tennessee State who was also an assistant at the Olympic trials. "I can remember him really discouraging us on Barkley," Sonju said.

The Mavs required size desperately. Pat Cummings, a six-foot-nine converted forward, was the player who most often passed for a pivotman in 1983–84, when Dallas was out-rebounded by a margin of more than 2 boards per game. "We needed the length of a guy who can play a four or a five," Sund said, using conventional basketball lingo for the power forward and center positions. He was quite certain back then that any and all of the top five picks would become major impact players. Motta and assistant Bob Weiss also backed the Perkins pick. "I just flat out like him," Motta said, before the draft. "He's going to be an All-Star in three years. He has the wingspan of a kid 7–7. He'll be our best shot blocker. He has started on a national championship college team, the Pan Am team that won the gold. He has already succeeded against a lot of NBA players. He knows what it takes to win, and he's a good kid." What convinced Sund were films of Perkins playing against Ralph Sampson and Patrick Ewing, particularly a game when he'd scored 37 points against Sampson and Virginia.

Nobody was quite so sure, though, about Dallas's second choice in the first round, which was the Mavs' own pick at the number 15 spot. Sund tried to move that pick, but there weren't any takers. "I wasn't a huge Stockton guy," Sund admitted. "I became a huge Stockton guy three, four years later, like everybody else." Brad Davis was the team's point guard, and his strengths and weaknesses seemed to overlap with Stockton's game. Both were unselfish and couldn't jump very high. Sund kept hearing that George Karl, who would be coaching in 1984 at Cleveland, liked Stockton. But Sund really had not seen enough of the kid to take the chance. "Scouting was not as sophisticated, and I never scouted Stockton until Portsmouth," Sund said, referring to the spring showcase game for draft prospects. Instead, the top contender for the Mavs' second pick was Terence Stansbury, the Temple guard who had torched North Carolina in the NCAA tournament.

The Mavericks opened Reunion Arena for a public draft party to watch the feed from New York. Thousands showed up, and Sonju was in a back room with his pack of Perkins cards. "We were all Perkins, all the time," Sullivan said about the affair. This was an era before cable feeds were common, but team officials set up a live telecast, and it was a really big deal. Sullivan printed out a list of all the players the Mavs were thinking of taking. John Stockton was not on it.

SMU coach Dave Bliss, a man headed for great disgrace down the road, was guest commentator, the emcee. Nearly twenty years later, Bliss would be involved in a recruiting scandal at Baylor of the most sordid kind. In order to disguise his own illegal payments to players, he would suggest to team members they tell investigators that Patrick Dennehy, a murder victim at the hands of another former Baylor player, had made this extra money by peddling drugs. The scandal would be a career destroyer for Bliss. But back in 1984, Bliss was still young and going places.

When the Mavs took Perkins, there was nothing but positive re- action from the crowd. Perkins was a brand name from a big school. But the Dallas organizers were a bit concerned about that later first- round pick, Stansbury. Nobody knew who he was, and Sund told Bliss right before the pick to say something nice about him. The Mavs had already bounced the pick off a couple local newspaper columnists, Skip Bayless and Randy Galloway, just so they would not be ambushed by the choice.

Dallas might have grabbed somebody else, perhaps Michael Cage, but Cleveland had been given the number 12 pick in this draft by Stern, dropping Dallas down to number 15. Cage, who had a pro- ductive NBA career, went to the Clippers at number 14. Stansbury was thrilled at the time to be picked by anybody in the first round, since his status had been uncertain. He was the first player from the state of Delaware ever taken in the first round of the NBA draft, and he would head down to Dallas the next day to meet the media and the triumvirate who tabbed him. This whole adventure did not turn out well. Stansbury would be headed for a different place, Indiana, after a self-destructive holdout.

Perkins was at the Olympic trials, meanwhile, and would go on to Los Angeles to win the gold medal with Jordan and Knight. Perkins was disoriented when he finally came down to Dallas with his adopted family, the Elacquas, to meet the Mavs. "I zoomed away from L.A., went to Dallas, and it was a strange trip," Perkins recalled. "I'd never been to Dallas before, and I was looking for a place to live. That was a really eerie feeling, staying in L.A. so long, and then the next day, it's over." He kept leaving his gold medal everywhere he went. He even forgot it once in Sonju's car. That was as close to a major title as Sonju would ever get in Dallas.

12

The Imperfect Fit

Charles Barkley never wanted to be a Philadelphia 76er, and the Sixers never really wanted much to do with Barkley, for that matter. In the weeks leading up to the draft, the two sides danced a particularly clumsy waltz of approach-avoidance. Neither party was pleased with this impending match. Each one aggressively shopped around for better options, hoping to subvert what eventually would turn into a very productive shotgun marriage. This situation was the opposite of the one in Portland, where the Trail Blazers and Sam Bowie liked each other a good deal from the start but were headed for a bad ending. It all just showed you that draft infatuations, and repulsions, were highly unreliable.

The Sixers coveted Michael Jordan and thought he was the true prize in this draft. Meanwhile, Barkley feared Philadelphia did not have the money to pay him his deserved millions under the new salary cap rules. Team officials weren't sure where Barkley fit on a basketball court or on their roster. He was the rotund embodiment of a "'tweener," a center in college who was too small, on paper, to play forward. Always with Barkley, there was a question of dimensions, not only regarding his width. He went through periods of his career passing for six feet, six inches, but in the end everyone arrived at the conclusion he probably was no taller than six feet, four and seven-eighths. He played much, much taller. But surely the tape measure didn't lie. How could he possibly be a power forward in the NBA, where minimum height standards were generally regarded as six-foot-two for a point guard, six-foot-four for a shooting guard, six-foot-six for a small forward, six-foot-eight for a power forward, six-foot-ten for a center?

The Sixers also did not trust Barkley's out-there personality and were not comfortable drafting such a round publicity hound. This was a rock-solid franchise built around steady, classy veterans like Julius Erving and Bobby Jones, still just one year removed from a 65–17 mark and an NBA championship in 1982–83. The team had posted nine successive winning seasons, with 50 or more victories during seven of those years and more than 60 victories on two occasions. Curiously, the city of Philadelphia never completely embraced this successful franchise. Its populace seemed more obsessed with football and hockey, with the beloved Eagles and Flyers. Through much of the '70s, the Sixers had played second fiddle to the Broad Street Bullies, those rowdy, champion Flyers of the National Hockey League. Matters did not improve much after that for the basketball team, even with all the victories. On Easter Sunday, April 19, 1981, when the Sixers were very much a title contender, only 6,704 fans showed up at the Spectrum (capacity 18,276) for victorious Game 7 of a dramatic Eastern Conference semifinal series against Milwaukee. "I think the attendance merely reflects how Philadelphians feel about the 76ers," said coach Billy Cunningham. "It's a shame, isn't it?"

The team deserved much better support, if quality of performance and character were the measuring stick. Erving, of course,

was a living icon, his reputation already assured as the most entertaining player of his generation. People around the league like Rod
Thorn would lament that the larger NBA audience had not seen
Dr. J in his most glorious American Basketball Association years.
Back then with the New York Nets, when Thorn was an assistant
coach on Long Island, Erving would dominate entire playoff series.
He single-handedly led the Nets over Denver for the last ABA title
in 1976, after averaging 29.3 acrobatic points per game during the
regular season. He was traded to Philadelphia that same year because of the Nets' eternal chaos and financial crises, reversing the
fortunes of the two franchises.

Bobby Jones was considered the consummate team player, a Bill
Bradley–type forward, a guy who might have fit in perfectly with
those championship Knick teams. He owned a sweet jumper for a
man his size. Moses Malone was the sturdy center, a boarding machine who led the league in that department for 1983–84 with an
average of 13.4 rebounds. When Malone made his famous prediction of three playoff series sweeps in 1983—"fo', fo', fo'"—there
was considerable skepticism around the league. But he correctly
gauged the talent on that team, and the 76ers nearly made him look
like a genius as they sprinted through the postseason. Philadelphia
lost only one game along the way—to the Bucks. Malone was not
the world's most prolific quote machine. He was a pioneer, having
come out early straight from Petersburg High School in Virginia,
and that lack of seasoning left him brusque and somewhat defensive
with the media. But Malone was a player's player, unselfish with his
time, willing to work out with any teammate and teach the lessons
learned from decades of shoving under the glass. Maurice Cheeks
was a prototypical point guard, smart and fluid and professional.
Andrew Toney was probably the most enigmatic starter of the
bunch, a pure, streak shooter out of Birmingham, Alabama, with a
naïve, provincial nature.

Even with this incredibly potent and balanced roster, Philadelphia was hardly perfect. The team was getting old. After years at or near the top, the performance arrow definitely was pointing down. There was a real sense the Sixers had peaked in 1983, when they won those 65 games after acquiring Malone to replace their erratic center, Darryl Dawkins. In 1984, the Sixers were eliminated in the first round of the playoffs by the upstart Nets, when New Jersey guard Micheal Ray Richardson briefly flashed the sort of form everybody had expected from the troubled player for most of his underachieving career. After that debacle, it was clear the Sixers required a burst of youth and energy, without completely toppling the proven chemistry. They desperately wished to remain competitive with the ruling elite, the Celtics and Lakers. Though they needed a power forward, the Sixers were hoping this draft would net them a franchise cornerstone, a Jordan or an Olajuwon. They fully expected to be in a high draft position to get one of these great athletes and to avoid the obvious risks posed by Barkley. The lessons learned from Dawkins, another flamboyant, unusually large player, were still fresh in everybody's minds. And Cunningham was a discipline-first kind of guy, a no-nonsense coach who might not mesh with Barkley, the Auburn cut-up.

For some time, it appeared the Sixers might get one of those top two draft choices. Philadelphia general manager Pat Williams had traded for the San Diego Clippers' 1984 first-round pick six years earlier, giving up Lloyd B. Free, a colorful gunner of great fame. Free went on to lead the woeful Clippers in scoring for two seasons, before he was shipped off to Golden State in 1980—the same year he officially changed his name to World B. Free. "I'm sure the Clippers thought that day of the 1984 draft would never come, but it came," Williams said. He observed the standings closely as the 1983–84 regular season chugged to a close and as

the Houston Rockets and Chicago Bulls collapsed badly enough
to claim two of the three top picks. "Suddenly, mysteriously,
Houston goes downhill," said Williams, who accepted this phenomenon with a bit more humor than Dallas coach Dick Motta.
"Bill Fitch is playing Elvin Hayes 53 minutes one night, the guy
can barely stand up he's so old, and our coin flip goes out the window." This was a time before the Internet or NBA TV, so
Williams would follow these out-of-town games by telephone, by
telex, by newspaper. On the final day of the season, he got the bad
news that the Sixers had sunk to the fifth pick in the draft. At the
time, Williams was getting ready for a Sunday game at the Spectrum. Jimmy Lynam was coaching that same day in San Diego
against Utah, and the Clippers had no incentive to lose since they
did not own their own pick. Not only did the Clippers win, they
scored 50 points in the second quarter to beat the Jazz, 146–128,
which represented the most points ever scored by that franchise in
a game. "They were driving to the finish as hard as they could,"
Williams said. "No experimenting. They win their last game, and
we're devastated. We're sitting there with pick No. 5, knowing
both Olajuwon and Jordan will be gone."

For a while, the Sixers weren't sure whether Dallas would take
Sam Perkins, the safe pick, at number 4. Maybe they would grab Mel
Turpin. If the Mavs passed on Perkins, Philly planned to take him
over Barkley, over Turpin, over everybody else. But then it became
apparent that Dallas was going the Perkins route and that Philadelphia would need to choose between the two fatties, Barkley and
Turpin. "We were on the horns of a dilemma," Williams said.
"We're sitting there with two guys who clipped their toenails by
memory. What to do? What to do?" Williams had seen Barkley
dominate the first week of the Olympic trials, and a couple of other
guys in the organization were also higher on Barkley than Turpin.

Jack McMahon, an assistant coach and a respected talent scout, had seen Barkley play as a freshman at Auburn and categorized him as "a ball-handling Wes Unseld," akin to labeling some hybrid mammal "a graceful hippo."

Harold Katz, the NutriSystem diet magnate and hands-on owner of the Sixers, fancied himself a basketball guru ever since he purchased the team for less than $13 million from the more aristocratic Fitz Eugene Dixon Jr. on July 15, 1981. Katz had scouted Barkley by watching Auburn games on his own personal satellite dish—a relatively new plaything only available to the very rich and equally eccentric. Katz was fascinated by Barkley and encouraged Williams to go in that direction. Katz still demands most of the credit for this pick and says that the late MacMahon was never really involved in the discussions. In the spring of 1984, the owner took the unusual step of accompanying Cunningham and assistant Matt Guokas on a trip to Bloomington, hoping to scout Barkley in person.

"We got there just in time to hear that Bobby Knight had cut him," Katz recalled. "But to me, drafting Barkley was still a no-brainer. Here was a guy who went after the basketball, knew where it was, and knew what to do with it."

For middle management, Katz's endorsement removed a bit of the risk from the venture. So it would be Barkley, the Sixers figured—maybe. Six weeks before the draft, the Sixers brought in Barkley for a workout, a rare event at the time but a session that Philly thought was necessary considering the question marks surrounding this particular option. The Auburn player showed up and was measured at a little over six feet, four inches, and 292 pounds. "It was right at that point that the whole draft began to fall apart," Williams said. "If we'd been smart enough to know how good some of the other guys were later—like Stockton, Thorpe, or Kersey—we would have gladly taken one of them." Williams had a talk with

Barkley, telling him to return to Philadelphia for a weigh-in before the draft and to lose twenty pounds in the interim.

"Go back and get in shape," Williams told Barkley.

"Round is a shape, Mr. Williams," Barkley retorted.

Barkley's version was similar to Williams's, with a few numbers rearranged. Barkley remembered he weighed around three hundred, and that the Sixers wanted him to lose ten pounds. For a short time, he thought it would be a good thing to be drafted by the Sixers and made a real effort to reduce his girth. There was an intermediate weigh-in a month before the draft, when he came in at a remarkably trim 277 pounds. "I was below weight," Barkley said. But then two days before the draft in New York, Barkley's agent, Lance Luchnick, projected some very different math that changed everything. Luchnick figured out that the Sixers were above the salary cap, and informed his client they could only offer Barkley the league minimum of $75,000 for his rookie season. This was not what Barkley had in mind when he came out early from Auburn, and it surely was not what Luchnick had in mind in the way of a standard agent's commission, which was 4 percent. Barkley was down in Houston at the time, about to head to Philadelphia for a final weigh-in, when he and Luchnick decided the player would simply eat his way out of the Sixers' immediate draft plans.

"We went out to eat dinner, and I had three desserts," Barkley said. "We got up the next morning, I had three or four servings of pancakes, plus milk shakes. Then I ate on the plane the whole way and when we landed at the airport, I ate one more time. I weighed in at 296. I gained 15 pounds in 24 hours. Harold Katz looked at me and said, 'Are you nuts?'"

Katz remembered only that Barkley was overweight. The former owner insisted there was never much doubt the franchise eventually would clear up enough money under the cap to sign Barkley. "As normal, he gets things a little mixed up," Katz said of Barkley's narrative. Looking back to all this pre-draft nonsense in '84, Williams said he never suspected Barkley did not want to be a 76er. Who wouldn't want to join a team like this, with a cast of superstars in a fairly large Northeast market? But for Barkley at the time, after all the energy he'd invested to manipulate the situation, title contention was not the top priority. Money was what mattered for now. And when he stepped on that scale, overweight again, he figured Philadelphia would be looking elsewhere. He might have been right, too, if only the Sixers had been able to trade up or down. Cunningham, still regularly in touch with Dean Smith, remained sky high on Jordan. Williams tried to pry that number 3 pick from the Bulls. Toney was the main bait, along with the Sixers' own draft pick at number 5.

That didn't work. And then the Sixers, still actively looking to revamp their lineup, were caught in some unexpected turmoil, the most embarrassing situation imaginable. Hoping to pick the pockets of the Clippers yet again, Philly tried to deal for twenty-three-year-old Terry Cummings, NBA Rookie of the Year in 1983 at power forward. Katz himself took an interest in this transaction, which he believed could be of great benefit to the team. The Clippers, however, wanted in return Julius Erving, along with the Sixers' second pick in the first round. This was a terrible dilemma for Williams, and it quickly became a public relations nightmare when the story of these talks was leaked to the media out on the West Coast. Erving was more than a basketball player; he was a source of great civic pride. The deal made perfect basketball sense for Philadelphia, which was trying to get younger and faster. Cummings, Barkley, and Malone would be a formidable frontcourt. Erving, thirty-four, had one season left at $1.7 million on a contract scheduled to expire in 1985. The team figured to endure no-win bargaining sessions at that time, because Erving would command more money as a legend than he was now worth as a small forward. So Cummings-for-Erving would have been a helpful trade in many ways, but nobody in Philly would pull the trigger unless Erving himself gave the official okay. Katz spoke directly with Erving, who heard about the impending deal late at night on the eve of the draft. Erving instantly became a very unhappy man. "I was hit with a bombshell," Erving said. He warned the Philadelphia owner, "It would not fly too well throughout the city if I approved the trade."

He was right, too. Though the Sixers, as a team, received only lukewarm support from Philadelphia residents, Erving was another matter. The city's mayor, Wilson Goode, said, "If he went, I'd probably go with him."

The Sixers backed off in a hurry, even denying the deal was close to being done. "Julius Erving was the Philadelphia 76ers at the time," Katz said. Yet Katz said there was one trade he tried to make involving Erving, and he would gladly have accepted the consequences. In a direct conversation with Kovler, the Bulls' CEO, Katz offered Erving and a future draft pick for the right to draft Jordan. "That was the only deal I would have made, and it didn't get anywhere with the Bulls," Katz explained. It surely would have been a historic day if these two superstars had been swapped, but of course Erving was far on the downside by then and Kovler didn't even bother to discuss the proposition seriously with his own officials.

With messy headlines of betrayal still on the newsstands, draft day arrived at a highly inconvenient time for Williams, for his own personal reasons. Williams's wife gave birth to their son Michael that morning. Better the morning than the afternoon, Williams figured. He was able to witness the blessed event and then drive straight from the hospital to the Quality Inn in South Philadelphia, which was set up as draft headquarters for the Sixers. One birthing had led to another. "I rush into the room and announce with great fear and trepidation we're drafting Charles Barkley," Williams said. In New York, Barkley was at the Felt Forum, still hopeful he would be going to Washington or some other team with money to spare under the salary cap to make him a millionaire.

"They call my name," Barkley said. "And I'm thinking, 'Oh, fuck.'"

13

Sweet Sixteen

Friends, family, and acquaintances kept whispering in Frank Layden's ear about this kid John Stockton from Gonzaga, and the whispers were coming from people who knew basketball. The first time Layden ever heard about the plucky point guard was from the coach at Weber State, Neil McCarthy. "He's going to be a good one," McCarthy said, after Stockton's sophomore season. "He's quick, he's strong, he's passing the ball." This was over lunch at McCarthy's basketball camp, after a morning session. Layden knew that if he listened to everyone's unsolicited advice he would go nuts and probably make more mistakes than he already did. "It went in one ear, out the other," Layden said, of McCarthy's recommendation. Layden, acting as both general manager and coach for the Jazz, barely kept the name in mind and forgot about Stockton until he ordered up some amateurish films from Gonzaga during the playmaker's senior year. "I look at the tapes, I don't think much about him again," Layden said.

But the whispers kept coming, this time from Ladell Anderson, the long-time Brigham Young coach. Anderson was on the selection committee for the Olympic team, and he told Layden that Stockton was so good, he should have made the squad if Bob Knight hadn't been so committed to his own guy, Steve Alford. Another voice: Jack Gardner, the former University of Utah head coach, was scouting for the Jazz on the West Coast. He watched Stockton play in a college All-Star Game and whispered some more. "There's a kid, absolutely terrific," Gardner told Layden. David Fredman, a jack of all trades for the Jazz, said more of the same. "It was still fairly quiet," Fredman said. "Not a lot of [Gonzaga's] games were on TV, but you could see this guy was very quick, and he could shoot the ball. We just didn't know his mental toughness yet." Layden's son, Scott, was one of his father's assistants and was ultimately in charge of researching the first-round pick and making a recommendation. He went along with his dad to the Chicago pre-draft All-Star game, scouting Stockton. Stockton was teamed with Kevin Willis in scrimmages, and they made a good combination, a precursor to Stockton and Karl Malone. Scott Layden watched Stockton run up and down the court, leading the break, feeding Willis in stride. Scott was sold, and now he had to sell Stockton to his dad, who was not nearly so impressed.

"I saw him in Chicago, but you lose all perspective there," Frank Layden said. "The guys who can run and jump, they're the ones who jump out at you. Athleticism is what counts. I thought, 'He looks like a nice player, but . . .'" Then came a random meeting, a turning point. "We met in an elevator inside a Chicago hotel," Frank Layden said. "John introduces himself to me, and I shake his hand and grab his arm to see how thick he was. He doesn't look very big. He looks small and pale. But you grab his bicep, it's like gripping iron." That stuck with Layden, who didn't really hang around long to watch the college kids play in Chicago. He left that up to his son and the scouts. Scott eventually returned to Utah and told Frank what the father already knew was coming but really didn't want to hear: Scott told

Frank he should draft Stockton with the number 16 pick. "I'm figuring, if I pick a guy from Gonzaga . . . ," Frank Layden said. "I mean, the last famous guy from there was Bing Crosby. And if it doesn't work out, if they don't hate me now, they'll really hate me."

Frank Layden heeded the whispers of his staff, finally. The Jazz settled on Stockton, and they wanted to keep him as much of a secret as possible, because fifteen teams were picking before Utah. At least one of them, Cleveland, had also expressed an interest in Stockton. The Jazz went into secret agent mode, erasing Stockton's name from the potential draftees on the blackboard at their headquarters. Even before Stockton's appearance in Chicago, Fredman had tried to talk the player out of appearing at the pre-draft showcase in Portsmouth, Virginia, through Jay Hillock. Stockton went anyway. The Laydens figured few people would suspect that they would use their pick on such a small prospect, if only because they had one of the best playmakers in the game on their roster, Rickey Green, who was peaking now at age twenty-nine. The Jazz had done fine the previous season with Jerry Eaves as a viable backup, though Eaves had required knee surgery immediately after the playoffs and it was not clear if he would be ready in the fall. "It's just that we didn't seem like the type of team to take John, because we had a point guard already, just off the All-Star team," Scott Layden explained. "But we were genuinely excited about him. John was the guy we locked in on."

While Stockton didn't exactly fit Utah's depth chart, he certainly matched the team's demographics. In 1984–85, the Jazz would have seven white players passing through its twelve-man roster, playing in a city that was less than 2 percent African-American. The league was nearly 75 percent black at the time, but not many of these athletes were comfortable or had much desire to reside in Salt Lake City, considered a remote outpost if not an extraterrestrial experience for inner city ballplayers. After a brief stint with the Jazz in

1987, Darryl Dawkins said he would rather play for "the Afghanistan All Stars" than in Utah. This was a time just before the Mormon Church openly welcomed and recruited minorities, when its doctrine was still abhorrent to people of color. The result was a great disconnect between minority players and the local citizenry. There had been several ugly or distressing incidents already involving black players, well before the 1984 draft. On New Year's Day, 1980, Bernard King was arrested in Salt Lake City and charged with five felony sex charges. Less than half a year later, shortly after coming to Utah from Atlanta, Terry Furlow died in a car accident, and an autopsy showed cocaine in his bloodstream. In September 1982, after finishing his season as a reserve with the Jazz, Bill Robinzine committed suicide in Kansas City at the age of twenty-nine. In November of that year, John Drew was assigned to a drug rehab center after one of his several setbacks.

So Stockton figured to be a safer pick in this regard, at least. Frank Layden certainly felt comfortable with the kid's background. "It doesn't hurt that he's Irish Catholic and his father owns a bar," Fredman remembered Layden joking. But both Laydens felt a lot of pressure over this decision. The Jazz had been so bad for so long, and some of the recent drafts had contributed greatly to the suffering. "You have to be 75 percent lucky," Frank Layden said about the selections. "We didn't do psychological testing, we hardly looked at films. I mean, like anybody could have told you that Kevin McHale would be a Hall of Fame player? Come on. . . ." Layden himself had been about 50 percent right, 50 percent very wrong. There was an extremely unfortunate decision back in 1976, when the Jazz was still in New Orleans and Layden was one piece of the brain trust. The team acquired a washed-up, thirty-three-year-old guard, Gail Goodrich, from the Lakers in exchange for a 1979 first-round pick. That pick turned into Magic Johnson, who would have significantly altered the history of the franchise. Thurl Bailey and Darrell Griffith were spot-on choices, and Frank Layden had somehow stolen a seven-foot-four car mechanic by way of UCLA named Mark Eaton with a fourth-round pick in 1982. But in that same draft, Utah chose the spectacular Dominique Wilkins at number 3 overall, then immediately traded him to Atlanta for John Drew, Freeman Williams, and $1 million. There were some serious financial issues at the time, but that was really no excuse. Wilkins was a dazzling player who could have had an enormous impact at the gate, if not on the scoreboard.

Frank Layden was particularly sensitive about this Stockton pick, because everybody would take one look at the player and know he was the antithesis of Wilkins. Stockton was not going to win any NBA All-Star dunking contests. Layden could not be sure about him. He generally liked to draft taller players, he said, because "you can't teach height." He also liked to check with as many coaches as possible from the draftee's conference. When Layden drafted Thurl Bailey out of North Carolina State in 1983, he had talked not only to Jimmy Valvano but to Dean Smith, to reporters who had covered Bailey, to trainers. Smith had recommended Bailey. "It's all ahead of him," Smith had said. "He's just a baby." That was good enough for Layden. When he picked Bob Hansen out of Iowa, Layden called Lute Olson, the former Hawkeye coach, for a scouting report. But Layden was not so well connected with the West Coast Athletic Conference, which Gonzaga had joined after leaving the nearby Big Sky Conference in 1979. Layden looked twice, three times again at those choppy films from Gonzaga. "I never saw him play live, and this seemed like an awfully big risk," he said.

The more Layden looked, the smaller Stockton got. He was listed at six feet, one inch, 165 pounds. Layden was not sure; he couldn't rely on that handshake in the elevator of a Chicago hotel. He phoned Gonzaga athletic director Dan Fitzgerald, double-checking one more time, almost seeking some kind of guarantee. Fitzgerald couldn't do that, but he reassured Layden that Stockton was the real thing. Surely he would be an effective trainee under Green, which was all the Jazz was looking for at the moment. Then four days before the draft, Layden called Hillock. "The Jazz was very secretive, and I hadn't heard from them at all," Hillock said. "Then it was Friday, and Frank calls me with a long list of questions. He had a whole questionnaire. I was in the office with my two assistants, we were all single, we were ready to go out and have a beer or two, and this guy has a list of questions that takes 45 minutes to answer. It was a long day in Spokane."

Maybe because he was secure enough in his position, Frank Layden could make this kind of decision on a relative unknown. Layden was the one mainstay of the franchise, and he fit the team like a glove, despite his three hundred pounds and his smart-ass Brooklyn background. "Laughing makes the losing easier," he would always say, explaining how he survived the Jazz. His mom had died soon after Frank's birth, and he was raised by his father, a dock worker and former boxer, plus two older sisters. Frank cut his basketball teeth on the Bay Ridge playgrounds. "We fought more in the playgrounds than we did in the games," he said. Frank was a solid guard for Fort Hamilton High, where he was known as a gunner, a kid who liked to shoot the ball whenever it so much as grazed his hands. This was hardly a recommendation for coaching, but he got his first stint on the bench when a teachers' strike threatened the basketball schedule. Layden began playing for and coaching several teams at the local Christian Youth Organization, all at the same time. He borrowed celebrity names for himself, like Lash LaRue and Happy Daily, to disguise his relatively innocent double-dealings.

Layden got a scholarship to play at Niagara in upstate New York, where he roomed with another basketball lifer and raconteur, Hubie Brown. It must have been a great time to be a fly on the dorm room wall. He coached the Niagara freshmen, and Layden fell in love with the Xs and Os, with the whole idea of coaching, soon abandoning some very tentative plans to attend law school. That decision was made easier, he said, because he wasn't admitted anywhere. Layden coached at Seton Hall High School in Patchogue, New York, and eventually returned to coach at Niagara from 1968 to 1976. He led the school to its first NCAA tournament in 1970. Actually, Layden would tell you, it was Calvin Murphy who led the team; Frank was along for the ride. Layden had a self-deprecating humor that was perfect for a perennially struggling team like the Jazz, a franchise he helped to run for twenty-nine years as assistant coach, coach, general manager, and team president.

The 1977–78 season in New Orleans may have been his weirdest, the most disturbing of all. Pistol Pete Maravich, the true Jazz improviser, wrecked his knee. Ownership shares changed hands, and the team was planning a move. To kick things off that season, Layden had felt mischievous and entitled enough in June of 1977 to select Lusia Harris from Delta State with his seventh pick, the first woman ever selected in the NBA draft. "Then it turned out she was pregnant, so we'd really drafted two people," Layden said. It wasn't the last time Layden did something silly and inspired in a draft. In 1985, he would pick a Harvard kid, Keith Webster, in the final, seventh round as a personal favor. Layden wasn't even certain Harvard had a basketball team, but Webster was so impressive in training camp he would have made the roster if the Jazz didn't already own Green and Stockton. "Last exhibition game in Pittsburgh, before we cut him, we made him captain of the team and we have a picture of him with Michael Jordan," Layden recalled. "Then I tell him what I think is the bad news and he says, 'Coach don't feel bad. I graduated from Harvard, I'm going to UCLA law school. I'll remember you when I own a team someday.'"

The Jazz had moved from New Orleans in 1979, escaping with its equipment just before the doors of the Superdome were padlocked to keep the team from breaking its lease. The franchise retained the nickname to produce one of the more remarkable non sequitur team monikers in the history of sports. If there was jazz in Salt Lake City, it was not played loudly or on Sundays. Originally, there was a contest to rename the franchise. But Sam Battistone, part owner of the club, decided that the Jazz would keep its nickname and its gaudy colors as a constant annoyance to officials and politicians back in New Orleans who had bugged him with their lease demands. This was the smallest major professional sports market in America, and Layden figured the concept was doomed. For the first four seasons in Salt Lake City, it appeared his pessimism was justified. Utah's NBA team suffered through a series of mishaps and slapstick comedy routines, finishing well below .500 every season. When the team played its first-ever game in the Salt Palace back on October 15, 1979, Layden found himself playing the role of sidewalk sandwich board man in addition to general manager. Despite a flood of freebie tickets, the arena was more than half empty for the opener against the Milwaukee Bucks, and Layden did not want the commissioner, Lawrence O'Brien, to witness this fiasco firsthand. Layden screamed at the ushers to open the doors to everyone who was walking down West Temple. Still, few accepted the invitation. The Jazz averaged just 7,665 during the team's first three seasons in Utah. Things were so bad early on, Layden claimed that when a fan once called to ask the starting time of a game, he responded, "When can you get here?"

After all the tough seasons in Salt Lake City, the spring of 1984 was a comparatively heady time in franchise history. Utah posted a 45–37 regular season mark, 31–10 at home, captured the Midwest Division by two games over Dallas, and won a playoff series for the first time. The Jazz played an exciting brand of basketball, scoring 115 points a game, fifth most in the league. Adrian Dantley, already on his fourth of seven NBA teams at age twenty-nine, could get under Layden's skin. But he had led the NBA with an average of 30.6

points while shooting nearly 56 percent. Darrell Griffith was a pure shooting guard, averaging 20 points. Drew had recovered from his drug problems to become an effective scorer again, while Bailey and Eaton provided enough interior defense to keep the team from getting mauled under the glass. Eaton altered many opponents' shots, leading the league in blocks.

Yet despite this success and its status as the only pro team in town, the Jazz was not exactly an established attraction in the spring of 1984. The Laydens hoped to drum up some more interest with a draft party at the Salt Palace, the team's home arena. It would be a great celebration. "The popularity of the franchise wasn't where it is now, but we coaxed a couple hundred people into the arena with the lure of free hot dogs and Cokes," Scott Layden said. Jazz officials monitored by phone the early results of the draft and were quite pleased that nobody had stolen Stockton. The fans were informed of the picks, and then soon enough it was Frank Layden's turn at number 16. "Why don't you go up and announce it?" Frank asked Battistone, the owner. Battistone took the bait, went to a microphone, and announced to the crowd, "This year, the Utah Jazz select John Stockton from Gonzaga." Down from the stands came wadded wrappers from the hot dogs, the cups from those free Cokes. Lex Hemphill, a beat writer for the *Salt Lake Tribune*, remembered more than anything that there was complete, eerie silence from the crowd. "They had no idea who John Stockton was," Scott Layden said. "They thought at the time we'd drafted [TV announcer] Dick Stockton." Battistone, stunned by the reaction, retreated. "Now I know why you wanted me to make that pick," he told Frank Layden.

Others knew about Stockton, though, and wanted him. "Teams were throwing money at us, and we were a poor team," Frank Layden said. "But I remembered what Pat Williams would say. 'Never trade a first pick.'" Not long after the Jazz selected Stockton, the phone rang at Jazz draft headquarters. It was Stu Inman, the GM from Portland, who had been trying to trade up to grab Stockton. "Did you pick him to trade him?" Inman demanded. He couldn't believe the Jazz would want another point guard. The Blazers were picking at number 19 and badly needed a playmaker, much more so than the Jazz, as a replacement for Fat Lever. Frank Layden told Inman to forget it, maybe in part because he respected Inman's judgment enough to know that Stockton might just be a real prize. "I thought I was getting a good little Catholic school kid who'd have been great at Niagara," Frank Layden said. "We didn't know we were getting Joe Montana, just like we didn't know we'd be getting Jerry Rice in Karl Malone."

It turned out the whispers from the basketball people were right. It was the crowd at the Salt Palace that should have known better.

14

Portland Selects Sam Bowie

Considering the enormous stakes at hand, the 1984 NBA draft telecast on USA Network was a relatively bare-bones affair. The draft itself took place on June 19, 1984, inside what was then called the Felt Forum at Madison Square Garden, corner of Eighth Avenue and Thirty-Third Street in Manhattan. The draft had once been a very nearly private affair, conducted on a giant conference call among commissioner Lawrence O'Brien and team officials. Then it moved and for several years was held in a hotel ballroom. Now it was being staged inside an arena seating thousands. The place was not well lit and not particularly well attended, either by team officials or by the national media.

Even those crazy fans known as draftniks did not quite fill the seats. The draftniks were nerds, for sure, but they did their homework and had one hard and fast rule for franchise executives: a team should always pick the best athlete, the most passionate dazzler available. To choose by position or need was considered utter folly and in some ways a betrayal of all that was true and good about the sport of basketball. And if the draftniks' approach sounded a bit too simplistic, it often proved dead right in the short and long run. Just a year earlier, eleven teams with the thirteen top picks had passed on Clyde Drexler, a player beloved by draftniks everywhere for his sheer, physical talent. And at this 1984 draft, Michael Jordan was number 1 on their list. The crowd buzzed about the North Carolina stud. Eyes rolled at the notion Jordan might not be one of the top two picks. Less cerebrum, more gut was clearly required from the men in charge.

The Houston management team was one of the few groups there in force, because this was the Rockets' show. A rather tacky "Miller Time" banner adorned the stage. A bespectacled, mustachioed David Stern would be the host and chief merrymaker. The league held a pre-draft party, playing host to rookies and their families at a small Italian restaurant near the Garden. Olajuwon was forced into a constant crouch at the place because the ceiling was too low for him. Then it was broadcast time, and Stern was ready. This was his first televised public appearance as the new commissioner on a grand scale, but he was not that nervous. Stern kept reminding himself that his predecessor, Lawrence O'Brien, had emceed the draft before, though it was from a hotel ballroom before a much smaller audience. "I think I got over my nerves by then," Stern recalled.

> I tried to keep it all in perspective. As soon as I became commissioner that February, Dan Patrick, who was the CNN anchor then, said, "We're going out on the street to ask people if they know who David Stern is." And he asked them whether I was the violinist Stern, or the radio shock jock Stern, and they didn't know. They had no idea. After that public humiliation, I knew my place. And then I was on a talk radio debate with Art Rust, Jr., an African-

American, who did a show asking whether the NBA was too black. So I was battle tested. Maybe I was still nervous in front of a lot of people. But I just kept thinking the camera there was showing us to an audience of about zero back then.

Nearly all the twenty-three franchises set up headquarters in their home cities far away, most often in hotel rooms, and kept an open phone line to their representatives sitting in the Felt Forum next to corresponding team logos. USA Network featured a play-by-play guy, Al Albert, and a couple of color men, Eddie Doucette and Lou Carnesecca, the local St. John's coaching legend. Steve Jones was "in the pit." There was a special live feed to Bloomington, where several of the draftees were practicing with the U.S. national team, in training for pre-Olympic exhibitions against NBA All-Star teams who were doubling as the Washington Generals. Things were clearly changing. There were nine undergraduates available in this draft, and Olajuwon was about to become the fourth non-senior in six years to be the number 1 draft pick. Still, these athletes were not kids. They were polished enough to make an immediate impact, for whichever team drafted them.

Scampering about the place, as always, was the omnipresent Marty Blake, super scout. Blake was the ultimate character, a chronic gym rat of the first order. He had been connected with the league already for about thirty years and would be around for many decades to come. Back in 1984, before all the game films, he was by far the most reliable source of information, other than an eyewitness scouting mission. If you were a reporter or a general manager, and you had questions about the draft, you would go to Marty, and he would give you an answer, even if he didn't really have one. Blake admitted to only the occasional fabrication, like the time somebody drafted an unknown Eastern European, a guy even Blake hadn't heard about, and he simply started making up generic facts : "Big, strong, not a great ballhandler, surprising touch . . ." Blake almost always knew the real skinny, though. He scouted and established contacts everywhere, in every dark corner of the globe, and he took his greatest pleasures in his most obscure finds in America and overseas. Over the years, he would be credited with discovering small-college stars Scottie Pippen (Central Arkansas), Dennis Rodman (Southeastern Oklahoma State), and Dan Majerle (Central Michigan). One contact would lead to another and another. Blake uncovered one player back in the '50s, J. P. Lovelady of Arkansas Tech, a sure thing, but he died in a car accident. At the funeral Blake met Arch Jones, who became athletic director at Central Arkansas. Years later, Jones was the one who called Blake and tipped him off about Pippen.

Blake figured this 1984 draft was top-heavy with amazing talent among the first fifteen picks before it thinned out quickly. He could give you the odds on these kids making it, round by round, because Blake studied the numbers. Of the 175 players drafted in the first round from 1976 through 1983, 144 of them had played at least four years in the NBA, a good measuring stick of success. That represented a hang-in-there percentage of .823. That percentage dropped to .342 in the second round, to .160 in the third, to .068 in the fourth, .029 in the fifth, .017 in the sixth, .018 in the seventh. Only one player drafted in the eighth round had sustained a four-year career, while none had done so from the ninth or tenth rounds.

More than twenty years later, Blake would go through his paperwork and find his limited list of impact prospects from 1984 ranked this way, by position:

Centers: Olajuwon, Bowie. "I never liked Turpin," Blake said.
Power forwards: Bowie, Perkins, Barkley ("He wasn't fat, he was an artist."), Otis Thorpe, Tim McCormick, Michael Cage.
Small forwards: Jordan, Kenny Fields, Tony Campbell, Michael Young, Jeff Turner.

Shooting guard: Jordan, Lancaster Gordon, Vern Fleming, Terence Stansbury.
Point guard: Alvin Robertson, Jay Humphries, Stockton. ("This
  was a very thin year for playmakers.")

At the time, like most others, Blake subscribed to the theory that
big was ultimately better. "Never take a flea if you can take a giant,"
was what Bob Cousy had once told Blake, and he never forgot. "You
get a great center once every twenty-two and a half years, so you better take advantage of it," Blake said. More than anything, Blake understood that there was no pure science in this scouting and drafting.
People made mistakes, big mistakes. The teams didn't have that
much funding for scouting, so there was a lot of guesswork. And
then there was the matter of pure, dumb luck—good or bad. Nobody was really an infallible expert on anything. A guy could write
three books on marriage just before his wife left him. Blake had another saying he used a lot about the random and rueful nature of life,
about how those things could sabotage even God's chosen people
back in Old Testament times: "If Moses had gone to his left, they'd
have got the oil, not the sand."
  At the Felt Forum on June 19, 1984, USA Network was intro-
ducing its broadcast with typical zeal. The voice-over screamed that
"six bona fide superstars will be going," leaving the audience to figure out who, exactly, that might be after Olajuwon, Bowie, Jordan,
Perkins, and Barkley. Was Mel Turpin a superstar? Apparently.
Surely nobody had conferred such status on John Stockton—not yet.
The network analysts also predicted that four centers and twelve
power forwards would go in the first round, suggesting team officials
were basing these picks on the successful model of the giant-sized
Boston Celtics. People were reminded that the 76ers had three first-
round picks, while the Knicks, Denver, Seattle, and Golden State
had none, and that all sixty-nine of the first-round picks over the

past three years were still playing in the league. Guaranteed contracts were likely to assure that, in any sport.

The announcers did their best to drum up some enthusiasm, which seemed justified. Carnesecca called this, "a great day for basketball," and Doucette called this crop of players, "a smorgasbord, the *crème de la crème*." There were some awkward moments early on as they waited for something to happen, and Carnesecca begged, "Get me some Gatorade, some soda."

The Lone Ranger theme sounded. At last, David Stern stepped to the mike and gave his opening address: "Welcome to the 1984 NBA college draft. . . . We wish Coach Knight the best of luck in the Olympics. . . ." Stern laid down the rules, kindly, in his favorite-uncle fashion: Each team had a maximum of five minutes to make a decision in the first round, two minutes in the second through fifth round, one minute in the sixth through tenth rounds. If there was a question about the eligibility of a pick, good old reliable scout Marty Blake would give his expert opinion on the matter, which would be considered gospel.

The first pick was a given, Olajuwon, the seven-foot center from Houston, to Houston. Charlie Thomas and his daughter, Tracy, the good luck charm, made the official selection for the Rockets at the Felt Forum. Olajuwon rose from his seat, wearing a black suit, white shirt, red bowtie. He walked to the stage, a big smile on his face, shaking hands. Tracy handed Akeem a number 34 jersey. Carnesecca, still thinking like an opposing coach, said it was a good thing Olajuwon had only started playing basketball five years ago. "Thank God, he'd be unbelievable," Carnesecca said. "He has tremendous control of his shots."

Olajuwon was positively beaming, a study in the purest sort of joyous expectation. "This is the best thing that ever happened to me," Olajuwon told Doucette. "My mom and dad flew in from Nigeria. I wanted them to see what's going on in the United States.

I'm just very lucky to stay in Houston." Olajuwon talked a bit about receiving eloquent advice from mono-syllabic Moses Malone, which was hard to picture, and then he said he looked forward to playing in the Twin Towers setup with Ralph Sampson. "That's a good combination. I can't wait." He drew a line right there, however. Minutes after getting drafted, he pretty much told the world, and Bill Fitch, that he was the Rockets' center, that Sampson was now a power forward. "I think I like to play in the paint," Olajuwon said. Fitch had the same idea, anyway. Ray Patterson gave a ringing endorsement of this notion as well. "There is no question both those players can play together, and I'd like to add Rodney McCray can play together, too." Patterson was asked whether he would trade either guy. "Can you think of anything that can pry them away?" he said.

The clock was running, and now it was time for one of the biggest mistakes in the history of sports to occur in clear public sight and earshot. "Portland selects Sam Bowie, University of Kentucky," said Stern. The commissioner generally used the whole franchise name at these affairs, including the nickname. He shorthanded this one, turned basketball's worst blunder into a very brief pronouncement. It was as if Stern, with great prescience, had wanted to speak the words quickly, sweep this disastrous pick under the rug for Inman's sake.

The crowd knew better than the Blazers. The draftniks booed the choice. The announcers came to the defense of this disaster. "He'll fit in with Jack Ramsay," Carnesecca predicted. Al Albert added, assuredly, "There's no doubt he's recovered from those two years he sat out with stress fractures." Later, though, the commentators were admitting that this was not quite a no-brainer, that perhaps something might go awry. Carnesecca called the Bowie pick "a calculated risk," and Albert said there were "questions whether they should go with great talent," which of course would be Jordan, about to become pick number 3. Bowie walked to the stage wearing a gray suit, purple tie. "I had a two-year layoff," Bowie said. "If I didn't have the support of the community of Lexington and state of Kentucky I wouldn't be able to do it. Thanks a lot, Coach Hall. Mom, I made it."

Bowie was immediately interrogated on the frailty of his legs. "They gave me a seven-hour physical," he said, meaning the Blazers' staff. "They didn't leave anything out. I don't know if that was referring to Bill Walton. He had a stress fracture." Like Olajuwon, Bowie already had ideas—make that a strong opinion—of how he might be implemented in Portland. "I think they're thinking of moving Mychal Thompson to forward and me at center," he said.

Now, at last, there was a buzz in the Felt Forum, some real electricity. Two low-level Bulls' officials were on the phone to Rod Thorn in Chicago, in what passed for a few seconds of suspense. "Everybody's excited about that one," Carnesecca commented, previewing the inevitable Jordan pick. "He captures the imagination." Stern officially pronounced the marriage that would change everything, that soon would make sneakers cost $100. "The Chicago Bulls pick Michael Jordan," Stern said. The place broke out in wild cheers. "This man is a can't miss, whether at the guard spot or forward," Albert shouted, above the din. Carnesecca called Jordan, "A great creator in the mold of Dr. J . . . a people's player. He's going to help my man, Kevin Loughery, right away."

Jordan was one of those players in Bloomington with Knight, who really didn't care one way or the other what USA Network wanted from his training schedules. His guys were set to practice that day, and they would stick to the original plan. If this had been twenty years later, Jordan surely would have been on a video conference within seconds. But back then, Knight was very much in charge, and he wasn't about to let go. With the pro futures of all these players on the line, with their minds on the draft back in New York, Knight would not budge. "We couldn't even see the draft,"

Perkins recalled. "Then after practice, we went to a broadcast station to find out where we got drafted. By the time we were through the door, we kind of heard where we'd went. We didn't have the traditional going-on-stage event." Jordan was not immediately available, and there was hardly time to consider the weight of this moment. The pick was made, and he would be interviewed whenever it was convenient, later in the show.

By now, most insiders understood that the number 4 pick was clearly going to be Sam Perkins. It was something Dean Smith knew long ago. But there was still some debate among the announcers whether the Dallas Mavericks would choose Turpin from Kentucky or Perkins from North Carolina. "Either way, you can't go wrong," Carnesecca said. "Turpin's a banger. Perkins is more like a surgeon." The pick was Perkins. "He's able to play two positions for Dallas," Carnesecca said. In the course of just four years, the Mavericks would have eight first-round picks, and Carnesecca made a prediction right then that never came true: Dallas was destined to become "a great dynasty, like Boston or the Lakers."

The Sixers were next up, with the number 5 pick they got in the deal with the San Diego Clippers for World B. Free. Quickly they chose the SEC player of the year, Charles Barkley. "He can score," Carnesecca said. "They'll bring him along slowly." The draftniks approved, heartily. Here was a colorful soul, a kindred spirit. Barkley was in attendance at the Felt Forum broadcast, wearing a maroon suit, ready for some face time. He was beaming, reaching out, and shaking hands with Stern. You would never have guessed he was cursing under his breath. Everybody was talking about his weight, throwing around numbers, how he was listed at 272 pounds, how Knight wanted him down to 215. They mentioned that Barkley once said, "I don't eat a lot . . . just all the time."

It was the humble Barkley on stage this day, though, the self-effacing Barkley. "They already have a great team," he said of

Philadelphia. "Hopefully, they'll play me at the power forward position." Sensing this comment might seem a bit brash, he quickly said he intended to "learn a lot from Marc Iavaroni," one of the more disingenuous comments ever uttered by Barkley in his long playing career. Barkley had more moves in twenty-four seconds than Iavaroni had in a season. On another delicate matter, Barkley said he didn't blame Knight at all for cutting him from the Olympic team. "No, sir, it was my inability to play defense," Barkley said. "We played primarily zone at Auburn." When the issue of his weight was broached, Barkley seemed honestly concerned, almost hurt. "I get a lot of talk about my weight," he said. "I feel I can control my weight. I don't worry about what people say about my weight. I'm going to try to play around 260, 265." Barkley thanked God. He thanked his mother and his grandmother, "the two greatest ladies on earth." There was so much to ask him, so little time. The clock was ticking down, and the Washington Bullets were about to choose Turpin, beginning one of the more painfully embarrassing few minutes in draft-day history.

First, the draftniks booed this choice with considerable conviction. Turpin was arguably overweight, like Barkley. But that was where the similarity ended. The draftniks didn't think Turpin had the athleticism to become a star. Turpin good-naturedly ignored the jeers and walked to the stage in a three-piece gray suit and striped tie. A charade began. The Bullets clearly had no interest in Dinner Bell Mel. They already had too many big, slow guys in Rick Mahorn and Jeff Ruland. They had drafted Turpin to position themselves for a complex, three-team trade with Seattle and Cleveland. The Bullets would send six-foot-eleven Turpin to Cleveland for Cliff Robinson, the rights to Tim McCormick, plus cash. Then Washington would send McCormick and Ricky Sobers, a starting guard, to Seattle for aging great Gus Williams, a thirty-year-old guard. Frankly, none of the three teams made out like bandits.

The announcers either were not clued into this forthcoming transaction or chose to ignore the rumors for the sake of decorum. For the moment, Turpin was a Bullet, and Turpin seemed to believe he would remain one. "They're going to have to enlarge the court," Carnesecca said, projecting a forecourt of Turpin, Mahorn, and Ruland. Turpin said he looked forward to playing for Gene Shue, the Washington coach. "I can learn a lot from him," he said. "I hope he'll work with me. I like to work behind the basket, use power moves." None of this was ever going to happen.

The rest of the top ten picks went along smoothly, uneventfully. With number 7, the Spurs chose Alvin Robertson, a top defensive guard said to be cut from the mold of Sidney Moncrief, a long-time mainstay in Milwaukee. Robertson would have a tough backcourt to crack in San Antonio, but he would certainly find his niche. At number 8, the sorry Clippers became no less pathetic by drafting Lancaster Gordon out of Louisville. The Clips might have drafted Barkley at number 5 if only they had kept their own pick. Instead, they chose Gordon, another disappointment-to-be. The franchise was in disarray. The Clippers were trying to move to Los Angeles at the time of this draft, but they were still using the San Diego Clippers logo. They were trying to figure out what to do with one-time great Bill Walton, an expensive acquisition who had signed with San Diego in 1979. He proved to be badly damaged goods and eventually would be shipped out in 1985 to Boston—where he would enjoy a brief renaissance. It was no wonder that college coaches like Dean Smith worried for their players, viewing a stint with the Clips as an unwanted stay in purgatory. Gordon was in Bloomington, one of sixteen players with Knight and the national team, though he would later be released in the final cut down to twelve. He became the first Olympian to pop up on a video conference to the Felt Forum. Doucette broke the bad news to Gordon, in a happy-face sort of way: "Congratulations, you are now a member of the Clippers," he told Gordon.

At number 9, the Kansas City Kings selected one of the purest of big forwards, Otis Thorpe out of Providence College, a wonderful player who had consistently out-rebounded Patrick Ewing in the Big East. "He must learn to come out and face the basket," Carnesecca said, a bit too disapprovingly. Thorpe seemed pleased and honestly surprised at this early selection, which would translate into more money ($215,000 in his rookie season) than he expected. "I had no idea," he said. "They were saying somewhere in the middle. . . ." Philadelphia then chose Leon Wood, who seemed at the time to be the logical solution to an aging backcourt. The draftniks agreed. They cheered the selection. Wood was a playmaker who could bring some offense, at least at the college level. He was on the video screen from Bloomington, wearing a shirt that read "CSUF" for California State University–Fullerton. He was happy to be with Barkley in Philly, he said. Wood asked people to hold off, though, on those comparisons between himself and Isiah Thomas. "It's a nice compliment, but I've got a lot to learn," Wood said. "I can learn a lot from Maurice Cheeks."

The Atlanta Hawks wheeled and dealed with pick number 11. They sent Dan Roundfield to Detroit and picked Kevin Willis from Michigan State. Willis, who could swing effectively between big forward and center, had suffered an ankle injury his senior year, then came on strong when it counted, when the scouts were there at the Great Aloha Classic and at the rookie showcase in Chicago. Willis looked marvelous at the Felt Forum, a fancy purple hanky sticking out of his gray suit pocket. He had been given a pep talk by Magic Johnson, and he announced that he enjoyed the physical game. "I can strengthen my defense, my ball handling," Willis said. He would be a fine player for years to come.

Cleveland owned the number 12 pick, a freebie from the commissioner jammed into the middle of the first round. The Cavs had been very bad for a very long time. The former owner, Stepien, did not help matters by trading away first-round picks as if they were half-price tickets to a Cleveland–Clipper game. This pick at number 12 was one of those giveaways that Norm Sonju in Dallas had so gravely disliked. The Cavs took McCormick at number 12, another charade. Some thought the Cavs would go for Kenny Fields at this position, but the Cavs had a deal worked out with the Bullets and needed McCormick to make it happen. Like Turpin, McCormick sounded clueless about this in front of the microphones. He was a Midwest kid, raised in Clarkston, Michigan, who had stayed in the area at the University of Michigan. "It's nice to be close to home," he said, on a feed from Bloomington, where McCormick would become another final cut by Knight. Eventually, he would be sent far, far away, traded from Cleveland to Washington, then Washington to Seattle in the three-way deal.

The Phoenix Suns chose Jay Humphries at number 13, a guard slotted to replace Dennis Johnson, who had been traded to Boston in yet another great deal for the Celtics. Humphries was supposed to be a good ball handler; he would feed Walter Davis, and there would be a harmonic convergence in the Suns' backcourt again. Except that Humphries was no Johnson, and the draftniks knew it right away. They chanted, "Who?" from the stands.

Now, finally, Michael Jordan appeared on a video screen from Bloomington. He had a tiny microphone in his left ear, the wire clumsily dangling down across his beige polo shirt. The interview was basic, meat-and-potatoes stuff. Jordan was self-confident without appearing arrogant. Unlike some of those who went before him, he was not about to dictate his playing position on draft day. "If I have to play small forward, guard, whatever the team needs," Jordan said. "I'm not looking forward to going in, living up to everyone's expectations. Just doing the best I can. I'm looking forward to meeting Coach Loughery, and looking forward to his coaching ability. Hopefully, I can go in and contribute, turn it around."

That was it from Jordan. There was no time for further reflection, because those woeful Clippers were up again, ready at pick number 14. They chose Michael Cage, the local kid from San Diego State, a solid choice and a bit of a surprise. Cage was a six-foot-nine forward, 220. But the Clippers already had Terry Cummings, which seemed to suggest a deal was in the offing.

Before there was too much speculation, however, Sam Perkins popped up on the video feed from Bloomington. He wore a white sleeveless shirt and a big smile. "You could be that last piece," Doucette remarked about Perkins's fit with the Mavericks. "I feel very fortunate about the pick," Perkins said. "I talked to Dick Motta, he told me what I can do. I don't know if I'm the missing link. They have a nice program down there. Either position will do, I'm capable of playing center and forward. . . . I'll probably be a center because of my bulk [compared to Barkley and Turpin, Perkins wasn't really what anybody else would term 'bulky']. I'll have to do a lot of work when I get down there." The Perkins interview ended abruptly so that the Mavericks could pick again, at number 15, and this would prove to be a terrible choice. With John Stockton still available, the Mavs instead picked Stansbury. Carnesecca loved the selection. "I remember him taking the last shot that beat me in the NCAA tournament," Carnesecca said. "He reminds me of Dave Bing. An excellent choice. He can see the whole court. He's a good backup for Rolando Blackman."

A remote interview with Alvin Robertson from Bloomington was cut short again by surprise pick number 16. "The Utah Jazz select John Stockton of Gonzaga University," Stern announced. There were audible murmurs from the crowd. The draftniks were baffled by this one, a real mystery. "Not many know about John Stockton," Albert said. "His name is certainly not on the lips of the fans here in New York. His star is rising." There was some quick paper shuffling by the announcers. Stockton had just been picked fifth among the guard prospects in this draft but was ranked nowhere near that high by conventional wisdom. Carnesecca and Albert kicked around the pick a bit more, which made little sense on those annotations in front of them. The Jazz already had a solid backcourt in Rickey Green and Darrell Griffith. "Frank Layden is certainly sticking his neck out," Albert said. Everybody just figured the Jazz had wasted a pick on a diminutive project, a backup point guard. Stockton himself watched the draft on television and smiled when he saw Carnesecca and Albert struggle to identify Utah's odd sixteenth pick. "The best thing about the draft," Stockton would recall, "was watching the guys on TV flipping through their notes trying to find something on me."

The draft droned on. The Nets waited until the last minute and then picked Jeff Turner, the Vanderbilt forward highly touted by Knight. The draftniks booed, correctly. Detroit picked Tony Campbell at number 20. Michael Young out of Houston was the last pick in the first round, by Boston. Portland owned two second-round picks. The Trail Blazers chose Victor Fleming at number 26 and then plucked Jerome Kersey out of Longwood College with the forty-sixth pick overall. Not many had heard of Kersey. Blake had. "Scouted him at a game, he had 20 rebounds," Blake said. "Then I brought him to Portsmouth, he didn't play well. I thought he was loafing."

The draft broadcast was done, its educated guesses and random acts now history. There was an alternative NBA universe out there, somewhere, with Jordan in Dallas or Houston, with Olajuwon in Portland, with Stockton a San Diego/Los Angeles Clipper. It was easy to imagine several scenarios in which the Bulls might have lost Jordan at the number 3 pick:

1. If Portland had won the coin flip, the Blazers planned to choose Olajuwon while the Rockets would have taken Jordan at the number 2 spot to complement Sampson.

2. If the Rockets had offered a deal sending Ralph Sampson to Chicago, the Bulls were willing to trade away their number 3 pick.

3. If the Cavaliers had lost just one more game during the regular season, or if the Bulls had won one more, the two teams would have finished in a tie. A coin flip might have awarded the number 3 pick to the Dallas Mavericks, who owned Cleveland's draft choice.

4. If Sam Bowie's frail legs had failed a physical exam with Portland, the Blazers would have settled on Jordan.

5. If Bowie had come out after his sophomore year, when his mother hung up the phone on that notion, the Blazers would have tabbed Jordan.

6. If the Rockets had grabbed local hero Clyde Drexler in the 1983 draft with their second pick, number 3 overall in the first round, then Portland would not have been able to choose Drexler much lower, at number 14. Without Drexler, the Blazers would have lacked a young shooting guard and would have picked Jordan in 1984.

7. If Jonathan Kovler, the Bulls' chief operating officer, had insisted on accepting Harold Katz's offer of the established, aging superstar, Julius Erving, then Thorn might not have been able to retain the number 3 pick.

You never know. If only Moses had gone left . . .

15

Not Twins at All

Hindsight isn't just 20–20; it's also rose-colored. And so when a retired Bill Fitch looked back on his first days with Olajuwon, he recalled that the big man made this transition from the University of Houston to the Houston Rockets as seamlessly as the geography suggested. "He was running back doors, doing drop steps like he was still in college," Fitch said. "He was much better than we thought, and we thought he would be very good." Fitch always had a soft spot for Olajuwon, always forgave the seven-foot Nigerian his early follies far more easily than he excused the very different flaws of Ralph Sampson. In this way Olajuwon was for Fitch what Magic Johnson was for Pat Riley, what Michael Jordan would be for Phil Jackson, what Patrick Ewing would be for Jeff Van Gundy. Fitch would tether his wagon to Olajuwon, the big horse, go along for the ride. But when Olajuwon arrived for training camp in September 1984, with a fresh six-year contract worth about $6.3 million, he was not quite ready to carry such a load. Olajuwon, in truth, didn't really know the definition of a drop step.

His college coach, Guy Lewis, had been right. Olajuwon could have used another year on campus.

Fitch joked that Olajuwon liked sometimes to run the whole Houston offense, which was fine except that it was the Houston Cougar offense. There were definitely some adjustments to be made, and not just on the court. This was still very much the party-animal version of Olajuwon. After signing his deal in August, he had spent much of his time tooling around the streets of Houston in a new Mercedes and precious little time training in the gym. Friends advised Olajuwon to change his habits. He advised them to take a ride in his Mercedes. Then he came to the Rockets and paid a quick price for such arrogance. These NBA players were much faster than he had thought, when he was watching the games on television. He could no longer "donk and donk and donk," as he liked to say in college. Olajuwon soon came to realize that considerable work, and some nuanced moves, were necessary to avoid embarrassment. Avoiding such humiliation was one of the great motivating factors in the proud life of the young Olajuwon.

The first matter during Rockets exhibition season was to shove Sampson over to power forward. For his cooperation in this matter, Sampson received precious little praise from Rockets' management. His concession was simply taken for granted. "I contended at the time that if Hakeem had been there first, and then they'd drafted Ralph, that Hakeem wouldn't have done it," said Fran Blinebury, the *Houston Chronicle* writer. "People overlook how damned good Ralph was, yet he was willing to go over there to the other position. He knew physically he had a high center of gravity, and he figured he could move over to forward and shoot some jumpers." More than twenty years later, Olajuwon still feels that this move by Sampson was not such a big deal. "Moving Ralph was not really a sacrifice because I don't believe there is a difference in the center position or the power forward position—they are both post positions. Our concept was not by 'position,' it was a concept of 'Twin Towers'—double trouble. Ralph and I always had a good relationship, and even though we don't keep in touch today, I still consider him a good friend."

In those early exhibition games, Olajuwon and Sampson were still uncomfortable and largely ineffective. Olajuwon was overmatched by Robert Parish of the Celtics and Artis Gilmore of the Spurs. He looked to Sampson for help. "I look up to him, I can't help it," Olajuwon said then. When Fitch told the team he was thinking of bringing Bill Russell to a practice to speak with the big men, Olajuwon stared blankly at him. He had never heard of Russell and never heard of Red Auerbach, either. Fitch got a kick out of Olajuwon, though, even as he boiled about Sampson. "He's such a good person, no one seems to mind," Fitch said, when asked about Olajuwon's confusion over the coach's system. He was mostly mad at Sampson, the same Sampson who had been named Rookie of the Year for his 21 points per game. As the preseason came to a close, Fitch was just starting to feel the heat about not choosing Michael Jordan, already anointed a superstar in Chicago. And in an interview with the *New York Times*, Fitch was now blaming Sampson for the decision to take Olajuwon.

If Ralph had been ready, I might have thought about taking Michael Jordan. Ready to be the tough, serious-minded, hard-nosed center he has to be. It's not his fault, I know, that people said he was so good. He wasn't. But now, he's been through a year and he's had all the nights when I've patted him on the butt and said, 'That's okay.' This year I'm gonna' be on him every night because he's the guy. He has to be dominating. He's got to eliminate the mistakes. On their bad nights, superstars are usually as good as the average player. Ralph wasn't like that. On his bad nights, he was awful.

There was another reason, Fitch says now, why it was important to choose Olajuwon in the draft. It was a reason that sounded particularly absurd in retrospect, considering Jordan's commercial successes. "We're in a business. We have to put people in the seats," Fitch said. "If we'd taken Jordan, [Rockets' owner] Charlie Thomas would've probably had to leave town."

This Olajuwon–Sampson marriage was going to have to work, and Sampson was struggling even worse than Olajuwon. He sprained an ankle, and he could not quite figure out where to go to get the ball at his new power forward position. Sampson was fine on the fly. But out of the halfcourt set, he was drifting too far on the wing, forcing long-distance jumpers that were outside his range. He was too worried about getting in Olajuwon's way. Sampson was making all his critics look good, playing like a point guard, and a lousy one at that.

Then the regular season started, and suddenly Fitch was a genius. Who needed Jordan? The Rockets, aided by a reasonably easy early schedule, stormed off to an 8–0 start. The opener was a signal of things to come, in many ways. Sampson deferred to Olajuwon from the start—from before the start, actually—waving his smaller team-mate into the center circle to take the tip-off on opening day. Olajuwon at center scored 24 points; Sampson at power forward added 19 points and 14 rebounds. Fitch was positively beaming. "I guess the court was big enough for the two of them, after all," he said. Here was redemption, too, for the whole organization, which had sent Moses Malone packing in 1982.

The Rockets' early streak continued, with good feelings all around. "He's always protecting me on the backside," Olajuwon said, about Sampson. "If I go for a block and miss it, I know that he's going to be there to get the rebound." In their eighth game, the two players combined for 37 points in a victory over Cleveland. The Rockets were now the only undefeated team in the NBA, though on the same day Michael Jordan scored 45 points to lead the Bulls to their fourth straight victory. This was very clearly a new NBA, and the Rockets were going to be a big part of it. The team wasn't just

Olajuwon and Sampson, either. The top four scorers were all shooting over 50 percent. Rodney McCray, twenty-three years old, was a prototypical small forward at six feet, seven inches, averaging 14.4 points on 53.5 percent shooting. Lewis Lloyd, twenty-five, was a pure six-foot-six scoring guard, an awesome finisher on the break, who would average 13.1 points on 52.6 percent shooting that season. There was good depth in Robert Reid, Mitchell Wiggins, and Lionel Hollins. But there was a big problem at point guard, where the talented John Lucas was in the midst of his worst drug problems.

Lucas was dropped from the team in December after testing positive for cocaine and then was reinstated in late February. The Rockets did not adjust well to his absence. In January they skidded to a four-game losing streak, as their record fell to an unremarkable 21–18. They had gone 13–18 since that explosive start. Though they would right themselves somewhat and finish at 48–34, Fitch was no longer in a great mood. And an angry Fitch was not a pleasant one. He was known to be a fine game coach, a strong strategist, and a hard worker. But he was not for everyone. Fitch was a determined taskmaster and control freak, not a players' coach in the mold of a K. C. Jones who followed him with the Celtics back in 1983. Fitch had been forced out of Boston that year, just two seasons after winning an NBA championship. That was a veteran, self-driven team in need of no further motivational speeches. Several Celtics had reached their limits with the man. And here in Houston, Fitch had not changed his caustic ways.

Fitch was ultrasensitive about reports in the local newspapers. Many coaches felt that griping to the media was a form of betrayal by players, but Fitch took this a step further. The previous season, he had ordered Sampson to read an article aloud to teammates in which Sampson had complained that practices were too lengthy. This time, Fitch forced Wiggins to stand and recite a story by local reporter Robert Falkoff, in which Wiggins commented that the team's offense had become too predictable and stagnant. Wiggins, like Sampson, was a vulnerable soul. He would be expelled from the league in 1987 for drug problems. Fitch could not abide character weaknesses and innately sensed them in players like Sampson and Wiggins. Humiliations inevitably followed.

Those two players, however, were not ultimately the cause of the Rockets' playoff demise that spring. Instead, Olajuwon's Shakespearean flaws, his raw temper and fierce pride, doomed the Rockets in the first round of the playoffs against the Jazz. This was a best-of-five series, knotted at two games apiece, and the rubber game was played in Houston. The Rockets appeared to have this contest won, after Utah's seven-foot-four center, Mark Eaton, hyperextended his knee and was forced to the bench late in the first half. Houston had two giant young colts, Olajuwon and Sampson, going against a smaller Jazz team with aging, creaky Billy Paultz holding down the paint. Paultz, nicknamed "The Whopper," had been in professional basketball for fifteen years, dating back to his days with the New York Nets of the ABA. Paultz virtually defined the term "journeyman" in sports. He was six feet, eleven inches, devoid of any God-given talents other than sheer pluck and a way of getting under opponents' skin. At age thirty-six he had been with five different teams in two different leagues. Sure enough, Olajuwon had his way with Paultz for much of the third quarter, scoring 14 points on the way to a 76–67 lead. But The Whopper was canny, and he had a few dirty tricks up his sleeveless jersey. Paultz kept working on Olajuwon, pushing him, shoving him, slapping at him. And Olajuwon was growing furious. "He punched me and I tried to get the referees' attention, and I couldn't, so I punched him back," Olajuwon said. "I didn't know if it fired them up, but he had already punched me in the stomach about four times."

The retaliatory punch had, in fact, fired up the Jazz big time, while Olajuwon lost his playing compass. Utah scored 37 points in the last quarter. Paultz finished with 6 points and 5 rebounds. Thurl Bailey outmaneuvered Sampson, and the Jazz fashioned a 104–97 victory to eliminate the Rockets. "The Old Whopper earned his money today," said Frank Layden, the Jazz coach. This would be Paultz's farewell spring, his good-bye to the pros, and the professional pest chided Olajuwon afterwards. "Either he can't punch or I can really take a punch," Paultz said. "It just shows what emotion and intensity can do."

Already in these playoffs Sampson was not the same player, starting to show signs of wear and tear. He had crash-landed while going for a rebound on March 24, 1985, in Boston Garden, smashing his head into the parquet floor and badly bruising his left hip. Under pressure to return quickly and prepare for the playoffs, Sampson ran awkwardly and began to do terrible things to his knees, which would deteriorate over the next two seasons and require surgery. Fitch closed practices to the media that spring, just so reporters would not see Sampson limp around the court, getting torched by Olajuwon in scrimmages.

Sampson enjoyed only occasional periods after that when his health was intact, but the maturing Rockets grew stronger the next season anyway, finishing with a 51–31 mark. On May 21, 1986, Houston eliminated the Lakers in Game 5 of the Western Conference final, 114–112. Sampson took an inbounds pass from McCray, spun, and threw up a spinning ten-foot shot at the buzzer. The ball banged off the front rim, then the back, then the front, and then dropped in for the winner. Olajuwon finished with 30 points, Sampson 29.

But even in his moment of glory, there were still signs that Olajuwon was not yet ready to handle this kind of pressure. Olajuwon was fine when he respected an opponent in a matchup. But he was a time bomb whenever a pest was assigned to him. In this case, the designated hacker was Mitch Kupchak. With just more than five minutes left in the game, Olajuwon and Kupchak were banging at each other under the Rockets' basket when Olajuwon suddenly started throwing right uppercuts. A referee and then Maurice Lucas pulled Olajuwon away. Players flew off both benches, because this was still a time when such an action was not punished by automatic ejection. Sampson tried to get at Maurice Lucas. Craig Ehlo of the Rockets tried to get at James Worthy. It was a terrible mess. Olajuwon was tossed from this critical game, along with Kupchak. Thanks to Sampson, the Rockets survived and knocked off the defending champions. The Rockets lost to Boston in the NBA Finals but were dubbed the team of the future by nearly everyone. All they needed was another year and another guard, everybody figured. It didn't turn out that way. "Our window was right there," John Lucas said.

Sampson would miss 41 games the next season, 1986–87. His wars with Fitch grew uglier. There were other problems, from the tragic to the supercilious. McCray's daughter, just five years old, was diagnosed with an inoperable brain tumor. There were rumors that Sampson and Wiggins hated Fitch so much that they were tanking games to get the coach fired. Patterson said that would never happen, backing up Fitch with a contract extension. Soon, Wiggins and Lloyd were expelled by the league for violating rules of the NBA drug program.

"History books get changed," said Rick Sund, the former director of personnel for the Dallas Mavericks. "But if Sampson doesn't get hurt, we'd never have beaten the Rockets. We were something like 3–17 against them, against the Twin Towers. But Sampson, because of injuries, never got to be the player he might have been." Through all this upheaval with the franchise, Olajuwon was himself a handful. "He was wild and crazy, among the league leaders in technicals," Blinebury said. "He was 'motherfucker this and that.' He was ready to hit anybody at anytime, and at the rate he was going, he was likely to get blown right out of the league. His transformation into an MVP statesman had as much to do with his religious awakening as anything." This was not a sudden, revelatory conversion. Instead, Olajuwon slowly, sincerely, began to believe that it was time to find himself in the ways of his family and culture. "I grew up in a Muslim family and my parents were very religious people," Olajuwon wrote recently from his home in Jordan.

My generation was of the mindset that religion was for the "elders." If you were young, you should be outside playing and looking forward to studying abroad in the U.K. or U.S. Religion was not a concern for us. If you were young AND religious, you were considered "not cool." I don't remember exactly when I decided to get serious about my religion but it was a few years after entering the pros. Islam is a way of life and once I had the opportunity to gain more knowledge about my religion, it made it easier to begin living that lifestyle and fulfilling my religious obligations. That knowledge also contributed to my behavior by teaching me the importance of patience and tolerance.

If there was a moment when this rededication became most obvious to the reporters covering the team, it was when Olajuwon decided that he could no longer be referred to in writing as "Akeem." His parents were in town for a visit, and he wanted them to see his name appear correctly in the newspaper. Blinebury was in the press work room, writing a game day story, when the Rockets' public relations director at the time, Jay Goldberg, informed reporters that the spelling from now on was "Hakeem," not "Akeem." That was the proper spelling all along, but Olajuwon had allowed everyone to spell his name incorrectly. The "H" at the start of the name was very soft, nearly unpronounced. "It is a name that comes from the Qur'an and was really just a mispronunciation (Akeem) rather than the correct spelling and pronunciation of Hakeem," Olajuwon explained. "Again, when I became more knowledgeable, I decided to correct it." Hakeem means literally "wise man, a doctor," in Arabic; Akeem means nothing. When he first changed it back in 1991, Olajuwon said this was "no big deal."

"I just want to go back to using the original spelling. Akeem is just the way that many people write my name when they are putting it into English," he explained. "Even back at home in Nigeria, some of my teachers in high school spelled it one way, some the other. I didn't think it mattered when I first came here and they spelled it that way at the University of Houston. But when I would go back home or when I would talk to my mother, she would ask me why my name has changed. I always thought it would be something very complicated to change." It wasn't complicated at all. The writers started writing "Hakeem," and that was that. The only one who had trouble with it, at least for a while, was Olajuwon himself. For some time, he still would sign autographs "Akeem."

Olajuwon's transformation with the Rockets was obvious. He was now calmer, a reliable and poised leader in the face of great pressure. Fitch was gone. Sampson was gone. With a new coach, Rudy Tom-janovich, and new teammates in place, he captured two titles in 1994 and 1995 during the span when Jordan was retired or just coming out of retirement. Olajuwon played 17 seasons in Houston, plus one unfortunate season in Toronto. Over 1,238 regular season games, he finished with averages of 21.8 points, 11.1 rebounds, and 3.1 blocks.

Olajuwon became a naturalized American citizen in 1993, capturing a gold medal with the U.S. Olympic team at the 1996 Summer Games in Atlanta. When he retired in 2002, Olajuwon surprised many people by moving his family to Jordan, returning to Houston only during the summers. "I started coming to Jordan [in 1996] and always enjoyed my time here," he explained recently.

It was my summer home for many years in which I would enroll in an intensive 6-week Arabic program. I always said when I retired, I would like to continue my studies on a full-time basis if I had the opportunity. My day is probably like many other people's days. I drive my children to school and then I go to class. I exercise regularly, check my emails and do my homework. I also spend time taking care of my business back in Houston. I don't really think my philosophy has changed, because you can apply the same principles on and off the court. I had a fulfilling career and was grateful to have accomplished a lot during my career. That chapter is now closed and I have the opportunity to accomplish other goals in life.

Olajuwon and Sampson took very different roads after their four years together. Sampson's path was a rocky one that would lead to sad consequences all around. He would play for nothing but bad teams after he was traded by Houston to Golden State in 1988. His can't-miss career lost steam because of knee problems. In his final four seasons in the NBA, Sampson's per-game scoring average sank to 6.4 points, then 4.2, then 3.0, and finally 2.2 in Washington. After he retired, there were worse problems. The extraordinary money that these modern players earned during their careers was supposed to allow them to live financially solvent, even luxurious existences well past their retirement. Yet in 2005, Sampson pleaded guilty in Richmond for failing to pay about $300,000 in court-ordered child support for two kids with two different mothers who were living in northern Virginia. Before he could be sentenced, he was indicted on perjury charges in 2006. Prosecutors charged that Sampson, then forty-six, had lied to them during investigations on the child care case. He had allegedly hidden income as a consultant and endorser for two companies as well as his ownership of a sport utility vehicle. Sampson was freed on bond but faced travel restrictions. In September 2006, the federal prosecutors dropped perjury and false claim charges, in exchange for Sampson's guilty plea to mail fraud. He was sentenced to two months in prison.

Olajuwon is quite busy doing charity work and helped to establish a mosque in Houston through his contributions. In February 2005, it was revealed that the mosque, the Islamic Da'Wah Center, had donated more than $80,000 to charities, including the Islamic African Relief Agency and Holy Land Foundation for Relief and Development, which the U.S. government claimed had ties with Al Qaeda and other terrorist organizations. Olajuwon was horrified by this report and initiated a forty-minute teleconference call with reporters to deny any knowledge of such connections. He said the money was targeted for medicine and schools.

"It took my whole career to build my name and the causes that I choose to support," Olajuwon, while in Amman, Jordan, told reporters.

> It's difficult to accept when my name is linked into anything such as terrorism. At the time they were raising the money in 2000, we didn't even know anything about a terrorist. It was reported in our tax return. This wasn't something that was secretive. It was very open. That's what I'm referring to. This was clear. This was not something underground. It was clearly a fund-raising for the relief organization. You see their work, you see their brochure, they've been doing it for years and they're approved by the government. And it's not just us. And they go to different communities to raise funds, because they have this permit. We don't want to give the money where most of the money is spent on the administration.

The call done, Olajuwon retreated to his studies and his private life. In August 2006, Olajuwon returned to Houston to help coach the Nigerian national basketball team as it prepared for the world championships in Japan. He had invited the twelve-member team to his American base city, where he gave the players a three-day tutorial. At that moment, Olajuwon was a U.S. citizen, residing primarily in Jordan, coaching his native African countrymen. He was a citizen of the world, of three continents.

16

After the Fall

Sam Bowie quite correctly found little shame in his odd, uncomfortable place in history. He preferred to think of himself not as arguably the worst NBA draft pick ever, but instead as a player who once earned the right through wearying perseverance to be chosen ahead of Michael Jordan in the extraordinary 1984 draft.

"Believe it or not, I still take it as a compliment," Bowie said. "And that's the way most people view it. I don't think anyone kicks anyone when they're down. Nobody knew I'd have more setbacks with my leg. Nobody knew Michael would become the kind of player he did. I feel very flattered when I hear my name mentioned with him and know that I was drafted before him."

For about two decades, Bowie has said more or less the same thing at dinner parties, at basketball games, and on the air as a commentator. His four-year stay in Portland and his ten-year NBA career were surely honorable, though they were neither smooth nor exceptional. From the start there were problems. Contract negotiations required more time than expected, several weeks beyond what either side desired. Bowie's agent, Larry Fleisher, also represented Portland free agent Jim Paxson and needed to get Bowie signed first so that the Blazers could then match any offer to Paxson from another franchise and still remain unfettered by the complex rules of the salary cap. If the Blazers went over the cap too soon with Paxson, then Portland could only offer Bowie the NBA minimum salary of $75,000. The whole process was delayed by regularly scheduled league meetings, and then it took a while for Fleisher to get into the meat of talks with Alan Rothenberg, the Blazers' attorney who was still, inexplicably, president of the San Diego Clippers. Despite public hints to the contrary, Fleisher did not want to sign his client to a one-year deal and then test the free agent waters. Who could know the fate of Bowie's shin? A multi-year guarantee was essential. "I was kind of worried about what the people in that area were thinking: 'Is Sam holding out and would he be there for fall camp?'" Bowie recalled. "I definitely did not want to come in on a bad note. I was packed and ready to go, but I'm paying a guy like Larry Fleisher to negotiate my contract and I had to do what he said."

Bargaining dragged on, even after first and third picks Olajuwon and Jordan were signed by Houston and Chicago, in part because Bowie had his own personal financial adviser. Bill Wilcox was required to sign off on any pact, and he did not like the contract language on some deferred payments. But Bowie finally agreed to a six-year deal on September 25, 1984, worth about $5 million—fine money for those days, salary cap or not. At the time, only two other rookies, Olajuwon and Ralph Sampson, ever had larger, per-year salaries. "I knew it was just a matter of time," Bowie told the Associated Press then, from his home in Lexington. "I was just waiting for the phone call." He was in Portland two days later for the team's first practice. This was especially important to the Blazers, because Drexler had missed weeks of training camp the previous season during a holdout. Drexler then required longer than expected to adjust. Bowie said he was ready to contribute, that he expected to fill a similar role with Portland as he had with Kentucky: he would block shots, rebound, and key the break. "A guy who can get the ball to someone who can score," he defined himself, espousing characteristically modest goals.

Just five days later, he was out with a cracked rib caused by a stray elbow to the back, between his shoulder blades, during a scrimmage with teammates. Over the summer, Ramsay met three times with Bowie and placed him on a thorough weight program to increase his strength. It didn't help, and that seven-hour, pre-draft medical exam by the Blazers' doctor now appeared hopelessly inadequate. It could not possibly foretell all of Bowie's brittle bones. Though he would recover quickly from this injury, it was a bad and accurate omen about problems to come.

People often forgot (though Bowie never did) that the Kentucky center appeared to be a solid draft pick for quite some time, for more than a season. When he returned from the broken rib after a couple weeks, Bowie's rhythm was off, but his body and mind were willing. He was embarrassed in one early November game by Kareem Abdul-Jabbar, when the Los Angeles Lakers' center outscored Bowie, 27–4, including a 17–0 trouncing in the first half. He was learning, though, he said. Just give him time. "I didn't like it, but in the sixteen years Kareem has been in the league nobody else has stopped him either so I guess you could say I'm in good company," Bowie said then, in an interview with the *Christian Science Monitor*.

> I also know I'll get better. The fact that I was injured and didn't have a training camp with the club is not a good way for a rookie to start. At least during that period you are going to learn some of the things you need to know about your new teammates. But when you have to gain that knowledge and win at the same time, you are often apt to

be a little tentative. One of the first things that has struck me as a rookie is the talent level throughout the league. Every center I've played against so far has been big, strong, and smarter about the game than I am. I used to have to deal with maybe one seven-footer a game in college, but in the NBA they're all over the place.

Not at Golden State, however. A week later against the Warriors, when he was not faced with such an intimidating matchup, Bowie scored 14 points in the final period and pulled down 12 rebounds to lead Portland over Golden State, 109–97. Bowie eventually settled into a performance niche, somewhere between that Lakers game and that Warriors game. He had a reasonably promising NBA season, averaging 10 points and 8.6 rebounds in nearly thirty minutes per game, getting named to the All-Rookie team. He was called for a lot of sloppy personals, fouling out nine times. And he did not exactly transform Portland into an instant contender, as had been the most optimistic version of the master plan. Inman said there were signs almost immediately that Bowie was not going to take this franchise by the lapels and drag it anywhere. "He was a terrific kid, if you visited with him," Inman said. "If I were to describe Sam, I would have to say he would always be happiest as one member, one part of a team. His attitude was, 'I don't want to carry this team. I'll make a major contribution.'"

The Blazers dropped from 48-game winners in 1983–84 to 42-game winners in 1984–85. They clearly missed the toughness of Calvin Natt, and then Kenny Carr's knee surgery compounded the problem. There was now a pervasive softness to the team, personified not only by Bowie but by Vandeweghe and Paxson. Still, all in all, the future looked bright enough. The Blazers could score points like crazy, with four players averaging more than 17 points. Drexler was becoming a star. Portland upset Dallas in a tough playoff series that spring of 1985 before losing to the eventual champions, the

Lakers. A year earlier, pre-Bowie, the Blazers had been knocked out in the first round.

There was naturally a bit of nervousness in Portland, more than a trace of second guessing, because Jordan had averaged 28.2 points as a rookie in Chicago and was evidently a superstar in the making. Then it was Jordan, not Bowie, who went down first after only 18 games in the fall of 1985 with a foot injury. Bowie was playing quite well his sophomore year in the pros, improving to 11.8 points per game, learning the ropes. This was still not a bad draft decision, not yet. But Bowie started suffering pains again in his left shinbone, and another operation was required to correct a defect in the leg and to excise bone spurs in his big toe. He played a total of 38 games that season. The next year was worse. In November 1986, just five games into the new season, Bowie landed clumsily after a jump shot and broke his right shinbone, badly. Drexler remembered seeing the bone sticking out of Bowie's leg and his teammate writhing in agony. "He was beating the floor over and over with his fist," Drexler said. This was a terrible setback, and by now the writing was on the greaseboard. Bowie just wasn't built for this wear and tear. Doctors inserted three screws into the right shinbone, but then two of them loosened, and yet another operation was required to insert two more.

On it went like this, comeback followed by crushing setback. When he returned for another round in 1987, that right shinbone fractured again during warm-ups before an exhibition game against the Cavaliers. He needed another graft from his hip bone, surgery similar to the one on his left shin, only more complex. His right leg now was patched together with a bone graft, ten screws, and a metal plate. Bowie played 20 games that season and had by then missed 183 games out of 246 over three seasons. The sight of Bowie hobbling to and from the Portland locker room on crutches became a constant, painful reminder to management that it had not drafted

Jordan, who had recovered from his foot problem and was by now in full, glorious flight. Bowie felt guilty about collecting his large salary, but he was an eternal optimist, a man with a strong Christian faith. He believed things happened for a reason, that he was being tested. "You will never be put through more than you can handle," he said to himself. The Portland fans were not thrilled with the situation, but they did not hold Bowie responsible. They graciously voted Bowie and Jerome Kersey cowinners of an award for most inspirational player on the team. In this way, Bowie was fortunate not to be playing in New York or Philadelphia.

"My main objective is to play the game for the fun of it and the love of it," Bowie told the *Los Angeles Times*, as he came back for the playoffs against the Lakers in the spring of 1988. "Every time I go off the court, I'm thankful I didn't get hurt again. I think too many people take their health for granted. . . . I like that I can be some sort of inspiration for people during trying times, but what I've gone through and what I'm going through—the comeback—is nothing I consider heroic by any means. Sure, I've had my share of surgery and broken bones, but these things were meant to be. I'm a Christian and I've always felt that tomorrow is predetermined."

Bowie returned in time to meet his nemesis, Abdul-Jabbar, in Game 1 of the playoffs that spring of 1988. He had a decent performance, hitting 6 of 7 shots for 15 points. But Portland was swept in that first-round series, and the Blazers decided to cut their losses. They traded Bowie plus a first-round pick to the Nets in 1989 for Buck Williams, a move that did the franchise considerable good. The Blazers had dealt a porcelain doll for an NBA iron man. Williams missed only one game in his first six seasons with the Nets—because of a suspension for defending himself against Lonnie Shelton in a frightening boxing match. The Blazers got seven good seasons out of Williams, who was just past his prime as a premier power forward. They got eleven seasons out of Kersey. They reached the NBA Finals in 1990 and 1992, when they were within two games of a championship.

So the Blazers recovered, somewhat, from their famous draft gaffe of 1984. And yet to this day the franchise is struggling financially, not enjoying the same innocent love affair between city and team that existed in the late 70s and early 80s. Its owner, Paul Allen, dreamed on too large a scale by financing in part the grandiose Rose Garden Arena. The Oregon Arena Corporation declared bankruptcy, and Allen began demanding funds from city taxpayers, vaguely threatening in a 2006 interview with reporters to move the Blazers elsewhere if no money was forthcoming. An edited version of the interview was posted on the Blazers' official Web site, for public access and personal emphasis. Allen is a billionaire co-founder of Microsoft, and so it was a bit tough for him to plead poverty. But Allen said that he would rather give the money to civic or charity organizations and that a private-public partnership was essential:

> When the original deal was made for the Trail Blazers, the finances of the league were different. For example, the salary cap for the 1991–92 season was $12.5 million. For the current season, it is $49.5 million. In retrospect, we should have made a deal that was a sustainable one for the Trail Blazers over the long term, and that made sense for the city. It's hard. As a businessman, I'm out of pocket hundreds of thousands of dollars—each and every game. That's brutal. . . . I want the team to stay in Portland. If this all ends up in the courts or someone buys the team and moves it, it would be a shame.

Would any of this have been different if the Blazers had drafted Jordan? It is impossible to know, of course, but dynastic successes can do wonders for a team's mid-term finances. Championship seasons build a communal reservoir of good will, and there is usually a substantial grace period before fans lose interest or revolt. Jordan left Chicago after 1998, but the mediocre-to-lousy Bulls averaged more than twenty-one thousand fans per game for the next three seasons and drew well over eighteen thousand per game after that. The Blazers were once a red-hot ticket, selling out their Coliseum from the 70s through the 90s (the famous capacity number, for years, was 10,666). From 1995 to 2003, the new Rose Garden drew close to or above twenty thousand per game. In more recent years, average attendance had slid into the sixteen thousands—and that was the announced attendance, not always reflecting sparse reality inside the arena when the Blazers were abysmal, as they were in 2005–2006. Things became so testy between the team and the media that the communications department announced that all requests for interviews would have to be approved by the team and that transcripts of the taped interviews would be made available to everyone on the team Web site. This effectively destroyed any possible exclusive news reporting and placed an additional strain on relations between reporters and team officials.

A Jordan draft pick might have meant banners, buzz, jersey sales, enough fannies in the seats to keep any owner happy for a while. Inman liked to look at it a different way. He preferred to think of that draft pick in 1984 as a freebie, as gravy. If you wanted to go around pointing fingers, he figured, then one should be pointed at the Indiana Pacers for trading away their pick in the first place.

"You look back, of course you'd change," Inman said. "But that would be quite the parlay, maybe asking too much. You give up Tom Owens [to the Pacers] for a first round pick and get Michael Jordan? Michael was not where our thinking was, not where our needs were. I'm so happy that Michael Jordan helped the NBA as much as he did and I'm happy for everything he did in Chicago. He accomplished it with dignity. He was one of a kind. I'd put him in my starting five, all-time, certainly."

Bowie was in nobody's top five. He played four years with the Blazers, four with the Nets, two with the Lakers, then retired. He finished with a career average of 10.5 points and 7.5 rebounds, numbers that were not far out of line with his final season in college. He suffered many more bumps and bruises along the way in New Jersey and Los Angeles, but the screws in his leg held relatively firm. He moved his family to Lexington and coached his oldest girl in basketball. His wife, Heidi, had some personal problems with a prescription drug that became public in 2001. Bowie quit his job as color commentator at Kentucky games in order to focus on his family. Sam and Heidi Bowie worked through the crisis together. Again, he was a rock.

"Everybody will say the same thing about Sam," said Kenny Walker, his old teammate at Kentucky. "He was a great basketball player, but a better person. You won't find a more quality guy than Sam Bowie. You're going against big, strong guys, you want them to be mean, intimidating. That wasn't Sam. Sam just does what he has to do."

If that meant not being Michael Jordan or Bill Walton, so be it. Sam Bowie never asked to be drafted number 2.

"I feel bad for Sam Bowie," Charles Barkley said. "He's a great guy and he couldn't help getting hurt. Everybody in hindsight tried to rag on him, as if they knew Michael Jordan would be Michael Jordan. I was the only one who knew it."

17

A Different Kind of Star

When Michael Jordan arrived in Chicago from Bloomington the day after the draft, the city's institutional memory immediately suspected another ruse. The Bulls had been hopeless for what seemed like forever. This was not the big man, not the anchor at center, who was desperately needed to construct a championship team. Rod Thorn and Kevin Loughery posed with Jordan for local newspaper photographers, and the only one who looked truly confident in those snapshots was Jordan. It would be months before Jordan joined the Bulls' first practice, before Thorn would get a welcome phone call from Bill Blair, the assistant coach. Blair would watch Jordan scrimmage against some bedazzled teammates, many of them veterans, all of them completely outclassed. Blair's simple message allowed Thorn to exhale, finally. "Looks like you didn't fuck this one up," Blair told Thorn.

But redemption for Thorn was still around the corner, down the block from that acoustically wondrous bandbox, Chicago Stadium. First came the tricky matter of signing this hot shot to a contract, a process Thorn called "reasonably hard." Jordan was coming off the Olympics, where his stock as a player and a drawing card had risen substantially. He had intangibles and tremendous marketing potential that were impossible to quantify in dollars and cents. Fortunately, there were guidelines in place, a descending salary scale from the number 1 pick, Olajuwon. If Jordan had been a first pick overall, Thorn surely would have had a tougher time negotiating with future super agent David Falk. The talks went on for weeks, until finally Jordan signed the deal on September 12, 1984, for what would now be considered ridiculously little money, but then was considered a king's ransom. The whole city ogled vicariously at these negotiations, shaking its collective head, tut-tutting at the thought of such outrageous figures. When Eddie Olczyk, an eighteen-year-old hockey prospect, signed with the Chicago Blackhawks, he joked, "I know it's nothing near what Michael Jordan will sign with the Bulls for. Sometimes I felt like, 'Hey, I'll sign for an eighth of what Jordan gets.'"

Eventually, Jordan got less than a million bucks a year—just $550,000 plus incentives for his rookie season. The contract would escalate to about $845,000 by the 1987–88 season, after which the Bulls would tear the thing up and give Jordan a new, eight-year pact worth about $25 million, an average of $3.125 million per season. At the time he signed his first contract, Jordan was the third-highest paid NBA rookie in history, behind only Ralph Sampson and Hakeem Olajuwon. This seemed like an extraordinary investment, and the Bulls' operating officer Jonathan Kovler was less than confident that Thorn had negotiated a good deal. "We were having a drink at the Ambassador East Hotel, and Kovler, in a joking manner, says to me, 'This guy better be good, for what we're paying him,'" Thorn recalled. "When Michael became Michael, I always kidded him about that statement." Poor Kovler. By midseason, he was hearing it from Dean Smith, too. Smith would sit with Kovler at a Bulls game, watch Jordan do something magnificent, and then chastise Kovler for underpaying Jordan terribly. Soon enough, this fact would become evident to everyone. By the end of the season, total attendance at home Bulls games in 1984–85 had increased by 87 percent from its pre-Jordan standards. Ticket sales were now $3.8 million, an increase of $1.8 million, and the Bulls made another $200,000 from the playoffs. Jordan had paid off his lofty salary nearly fourfold.

The skeptical Kovler was in attendance when Jordan first arrived in Chicago to sign the NBA contract in September 1984, holding a press conference where he came off as the humblest rich man in Illinois. This kind of media gathering was a standard, clumsy affair around the league, whenever a first-round pick was inked. Kovler said the signing "shows ownership's commitment to bringing a quality product to Chicago." Thorn predicted Jordan would probably be a guard, not a forward, because of his size and quickness. For Jordan, this day was great fun, as much an adventure as an obligation. He went to a baseball game, Cubs versus Expos, at Wrigley Field and chatted with a local institution, announcer Harry Caray. Jordan loved to play baseball, always, but he had never actually attended a major league game before. There were no such teams near North Carolina, he explained. Jordan's parents, James and Deloris, came from Wilmington for the signing ceremony and were at his side to demonstrate their official support one last time. After this, he wouldn't need them at his news conferences anymore. "I won't try to carry the team—just fit in," Michael told the assembled reporters. "It's not the 'Michael Jordan Show.' I'm one of the Bulls' players, and I have to earn everything I get in the NBA. But if I can work with Bobby Knight, I can work with anybody."

The salary was a nice start, but already it was becoming clear that Jordan would tap streams of revenue never before imagined. Falk talked then about how Jordan had become a marketable figure because of the Olympics, and because, well, he looked fabulous. Jordan very much appeared the part of the great African-American sports hero, graceful in physique and handsome in countenance. Less than two weeks after he signed with the Bulls, Jordan was creating a photo portfolio, posing for a fashion layout in one of his size 44 long suits, and talking about himself in the third person to the *New York Times*: "The idea is to show the versatility of Michael Jordan," Jordan explained. "There'll be some shots in leisure clothes, some in business clothes, some in tuxedos—to show how I'd look in all types of commercials."

Though he never said a word in his early ads, Jordan looked very good, indeed. As Falk noted, Jordan had an edge over other Olympic stars from less glamorous sports because he would remain up front in the public eye. Falk gave that concept a name, calling it "ongoing visibility." The agent was considering endorsement deals with makers of electronic appliances, basketballs, and, yes, shoes. "We don't want him to be over-diluted," Falk said, coining another phrase in agent-speak. By 1989, five years in the future, dilution would not be a problem for this superstar. Jordan would have a seven-year contract worth more than $20 million with Nike, plus endorsement deals estimated at another $10 million with McDonald's, Coca-Cola, Wheaties, Chevrolet, Wilson Sporting Goods, and Johnson Products. If there were still experts out there who thought a black athlete was not a viable salesman in white America, they had been proved very foolish. Spike Lee's ingenious, artful commercials and Jordan's natural likeability created a marketing monster. "Michael did more than anything to change those perceptions," Charles Barkley said. "He and Spike Lee, I give them tremendous credit, because Nike was really the first company to do something like this and the commercials, they're the key. The shoe deal was everything. Magic and Larry, two of the greatest athletes ever, never took shoes to the level that Michael and Spike did."

Even before the 1984–85 season began, during exhibition games, everybody soon discovered what all the fuss was about. Jordan was far more entertaining even than advertised. He had a dynamism never seen before, outshining the brightest lights in the game, Magic Johnson and Larry Bird. Jordan wasn't so much about playmaking, though he was good at seeing the court and dishing off when necessary. He was all about the dazzle. "He can make the unmake-able play," wrote *Boston Globe* columnist Bob Ryan. And in Chicago, people were noticing. The Bulls were selling fifty season ticket packages a day. The crowd at Chicago Stadium was raucous, energized for the regular season opener against Washington. Attendance was 13,913. Loughery called it the best and biggest audience he had seen since coming to Chicago a year earlier. Opponents were already designing defenses to stop a rookie who had yet to score a point in the league. "We want Jordan to be a team player," Bernie Bickerstaff, the Bullet assistant coach, told the *Washington Post* on the eve of the opener. "If you play too far off him, he'll make the jumper; if you play him a little close, he'll break you down. If you play him close, but not too close, he'll pass. That's what we want, the ball in somebody else's hands as much as possible. Otherwise, he can take over a game."

That was the official plan. The unofficial plan was to allow the Bruise Brothers, Rick Mahorn and Jeff Ruland, to maul Jordan into oblivion. It worked to some degree. Ruland crashed into Jordan in the second quarter, and Mahorn blindsided Jordan early with another pick. Jordan played forty minutes, converting only 5 of 16 shots from the field for 16 points. But he also had 7 assists, 6 rebounds and 4 blocked shots, while the Bulls whupped woeful Washington, 109–93. Afterward, Jordan said he had played well, despite the rough shooting night. He took his lumps, didn't gripe about the rough play, and said things went exactly as he figured. Asked where he would go for a postgame party, Jordan said, "At home in my bed. Just me, a bottle of aspirin and an icepack." The Bulls' second game was less successful. In Milwaukee, a ninety-minute ride up I–94, Jordan missed a running baseline drive at the buzzer, and the Bulls fell, 108–106. But the third game at home against the Bucks would set the course for the rest of the season.

Quintin Dailey was already rebelling against his new backup role as sixth man behind Jordan. The volatile Dailey had been the team's second-leading scorer the previous season, and now he missed the game against the Bucks for "personal reasons." His older brother, Tony, called assistant coach Fred Carter just an hour before the game, to say Dailey had overslept. Tony called again half an hour later to tell the Bulls his brother was too sick to make the game. Back in 1982, Dailey had missed six games because of severe depression and then underwent a six-week rehab for alcohol and drug abuse in Baltimore. This time, he was fined for missing the home game against the Bucks, while Jordan completely took over. The rookie scored 22 of his 37 points in the fourth quarter, 13 of his team's final 17 points. His basket with thirty-one seconds left put Chicago ahead for good, and then the Bulls went on to win, 116–110, without Dailey and very much with Jordan.

These were now Jordan's Bulls, and Dailey would be lucky if he hung on for the ride. For the first time the team hired an outside advertising firm, Jack Levy & Associates, to work on TV and print ads that would star Jordan. After Jordan went off for 45 points on November 13 against the San Antonio Spurs, there were two successive sellouts at Chicago Stadium, an arena that had not experienced a capacity crowd for NBA basketball in three years. The whole league got an enormous boost from the buzz. Cable television ratings increased by 20 percent, while attendance soared nearly as much. By December, Falk at ProServ had negotiated a Nike deal for Jordan worth $2.5 million over five years and a promise from the company to create the first-ever signature line of shoes. "I don't think I'm big-headed because of the success I've been getting," Jordan told *Business Week*, between meetings with Chicago's corporate leaders. "I'm doing things I normally do and playing my natural game. Once I'm on the court, it's really fun."

The hype might have all exploded from its own bloat, except that Jordan just kept backing up all the endorsements and all the fuss with his game. On December 8, he hit a winning, twisting jumper against the Knicks at the buzzer, despite being double-teamed. Only the renowned contrarian, Knicks' coach Hubie Brown, could deny him his glory. "It's true Jordan's jump shot with two-and-a-half play-ers on him ended our hopes after a great comeback," Brown grumped. "But it's a shame Orlando Woolridge has to take a back seat to Jordan." Jordan scored 32 points in a rout over Boston on December 22, another wonderful night in Chicago. The Celts were ailing, playing shorthanded, and did not appreciate the pounding. A rivalry was born, along with a new superstar. Over the course of the season, Jordan would average 28.2 points on 51.5 percent shooting, with 5.9 assists and 6.5 rebounds per game. The flawed Bulls made the playoffs for the first time in four years.

And all around the league, Jordan was winning disciples. It was not just James Jordan, Charles Barkley, Billy Cunningham, and Dean Smith anymore. Other great players, like Bird, now under-stood that Jordan embodied the NBA future. The great Celtic for-ward was only twenty-eight and had another championship left in the tank. But after the Celtics held on to beat the Bulls, 110–106, in front of 18,061 fans at Chicago Stadium, Bird sat down at his locker with reporters to praise this next generation player, this pure energy force. It was not unusual for Bird to call an opponent the best player in the game. He had done it with Micheal Ray Richardson, among others. This time, Bird waxed in grander terms, about a kid who would carry the league on his shoulders long after Bird retired:

Best. Never seen anyone like him. Unlike anyone I've ever seen. Phenomenal. One of a kind ... At his stage in his career, he's doing more than I ever did. I couldn't do what he did as a rookie. Heck, there was one drive tonight, he had the ball up in his right hand, then he took it down, then he brought it back up. I got a hand on it, fouled him, and he still scored. And all the while, he's in the air. You have to play this game to know how difficult that is. You see that and figure, 'Well, what the heck can you do?' Best. I'd seen a little of him before and wasn't that impressed. I mean, I thought he'd be good, but not this good. Ain't nothing he can't do. I have never seen one player turn a team around like that. All the Bulls have become better because of him. Orlando Woolridge will probably be an All-Star for the rest of his career. And pretty soon, this place will be packed every night, not just when the Celtics come to town. They'll pay just to watch Jordan. Got to. That's good for this franchise, good for the league ... The first three seasons in the league, all I worried about was the Boston Celtics. But I realize the NBA is only as strong as its weakest link, so I'm concerned about more than us now. I still don't wake up and check attendances around the league every morning in the paper, but I feel like the sport is getting better all the time. Last year was the most competitive of the six I've been around. . . . The second half of this season, and then the playoffs, could be the best yet. The NBA is perking up all the time.

Bird had turned pitchman. Jordan was oblivious, ecstatic, completely in his element in the NBA. What could be better than a competitive game every two nights, except a game every night? In this way, he brought an infectious enthusiasm to his sport in a manner not unlike that other Chicago sports hero, Ernie Banks.

The fun had to end some time that rookie season. The Bulls were eliminated on April 26, 1985, by the Milwaukee Bucks in a four-

game, first-round series, but not before Jordan put on one last remarkable show in Game 3, just a glimpse of playoff theatrics to
come. He scored 35 points and buried the winning baseline jumper
with 17 seconds left, for a 109–107 victory. Even after the Game 4
defeat, Jordan was bubbling with anticipation. One year later he was
quite certain that he had made the correct decision, walking out of
that dorm room and away from Buzz Peterson, turning professional
after his junior year. His dad had been right. His coach had been
right: he had been ready. "I'm happy we did a little better than a lot
of people said we would," he said about the Bulls. "I did the right
thing coming out of school early. I never really thought it wasn't the
right thing to do, but maybe some other people did." He was heading back to North Carolina now, to finish up his degree, fulfill a
promise to his mother. "I'm going to go back down South, get a little education," he explained, smiling at the prospect. "I'll probably
talk to Dean tomorrow."

A rising tide lifts all boats, the saying goes. Jordan was doing just
that for the Bulls, but not in time to rescue fellow travelers from his
rookie season. They would all be left behind on this great adventure.
Jordan's first year in the league wasn't even complete yet when Jerry
Reinsdorf, the owner of the Chicago White Sox, purchased the Bulls
from the Wirtz family in March and began to make immediate personnel moves. First to go was Kovler. Thorn was called into a
lengthy meeting with Reinsdorf, basically asked whether he had
been responsible for the string of failures in the '70s and '80s. Reinsdorf gave Thorn a chance to blame it on Kovler, if he only suggested
his hands had been tied. Thorn refused to plead not guilty. It wasn't
true, for one thing. "I had a lot to do with the decisions, and I should
be held accountable," he said. Two weeks after Kovler was dismissed,
Thorn was axed on March 26, 1985, and replaced by Jerry Krause.
After the Bulls lost that playoff series to the Bucks, it was the coach's
turn. Loughery was fired in late May, along with assistant coaches

Bill Blair and Fred Carter. "The only thing that surprised me was that it took so long," Loughery said. Thorn and Loughery, working together over decades, had nurtured the early years of two legends: Julius Erving and Michael Jordan. Thorn, as general manager of the New Jersey Nets, would go on in the first decade of the twenty-first century to acquire two more superstars, Jason Kidd and Vince Carter. He generally found it more difficult to capture championships than to discover magical players.

Back in Chicago, there would be a complete housecleaning, from the trainer on up, and down. Not a single player from the 1984–85 team would remain a teammate of Jordan by the time the Bulls finally won their first title six years later. Krause purged the roster with amazing efficiency. Steve Johnson, David Greenwood, Ennis Whatley, and Wes Matthews were gone by fall 1985. Quintin Dailey and Orlando Woolridge, two top scorers, left in 1986, along with Rod Higgins and Sidney Green. Dave Corzine made it all the way to 1989 but not quite to the title. They were replaced by a cast of characters that ranged from useless to remarkable, over the course of Jordan's fourteen seasons with the Bulls—six of them resulting in championships. Krause's most important transactions included the acquisition of Cleveland's draft pick, Charles Oakley, in 1985; the draft-day trade in 1987 of Olden Polynice to Seattle for Scottie Pippen, Jordan's right-hand man; the drafting of Horace Grant in 1987; the hiring of Phil Jackson as head coach in 1989; the trade for Dennis Rodman from the Spurs in exchange for Will Perdue in 1995. Those became the cornerstone moves that gave Jordan just enough support throughout his remarkable career to contend with and then overtake the Sixers, Celtics, Lakers, and Pistons and to hold off the Rockets, Knicks, and Jazz. Jordan would alter the definition of greatness and of a championship team. No longer were NBA titles acquired necessarily by gargantuan bodies. No longer were players limited to the money they earned from their playing contracts. Here was the triumph of individualism over the sublimation of ego. What was good for the player was, by extension, good for the team.

Jordan would wag his tongue and hit the buzzer-beater again and again. But he was just a man, not without his cracks and flaws. That relentless, insatiable competitiveness that once led him to cheat Peterson's mother at Crazy Eights soon enough would lead him into real trouble. Gambling scandals tainted his reputation. There was a $57,000 check written by Jordan to convicted North Carolina drug trafficker Slim Bouler, reportedly to cover golf debts dating from October 1991. Richard Esquinas, another golfing pal, wrote a quickie book that detailed how Jordan dropped $1.25 million to him in a single golf binge in September 1991. Jordan said those numbers were outrageous. He was recognized and pestered everywhere, the most public of figures. Yet between playoff games against the Knicks in New York in 1992, Jordan rode to Atlantic City with his father. Together, James and Michael Jordan hit the blackjack tables until the wee hours of the morning. The NBA found no violations of its rules, but still the gambling was a real concern among league officials. Finally, there was Jordan's most heart-breaking tribulation. His father was murdered in July 1993, by a pair of teenagers in a robbery gone wrong. Jordan was shattered. He became embittered as the press incorrectly projected a link between his father's disappearance and possible gambling associations. From then on, Jordan was more distant with the media, cutting access to the bare minimum, often limiting communication to postgame clichés. He also kept his wife Juanita and their three children far from the cameras.

Jordan announced his first retirement in October 1993 to take a fling at baseball. "At least my father saw my last basketball game," he said. His flirtation with that game proved less than successful. Like golf, baseball was simply a sport he could not master at such an advanced age. Jordan, rededicated, came back to basketball in 1995 and still had enough left to win three more titles, the last in 1998. When his jumper rippled through the net with 5.2 seconds left in Game 6 on June 14 in Salt Lake City, everybody believed this was his final professional moment. That game-winning shot, the steely look on his face, were frozen in time, a look for the ages.

"Once you get in the moment, things start to move slowly," Jordan said, trying to explain how he pulled off his good-bye miracle. "You start to see the court very well. You start reading what the defense is going to do. I saw that. I saw that moment." Joyous and nostalgic at the same time that day in Salt Lake City, Jordan danced around the court after winning his sixth NBA title, pumping his fist, the same way he had celebrated after finally winning his first playoff series against Cleveland in 1988. He had scored 45 of his team's 87 points, making 4 big steals. And though Jordan always loved a challenge, this game was a strong argument to retire and leave as a champion at age thirty-five. He couldn't do it, though. He returned once again because of that competitive drive, the same compulsion that contributed to his many successes and occasional humiliations. It drove him to come back for two frustrating seasons with the Washington Wizards, from 2001–03, as a player and a less-enthusiastic executive. This stint finished badly, when Washington owner Abe Pollin sent him packing unexpectedly. If he wasn't playing, drawing fans, Pollin didn't want him. Jordan had been less than brilliant in his personnel decisions, hiring and then firing coach Leonard Hamilton after one season, using the first overall draft pick for high schooler Kwame Brown, a terrible bust, and trading future All-Star and NBA champion Richard Hamilton.

His Wizard years were a mistake, but they changed nothing, really. His fingerprints were on the sport forever. After he retired as a player for the third and last time in 2003, he went into near seclusion with his family in Chicago, emerging only for regular golf outings (his official U.S. Golf Association handicap remained over four strokes), must-do promotional endorsements, and an appearance on the Oprah Winfrey show to plug yet another book.

But again, despite insisting that he just wanted his private time, Jordan was restless for the game and the competition. He and Juanita would soon announce their divorce. In June 2006, he became part-owner and managing member of basketball operations for the Charlotte Bobcats, a dual homecoming to both basketball and North Carolina. Robert Johnson, an African-American businessman who bought the expansion Bobcats in 2002 for $300 million, had been lobbying Jordan for four years to do this. Jordan had been trying to become a majority owner of his own team. But there are only so many NBA franchises, and there was no guarantee he would secure the next one available. Larry Bird had tried and failed to purchase the Bobcats with his own group. So Jordan accepted Johnson's offer, a chance to right his reputation after his executive failings with the Wizards. He would be part of the management team, and the Bobcat players wondered aloud whether he could resist showing up for at least a practice or two.

He had had quite the glorious run, and now it was still going. Not bad for a third pick.

"We always knew he was good back at practice in North Carolina," Sam Perkins said. "But we all had this college mentality then. We didn't know Michael was as good as he was. I had to see it for myself in the pros, and then I did. It was maybe his second, third year, I saw him play in one game against us and he was a different player. Different than anybody on the court."

18

Far from Eden

Lee Fentress, the player agent, and Norm Sonju, the Dallas general manager, negotiated through the summer and well into the fall of 1984. Suddenly it was October 9, and Sam Perkins was the last unsigned NBA first-round draft pick. They would agree that day, finally, on a five-year deal starting at $500,000 and ending at $755,000. As always, all the hand wringing had led to a fairly conventional end, just another contract that fit the draft slot and the sliding scale. Jordan, picked right above at number 3, had a $550,000 salary to start, negotiated by David Falk. Dean Smith, who had encouraged these different representatives for his two stars, was quite pleased by both outcomes. Dick Motta was not nearly so happy. He didn't care about the size of the contract but was irate about the length of these stubborn bargaining sessions. Both his first round picks, Perkins and Terence Stansbury, were extended holdouts and had missed his valuable preseason training sessions. By the time Perkins arrived—eagerly—Motta didn't know exactly what to do with him. Perkins thought of himself as a power forward. Motta seemed to indicate Perkins was more of a scoring forward. "Then he stuck me out there at center," Perkins said. There was nobody else, really, to play the position. Perkins averaged 11.0 points his first season, with 7.4 rebounds per game. By his second year, back at power forward next to James Donaldson, those numbers would climb to 15.4 and 8.6, where they would remain for much of his career. This was not enough to make Motta happy on most nights, however, and soon enough Perkins was not all that thrilled with his situation, either. "As time went on, Motta just felt I wouldn't become a real player until my fifth, sixth year," Perkins said, in a rare, huffy moment during an interview with the *Hartford Courant* in 1991. "I just stuck with that and continued to do whatever he told me to."

Typically, Perkins was overshadowed in his regular season debut by the opponents. Dallas opened at home on October 27, 1984, against the Rockets. Perkins, starting at center against the new Twin Towers of Olajuwon and Sampson, had 12 points and 8 rebounds. The Mavericks lost. The world shrugged. On November 10, Perkins had 16 points and 9 rebounds during a victory over Seattle. But by mid-December he was averaging just 8.2 points on 7 shots per game and coming off the bench. Perkins was struggling in matchups against bulkier centers, dreaming about moving back to his more natural position of forward. Motta promised this would happen eventually. In the meantime the coach diplomatically expressed some impatience with Perkins's passive demeanor. Motta was finding out that the player nicknamed the Big Smooth was every bit as laid back as advertised, that all the yelling in the world wasn't going to light a mean fire or change his easygoing temperament. "He hasn't been aggressive enough as far as taking his shots," Motta said then. "We're trying to call his plays more to encourage him to shoot. He's a very sensitive young man and I think he didn't want it to look like he wanted to take over. That's a credit to him. I'd rather see that than have a rookie who thinks he knows it all."

Perkins wisely decided his path to success was not in bulking up, but rather in his innate quickness and soft touch. Things got better when everybody acknowledged these gifts and began to accept his limitations. There were nights that first season, like on February 19, 1985, when Perkins rewarded supporters with breakthrough performances. In that game against the Rockets, Perkins scored 28 points and held Sampson, seven inches taller, to just 2 points in the first half by consistently denying the ball to the bigger man. Unfortunately, these dominant performances were the exception with Perkins, not the rule. More often, he was content to play a subsidiary role. Perkins was not on the radar screen of major media outlets at the national level. They were too busy raving about Jordan, and back in North Carolina they were already worrying about the fate of the gutted Tar Heels.

When Perkins reviewed his six seasons in Dallas, he interpreted them differently at different times in his seventeen-year career, depending on the mood. Sometimes, he would praise Motta for his high standards and unending demands. Other times, Perkins would characterize his time with the Mavericks as "wasted." He truly did not feel comfortable among some of his teammates back then, with all their dissension and problems. "It really dampened my time there," Perkins said.

> From the way we were coming out of school, I thought this was the same attitude there would be coming into the NBA. Then I found out you lose a game or two in a row, nobody is upset. They're getting dressed, nobody is upset, and I couldn't believe it just two losses in. Then you had problem players. You find out all the little things they're bickering about—'I don't have enough shots,' for example. It takes a toll on you. I didn't really want to be there. It wasn't my favorite place. But I was committed to staying there.

This was no longer the peaceful Camelot of North Carolina, and Motta was certainly not Dean Smith. In many ways, Perkins's steady contributions guaranteed that the Mavericks would remain contenders in the Western Conference for the next few years. At the same time, his stable presence probably encouraged the Dallas franchise to take an imaginative gamble that backfired badly. In the spring of 1985, Dallas might have drafted Karl Malone. But the Mavericks figured they already had a player, Perkins, to fill that role of power forward. Instead, they chose Detlef Schrempf, a six-foot-nine German import who played more like a shooting guard and didn't truly find himself until he was traded to the Pacers. It was an outside-the-box decision that Motta would come to rue later, but really nobody could take this out on Perkins. He was more than a fine, all-around player. Perkins was one of the nicest guys anybody ever met. And on a team that would feature the likes of irascible Mark Aguirre and the troubled Roy Tarpley, Perkins was a valued asset for the purpose of community relations.

Aguirre fought with Motta constantly. Tarpley was suspended again and again for his drug problems. Then there was Perkins. "Perkins was a coach's dream," said Norm Sonju, the general manager. "You don't even know he's there. Like an old shoe." In this way, Perkins was very much like Sam Bowie; both were big, sweet guys who were not inclined to knock down opponents unnecessarily in the lane, who were content playing contributory roles on a winning team. Back at the Olympic trials, Leon Wood had noticed the same characteristic. Perkins appeared indifferent somehow, though the results were always greater than the game face. "Sam was dominant in his own right," Wood said. "Long arms, he could hit the jump shot. But he was not the guy who was going to hit you for 25 or 30. If you came into the middle, he'd block your shots. He also had that facial expression that said he's not playing hard, but that wasn't the case. He did as much as he could, considering he was 6–9." It's just that once he got to the NBA, Perkins suffered badly by comparison with his former college teammate, Jordan, and with the Class of '84 in general. He would not make that sort of splash, not have the same impact, as those other players. Nobody was Jordan. "I try to do whatever I can, and he's on a whole different plane," Perkins said then. "He's a superstar."

Before Perkins arrived in 1983–84, the Mavericks were 43–39 and in second place in the Midwest Division. They reached the second round of the playoffs. With Perkins playing 82 games his rookie season, starting 42 of them, the Mavs were 44–38 and in third place, before falling to Portland in the first round. Not much progress there. The Mavericks were already smarting about what happened with Stansbury, who had been expected to play a major role at shooting guard. That didn't happen, and the notion of choosing Stansbury ahead of Stockton and others was looking rather foolish. "Terence Stansbury's young agent [Bill Pollock] at the time did not work with us to get him signed," Sonju recalled. "He came late to training camp. With the Dick Mottas of the world, it was my way or the highway. You can't pull that off today with these players, but when he came to camp late, we felt he didn't have a chance with Dick and we traded him right away to Indiana."

That left Perkins to prove that Dallas management still had a coherent vision for the future, and he was not going to change his personality to match the pressure. "Perkins didn't have a mean streak, not like a Barkley," Sonju said. Perkins agreed with that and didn't see anything wrong with it. "When they say I'm laid back, I don't care," Perkins said. "Because, I mean, I *am* laid back. People say that I go through the motions, that I'm lazy. I work hard, as hard as anyone. It's just that sometimes it's not seen." If you talked to anybody in the Maverick organization, he would tell you the same thing: Sam Perkins was one of the team's most beloved players of all time. He also was not the fellow to carry a franchise, just to boost it a bit. "I've been in this league more than three decades, and Sam is still one of my favorites, along with Derek Harper," said Sund, who was the

Dallas director of player personnel. "He's also one of the best players to never make the All-Star team. Sam was with four teams in his career, and made it to the conference finals on all four as a starter. He was such a coach's player, he never got the stats as a result. He was all about winning, about playing multiple positions even though he was a true power forward. I look at him as one of my better draft picks, chemistry wise."

That chemistry was strained at times by the team's failure to win a conference title. Dallas would be eliminated in the second round of the playoffs in 1986 and the first round in 1987 before reaching the Western Conference finals in 1988 and falling in seven tough games to the eventual NBA champions, the Lakers. That would be as good as it got. The Mavs didn't even make the playoffs in 1989, and then Perkins's original contract was expiring. As a restricted free agent, he had limited options and asked for a five-year deal. Dallas offered three years. Perkins believed that this contract, when it expired, would leave him vulnerable in his mid- to late-career. He felt insulted and decided to sign for just one season, taking an enormous risk by agreeing to a contract worth only about $900,000.

As Perkins's second contract drew to a close in 1990, he was on the verge of becoming that rarest of commodities: a still-young big man, an unrestricted free agent. Both he and Dallas management were ambiguous about extending his stay with the Mavericks. Fentress and Dean Smith were talking up the Lakers, always an attractive home. His old Tar Heel teammate, Worthy, was waiting there to make him comfortable. The date was approaching when a decision would have to be made. Sund was afraid the Mavericks might end up with nothing if they didn't trade Perkins before his one-year pact expired. "We're playing in Milwaukee, I call Sam to take him to dinner," Sund said. "I told him, 'I have an opportunity to trade you. I don't want to. And I won't tell you which team it is. It would be a team you're comfortable with. But I'm afraid if we don't trade you,

you don't want to be here. And if that's the case, I'll move you. If it's about money, the Mavericks will give you comparable money.'" And Sam looked me in the eye and he said, 'I'll stay. If there's an offer that's better, I'll let you match it.'"

The trade deadline passed. Perkins became an unrestricted free agent, on schedule. Fentress called Sonju in Australia and told the Dallas general manager that Perkins had received an offer from the Lakers for about $18 million. Fentress said he wanted to take the offer, but that Perkins had promised Sund he would give the Mavericks a chance to match. If Dallas came up with $19 million, Perkins would stick with the Mavs. Sonju called the team president, Donald Carter, who refused to ante up the extra million dollars. Eighteen million was the limit. "Sonju called me," Sund recalled. "I hung up the phone, told my wife, 'That's the biggest mistake in Mavericks history, while I'm here.' To this day, I will always respect Sam Perkins. He did what he's supposed to do. You're supposed to go out and get the best you can. He turned it down to give us an opportunity. We lost him, and got nothing in return." Perkins received a fax from Fentress, saying the Mavs had decided to pass. The decision was a disaster for Dallas, made worse because the seven-foot Tarpley would play only 60 more games for the Mavericks between suspensions. The franchise buckled, suffering four of its worst seasons ever. Dallas plunged to 28–54 in 1990–91, 22–60 in 1991–92, 11–71 in 1992–93, 13–69 in 1993–94.

Perkins moved on, signing with the Lakers for six years and $19.2 million, the largest contract ever at the time for an unrestricted free agent. "It was a big gamble, but obviously it paid off," Perkins said of his one-year ploy. Because of this decision, Perkins could always boast he was teammates with arguably the two greatest basketball players in history, Jordan at North Carolina and Magic Johnson with the Lakers. Eventually, Perkins went to Seattle and Indiana before retiring in 2001, two months short of age forty. He never won a

NBA championship, which hit him hard inside despite the soft demeanor. He had sworn all along he would wait until retirement to get married, because there were too many temptations on the road. He nearly made it. He was married in 1999, to Dione, a Seattle police officer. His twin daughters by a different mother, China and Chyanne, had been born in 1995. Today he is divorced and has three kids. He performs charity work, sometimes on behalf of the NBA, sometimes on behalf of research for breast cancer. He has worked with an entertainment company in Seattle and has done part-time announcing for the Indiana Pacers. Ironically, he settled in Dallas, the place he said he didn't really like. Perkins was never a close buddy to Jordan, though the two remember fondly their days together in North Carolina, as part of that Class of '84.

"I think it was the best draft class," Perkins remarked recently.

> People will debate it. But we had a lot of guys from top to bottom, a lot of talent going through the second round. The reason people aren't polished today in the draft is they don't stay around four years to acclimate themselves. You have talent in the rough, but not consistently one through ten. Some fall by the wayside, and you don't hear from them anymore. My class, we went through games, through real college careers. Teams were more confident they knew what they wanted, and what they were getting. Now you're not sure. They're thinking, "He's a shooter, but is he a defender? Can he dribble the ball?" You have to develop them more when they get to the pros. That's not to say they're not talented. You just don't know what they have.

Perkins lasted seventeen years. If you look in the back of the NBA Register, he is not listed among the so-called "all-time great players." The fourth pick in the 1984 draft was never quite great, it must be conceded. He was just very good for a very long time.

19

Charles in Charge

When Charles Barkley arrived for his introductory press conference in Philadelphia on September 25, he was already determined to make a fresh start of things. His clowning days at Auburn were behind him, he decided. The weight jokes that gained him as much publicity as his play were no longer welcome, certainly not with his family in attendance alongside the press. "I can control my weight," Barkley said impatiently. Barkley was recasting himself as a great basketball player. He didn't need this other stuff to command attention, make him look like a carnival sideshow. But Pat Williams, a well-intentioned man, was forever in love with a good, wholesome punch line. He would not let the fat remarks go. Always the roastmaster, Williams rattled off a few light barbs at the event, as Barkley looked on unhappily, thinking that this was no longer what he had in mind. No more Sonny-and-Charles Show, please. Phil Jasner, an enterprising beat writer for the *Philadelphia Daily News*, approached Barkley's mother, Charcey Glenn, to ask what dinners had been like at home all these years. She also wanted no part of that angle.

The contract negotiations had not been easy, dragging on between the Sixers and Luchnick through the summer. It wasn't just the dollars and cents (the deal eventually was reached in mid-September and would come to about $2 million, starting at a bit over $300,000 and escalating over four years). Williams was also inserting weight clauses, to make certain Barkley stayed in shape. When bargaining stalled, Barkley took the unusual step of attending the Sixers' rookie camp at Princeton, New Jersey. He was still unsigned, risking possible injury to prove a point. Barkley wanted to convince Harold Katz and the Philly hierarchy he was worth a long-term deal, so that Williams would fiddle with the roster and free up some money under the salary cap. The player was determined to avoid a one-season minimum contract. "At this point, I still didn't know how good I am," Barkley recalled. "I needed to get some security. I'm not thinking one good year, then become a free agent. I had to take care of my family."

From the moment Barkley showed up at the rookie camp, Pat Williams was reassured that drafting the Round Mound was not the biggest blunder of his career. "At Princeton, we got the sense he was a different kind of player," Williams said. "He comes in unsigned, he dominates. That was telltale. He came into camp at 255, and he cared. The amazing thing was, from the time he reported in the fall, as far as I know, that weight clause in his contract was never looked at. He was a ballplayer." Williams cut Franklin Edwards and traded Leo Rautins, the team's number 1 pick from the previous season, to free up about $280,000 for Barkley under the salary cap. He had also traded away the team's third first-round pick for 1984, Tom Sewell of Lamar University, to the Washington Bullets for a first-round choice in 1988. The Sixers were one of just five teams at the time who were over the cap, and their plight was sabotaging efforts to sign the team's other first-round pick, Leon Wood. Wood and his agent, Fred Slaughter, filed a lawsuit in U.S. District Court challenging the validity of the salary cap, creating yet more headaches for Katz and Williams.

Once Barkley started playing with the Sixers, he was thrust into one of the most awkward situations imaginable. He was surrounded by accomplished stars on the downside, and Barkley was just starting to feel his oats. "I think Charles looked around and decided, objectively, 'I'm the best player here,'" Jasner said. On the surface, everything was fine. These were good guys on the roster, class acts, and they would welcome Barkley in appropriate fashion. And Barkley was deferential at first. "I was really nervous going into training camp," Barkley said. "I'm thinking, 'What do I call Dr. J? Mr. Erving? Julius?'" Erving walked up to Barkley on the first day, told him, "Hey, I'm Doc." That was the end of one problem. Moses Malone became Barkley's best buddy on the team, working him hard, teaching him the ropes. "I call him, 'Dad,' to this day," Barkley said. But there was definitely some friction between Barkley and the lesser players on the roster and between Barkley and the coach, Billy Cunningham.

Barkley was still doing some of the things that had driven Sonny Smith to distraction. He was knocking down teammates in practice, showing them up. On at least one occasion, he slammed a guy down and dropped a basketball on him—crazy stuff. Cunningham felt obliged to close practice to the press for the first time, just so he could rein in this new kid. There was a war of wills going on. The veteran coach was likable but would take no sass. Cunningham felt most comfortable around players like Erving and Jones, not this upstart forward with the boisterous playing style. Cunningham really didn't have much intention of relying too heavily on Barkley in his rookie season. "One thing we don't want to do is throw a great deal of responsibility on his shoulders," the coach said. "We're going to try and bring him along slowly. We want to see him develop defensively."

That was the plan, anyway. The plan went out the window when it became clear that Barkley needed to play substantial minutes if this team was going to remain competitive with Boston and Los Angeles. Nobody understood that better than Barkley. "Charles was humble when he first got there," Wood remembered.

> But once we were through training camp, he felt he fit in, and felt he should be on the floor. He was okay around Dr. J at first, all quiet, but he wasn't quiet for long. Back then, Cunningham wouldn't play rookies much, but before you knew it they traded Marc Iavaroni, moved Bobby Jones to the bench. You have to understand the clash of personalities going on. Doc was very professional—glasses and a briefcase. We didn't have a dress code. You could dress the way you wanted. Doc was in a suit and tie, anyway. Then we had a skid, and held a team meeting. Doc said what he needed to say. We went down the line, and I had nothing to say. I was just a rookie. Then it came to Charles, and he says, "I got something to say. No disrespect, but I need to be involved in the offense more. You're getting up in years." I had my head down, thinking, "Are you kidding? This guy's telling this team he should be one of the top two or three options on offense? We have legends like Doc and Moses here." Everybody says how Charles speaks his mind. Well, it started that first season.

Cunningham rode Barkley every minute of every waking day, as those closed practices with the Sixers became a test of wills. His teammates could have frozen him out; maybe they should have done so. There was something about him, though, that didn't insult anybody's intelligence, even when he was exhibiting his most prankish behavior. Barkley had a love/hate affair with authority, with the media, with almost everyone. From day 1 he would say or do something outrageous, and people would forgive him almost immediately, shaking it off with a simple, "That's just Charles." Bobby Jones, one of the elders on the team, said Barkley had "a teachable heart." Pat Williams, who would leave Philly for the Orlando Magic before that expansion team's 1989 debut, always thought Cunningham was the perfect first coach for Barkley. Cunningham had no insecurities. He was a Hall of Fame player himself, and he had a championship under his coaching belt. In later years, Barkley would thank Cunningham for his impatience that first season, for his straight-arrow guidance. Back then, it was a battle every day.

The 1984–85 season was a qualified success for the 76ers and for Barkley. Philly won 58 games, then cruised past Washington and Milwaukee in the playoffs before losing to the hated Celtics in five games for the Eastern Conference title. Barkley may have been a rookie, but he played more minutes that season than any Sixer other than Malone, Erving, and Cheeks. He averaged 14.0 points on 54.5 percent shooting and grabbed 8.6 rebounds. Cunningham quit coaching after that season. He said it was tough to walk away and hand the team to Matt Guokas, if only because he saw such great potential in Barkley. The Kangaroo Kid knew boundless, creative energy when he saw it.

What followed after the inaugural season was enough to fill several books—and Barkley wrote a few of them himself, only to deny parts of his co-written autobiography. Barkley would play sixteen years in the pros—the first half of his career in Philadelphia, then four years apiece in Phoenix and Houston—before a bad back and a torn quad forced him into retirement. While he was averaging more than 22 points and 11 rebounds in 1,073 games, he redefined the role of an NBA player, just as he stretched the limits of a six-foot-five-ish forward. His tongue loosened as he grew more comfortable with his position as a leader on the team, a very different kind of floor general from Julius Erving. Barkley was so many things: a corporate sponsor, a wild man, a quipster, a caricature, a politician, a generous philanthropist. There was never a dull moment, but many inappropriate ones. On March 26, 1991, Barkley became angry with a heckler behind the baseline who was being particularly offensive. The game was at the vacuous Meadowlands in New Jersey, where an individual's voice can carry from one end of the court to the other. Barkley spit at the guy and missed, hitting an eight-year-old girl, Lauren Rose. The league suspended him for a game and fined him $10,000. "I can't even begin to apologize," Barkley said. "It was just a bad, bad thing." He was less apologetic about the politically incorrect way he analyzed an overtime victory against the Nets on November 3, 1990: "This is a game that, if you lose, you go home and beat your wife," he said after the game. "Did you see my wife jumping up and down at the end of the game? That's because she knew I wasn't going to beat her."

On December 22, 1991, in Milwaukee, he reportedly broke the nose of a man, James McCarthy, outside a Milwaukee bar. A misdemeanor charge of battery didn't hold up in court. On July 7, 1996, in Cleveland, he allegedly punched a twenty-three-year-old man, Jeb Tyler, in the nose. Tyler filled out a police report but then didn't press charges. On October 26, 1997, in Orlando, a bar customer threw a glass of ice at Barkley, and the player reacted by hurling him through a plate-glass window. The only regret, Barkley would say later, was that the window wasn't a few floors higher. He was charged with aggravated battery and resisting arrest without violence, spending about five hours in jail before posting $6,000 bail. It was always something. Barkley was found guilty of failing to pay back promissory notes he had used to buy cattle, of all things. Barkley split in ugly fashion from Luchnick, and the NBA Players Association decertified Luchnick after an arbitrator found the agent guilty of overcharging the player. Barkley warred with Katz, with David Stern.

He was no picnic on the court, either. During a big game against the Bulls, Barkley could no longer tolerate the disappointing play of center Mike Gminski. He turned to Jimmy Lynam, then the coach, and growled, "Get him out of the game." Again, because of the source, Gminski didn't really take those comments as an insult. Gminski and Barkley would become good friends, hang out, go to movies. They went to see *Mississippi Burning* together (Gminski was white). Barkley, despite his occasional ethnic jokes, was practically color blind when it came to picking his friends.

In another game against the Lakers, the Sixers were getting beaten badly, and Barkley soared downcourt on a fast break. Jasner remembered how the forward tried to finish the play with a two-handed dunk but somehow the ball flew fifty feet in the air. Guokas was furious that Barkley had showboated away a sure bucket, but Charles insisted he hadn't missed that dunk, that something super-natural had happened. Sure enough, when Guokas punched up the tape, Barkley had thrown the ball down so hard and fast through the rim that it had rebounded off the top of his own head.

Stuff like that always happened around Barkley, who never knew a quiet news day. He lived a relatively normal, even altruistic private life. He performed magnanimous favors, like popping up unexpect-edly at birthday parties or banquets that honored friends of friends—people he hardly knew. But that would not be the headline in the paper. And all along, regardless of the nutty nature of his tres-passes, there was that sense again: "That's just Charles." The self-promotion and crazy antics never really got him in serious trouble with the public, maybe because he was a gracious, funny interview and a man known to donate both time and money to friends and worthy causes. Instead of disrepute, his antics landed him inspired commercial spots with Right Guard ("Anything less would be unciv-ilized") and Nike ("I am not a role model"). This was what he had had in mind all along, when he was plotting his lucrative career at Auburn and then in Bloomington, at those infernal Olympic trials. He had his own raucous style to sell.

There was never any doubt Barkley was a unique talent, packed solid for the long haul. When he retired, he ranked 13th on the NBA career scoring list and 15th in rebounding. He became a two-time Olympic gold medalist after Knight cut him. Even as Barkley proved himself one of the greatest players in the game, the Sixers did not take much advantage of his presence. The team's victory total was inversely proportional to his scoring average. In 1985–86, Philadelphia won 54 games while Barkley averaged 20.0 points. In 1986–87, the 76ers won 45 while Barkley averaged 23.0. In 1987–88, Philly slid under .500 for the first time in thirteen years, winning just 36 games while Barkley averaged 28.3. Barkley was peaking while his team was tanking.

For this great misery of losing, Barkley generally blamed the owner, Harold Katz. He may have had a point, too. Katz was a cigar-chomping tough guy from South Philly who went straight from high school to work in his dad's grocery story. Katz started out in the insurance business and then founded his NutriSystem concept in 1971 at age thirty-four. The company was a cottage industry in weight loss—complete with therapy sessions, prepared foods, medical checkups. It made a quick fortune and went public in 1981 on the New York Stock Exchange with revenues reported at about $167 million. Katz's personal wealth was then estimated at $300 million. He had a corporate jet, a suburban office in Jenkintown, Pennsylvania, and a yen to buy a basketball team. Katz fancied himself a basketball expert. He had played the game as a kid, and if a reporter did not know this fact, an interview might end abruptly with, "You haven't done your homework." By 1983 NutriSystem began to break apart. Individual franchises filed a class-action suit against Katz for alleged price gouging on food items. Revenues were shrinking. But 1983 was also the year the Sixers won a championship for Katz—just two years after he had purchased the team from Fitz Eugene Dixon Jr., a very different sort of gentleman owner who once failed to recognize the name "Julius Erving" when the superstar was first made available to Pat Williams.

This NBA championship empowered Katz even more. His insistence on obtaining Moses Malone and his scouting missions on Barkley were further proof he knew what he was doing. But when Katz backed down on trading Erving for Terry Cummings, it proved to be a rare and ill-fated display of empathy from the owner. In the end, Katz was as thin-skinned as the next guy. A smarter, tougher basketball man might have broken up the aging Sixers while they still held some trade value. Instead, Barkley was doomed to play with a declining roster for his entire eight-year stint in Philadelphia. Katz and Sixer management never found players to complement his talents, which were obviously eclectic and demanded a less conventional lineup. Barkley could forgive a lot of things but never this incompetence. On the April day in 2006 when he was voted into the Hall of Fame in Springfield, Massachusetts, Barkley was still complaining about the Sixers' old personnel moves to a *Philadelphia Daily News* reporter, Dick Jerardi. He remembered, not so fondly, the day he was told Philly had signed a recycled Charles Shackleford. "We needed a rebounder," Barkley said. "They told me he was a great player in the Italian League. When people want basketball players, they don't go to Italy."

Katz's biggest regret, he often said, was trading Barkley to Phoenix in 1992. But by then, Barkley was talking his way out of town, referring to the team as "purgatory," and forcing Katz's hand. Barkley later said there were no hard feelings and that Katz was a decent human being, just a lousy basketball talent scout. When Katz finally sold the Sixers in 1996 for about $125 million (an appreciation of $112 million in fifteen years) to go into venture capital, the owner admitted that he could be faulted for just one thing—caring too much. "If I made mistakes, maybe it was because I was too impatient to win," he remarked in an exit interview. As for his relationship with

Barkley, Katz says now that it is just fine and has always been that way. "I've never had an argument with him," Katz said. "I bumped into him in Philly in 2005, and we had drinks and were laughing." They have commiserated about the NBA, how it has changed. "The nature of the player is far different than it was," Katz said. "Now they have their best season at the end of their contract, then sign for a new, six-year deal."

With or without Katz—in Philadelphia, Phoenix, or Houston—Barkley never won an NBA title. That was a common affliction in this era, shared by great players like Ewing, Stockton, and Karl Malone. The player in Chicago, Jordan, was simply too stupendous and willful. But Barkley kept entire teams afloat at times and endured only three losing seasons during his entire career, in 1987–88, 1991–92, and 1999–2000. He probably came closest to winning everything in 1993, his first season with the Suns. Barkley was still strong as an ox then. Phoenix gave Jordan and the Bulls all they could handle.

Barkley was never jealous of Jordan, who had become a good friend and running buddy by the late '80s. He always understood that Jordan had something, an extra athletic gear, that nobody else in the game possessed, and Barkley was able to accept he was the second-best player in the universe. It was just important not to tell him he might be the third- or fourth-best player, because that would upset him deeply. Jordan was better, but he wasn't unbeatable. In 1993, Barkley came to believe the Suns were a better team, all-around, than the Bulls. Phoenix had a pure shooter in Dan Majerle, a fine playmaker in Danny Ainge, and enough of an interior presence in himself, Mark West, Tom Chambers, and Cedric Ceballos. The Suns won 62 games during that season, the most in the league and 5 more than the Bulls, then survived the deep, Western Conference playoffs with victories over the Lakers, Spurs, and Sonics.

The Bulls captured the first two games at Phoenix in the Finals for a huge edge, but the Suns won a triple overtime Game 3 at Chicago on June 13, 129–121, one of the classic postseason contests of all time. By Game 5, another Suns' victory, Barkley had gone on national television to declare, "God wants us to win the championship."

"I told Michael Jordan the other night that it was destiny for us to win," Barkley said.

He was asked how Jordan responded.

"He reads a different Bible," Barkley said.

In Game 6 at Phoenix, the Suns were up 4 points with forty-three seconds left and had the ball. It appeared the series would be carried to Game 7, which would also be on the Suns' homecourt. Frank Johnson, a Phoenix guard, missed a jumper. Jordan got the rebound, headed downcourt past all five Suns, and scored the basket in a maneuver that required all of five seconds. Phoenix missed a couple of shots, and then John Paxson buried a three-pointer for the Bulls' victory. Barkley's 21 points and 17 rebounds weren't enough. His last real chance at a title slipped away. He would often insist afterwards that it didn't really matter in the end, that his career and his life's work would stand on their own. He was right about his life's work but surely lying about the missing title not mattering to him.

Barkley remained front and center after retirement. He flirted with a run for governor of Alabama—he was at first an outspoken Republican, explaining that it was the party of the rich, which he happened to be. By 2006, he was announcing his intention to run for governor as a Democrat, in order to help the state's poor. Then he was an Independent, putting down both parties, hoping to reestablish residency in Alabama by 2007 in order to qualify for the governor's race in 2014. He was inducted into the Hall of Fame in September 2006, choosing old pal Moses Malone and former Suns' CEO Jerry Colangelo as his presenters. He thanked Malone, Erving, the late Sixers' scout Jack McMahon, his mother, and his grandmother. He said the proudest moment of his career, oddly enough, was making his ad, "I am not a role model."

"When I talked Nike into doing the commercial, I knew it was going to be a big deal," Barkley said in the induction speech. "We have a problem in the black community because all these young black kids think they are going to play professional sports. They are not going to. We've got to get more black doctors, lawyers, engineers, teachers, firemen, policemen. They've got to get 'real jobs,' as I call them. They've got to do better in school. They've got to stop killing each other. They've got to stop having kids they cannot afford."

Real jobs weren't for Barkley, though. The closest thing would be his role as a studio analyst on NBA games for TNT network, a career that was ideally suited to his talents. From the start, Barkley was very good at expressing half-serious opinions that made a good degree of sense, if you half-listened to them—perfect for TV. And if he insulted somebody, if he said something offhandedly cruel or crude, well, that was just Charles.

20

The Player's Player

You'd think the kid from Gonzaga would be grateful, Frank Layden remembered thinking. Instead, John Stockton—the accommodating, team-oriented, big-hearted, little-school John Stockton—decided to hold out for a larger, longer deal after the June 1984 draft. "In those days, I would not bring a kid in without a contract," Layden said. "We hard-balled him out of a little bit of money, and John was just counting on his friends and family back in Spokane to keep him going until he got a deal." Layden had his hands full that summer, and Stockton was far from his worst problem. Adrian Dantley became embroiled in a contract dispute that was becoming ugly. It would not be resolved until after the season began and would drive another wedge between the star player and Layden. Rich Kelley, the backup center, was a free agent testing the waters. Nearly lost in the margins of this commotion, Stockton ended up signing on September 26, 1984, for the grand sum of $125,000 his first season. Four years later, in 1988–89, he was still earning a salary of only $300,000, a cut-rate bargain even for those days. The Utah Jazz operated this way at every level, a small-market oasis of economic restraint in a sports world hurtling onward and upward.

Stockton reported to work finally, with great anticipation on all sides. The reviews were solid from the start, a great relief to all. Rickey Green told Frank Layden as much, immediately. "Coach, you got a good one," Green said. Jerry Eaves, the third-year backup guard recovering from knee surgery, came over to Scott Layden at the first practice and remarked, "He's really good, isn't he?" Eaves had mixed feelings about this, because his own job was very much at stake. "We knew already he was good," Scott Layden said. "We just didn't know he would be an immortal." Convinced that Stockton was ready for a steady reserve role, the Jazz reluctantly waived Eaves on October 11. This was a difficult move, because Scott Layden considered Eaves a friend. It all felt a bit cold, too, because Eaves was working his way back from an operation. But the Jazz had only so much money, and nobody required three point guards.

Stockton endured little pressure, learning behind Green in the league's smallest market. His location spared him a great deal of commotion. Two thousand miles away in New York, the Knicks had a half dozen beat writers traveling with the team. In Utah, the Jazz was covered by two newspaper reporters. Stockton also had the sense he was still close to home, in just another small city out West. Salt Lake City was really not that far from Spokane, in geography or mindset. "I couldn't have played anywhere else," Stockton said. "Comfort is part of it. Anywhere else, I would have been swimming upstream." The Jazz scheduled an exhibition game at Spokane for him and for the team's own coffers. Stockton debuted in the regular NBA season on October 27 at Seattle, where many of his college fans turned out to see him score 4 points and, more telling, get 5 assists in just seventeen minutes. "Stockton played well," Frank Layden declared at the time. "He did a good job. He got taken to school a couple of times, but what I like about him is his defense and he sees the floor. The reason he'll play a long time in this league is the word, 'unselfish.'"

Stockton was a valuable cog that first year, and then he became something much more than that in the first round of the Western Conference playoffs against Houston. The Jazz was the clear underdog in this best-of-five series against Sampson and Olajuwon. Utah's player payroll of $2.5 million was second lowest in the league, and the team would take a three-and-a-half-hour bus ride from San Antonio to Houston that season to avoid plane fare and save some money. Frank Layden liked to say "low-budget productions win Oscars," but it was repeatedly the bigger-budget teams in Boston, Los Angeles, and Philadelphia that captured the NBA titles. Somehow, the Jazz scrapped to a deciding Game 5 in Houston, where the Rockets appeared relatively safe with a 9-point lead going into the fourth quarter. Utah's starting center, Mark Eaton, had left the game in the second quarter with a knee injury and had not returned. Layden decided in that final period to do something quirky, bordering on ridiculous. He benched Dantley, surrounding Thurl Bailey with four reserves—Stockton, Billy Paultz, Rich Kelley, and Fred Roberts. With Stockton at the helm, threading passes to teammates in stride, Utah stormed back to win the game and the series, 104–97. "It looked that game like John had been playing for 10 years in the league," said Lex Hemphill, who was covering the playoffs for the *Salt Lake Tribune*.

Frank Layden absolutely loved Stockton, who was a throwback to his own days. Here was '50s basketball, alive and kicking in the '80s. Stockton was the embodiment of the pick-and-roll, the backdoor cut, and the short short pants, all rolled into one. Dantley was different. He presented an unfamiliar set of cultural demands on Layden. Dantley was a proud, strong-willed, authority-questioning African-American, in many ways the inevitable and bright future of the sport. Stockton, though, was right in the coach's wheelhouse. "He was all, 'Yes sir, no sir,'" Layden said.

It was Catholic school all over again. Older players would tease him, tell him, "Make sure you wear a tie on the plane," and he would go along with it, just because he was used to it. His whole career, I never saw him try a behind-the-back pass or dribble. He'd call me up on Sunday mornings, 7 AM, to make sure I was ready for church and then we'd walk over to Mass together. If I'd chew him out, he was always the same, always the same stoic look about him. He was there on time, ready to play. The only time I saw him get mad was when he sprained an ankle and I wouldn't put him back in a game. Most of the time, if you sat him, his attitude was the same. And it was infectious. It spread to the whole team.

After Stockton's rookie season, Layden called the player into his office for a traditional exit meeting. "Coach, what do I have to do to get better?" Stockton asked. Layden told him he had to increase his shooting range. "He's the kind of kid, he went home and shot a thousand shots a day," Layden said. Soon enough, his jumper became a weapon. In 1984–85, he tried only 11 three-pointers, making 2. By 1987–88, he shot 67 of them, converting 24 (35.8 percent). By 1991–92, Stockton was one of the top bombers in the league, burying 83 of 204 three-pointers, or 40.7 percent.

With the thirteenth pick in 1985, the Jazz drafted Karl Malone, the forward from Louisiana Tech whom Stockton had serendipitously met at the Olympic trials in Bloomington. This would, ultimately, become a magical pairing of small college workaholics. But it was not quite an instant Hall-of-Fame marriage made in heaven. When Malone arrived, Stockton was still playing behind Green and would do so until the 1987–88 season. Malone liked what he saw of Stockton but worried about him. "He's an awful little fella' to be out there playing," Malone recalled thinking, his rookie year. "He's going to get hurt." Malone was an instant starter, a true steal in the draft, yet was not one of Layden's favorites at the start. Malone was perceived more as an ally of the team captain, Dantley, in what was becoming a potentially volatile roster divided by race and agenda.

Matters came to a boil during a tight victory over Phoenix on March 7, 1986. With Malone at the foul line down the stretch, Suns' coach John MacLeod called a timeout to ice Malone, who was then a shoddy 48 percent free throw shooter. Layden was furious at this tactic, which he felt was a bush-league, college strategy. When the game was done, Layden yelled at Malone that this was what he got for being a miserable foul shooter. Malone yelled back. Dantley tried to play peacemaker, and the argument regained momentum in the locker room, where Dantley told Layden to stop picking on the rookie. Layden ordered Dantley to return to Salt Lake City, suspending the team's leading scorer for a game rather than allowing him to travel with the team to Portland. Later, after Layden and Dantley met with owners Battistone and Larry Miller, fines were announced as two pennies for Malone (for putting his two cents in) and $3.00 in dimes for Dantley, a more pointed, biblical allegory about Judas and thirty pieces of silver. Dantley was furious, particularly after the team announced he'd been suspended "for disciplinary reasons."

Stockton was not about to get involved in any of this mess, hoping to stay above the fray. Hemphill remembers climbing onto the team bus after the Phoenix game, and for a few minutes it was just the reporter and Stockton sitting there. Hemphill, like any good journalist, asked Stockton what had happened in that closed locker room, because he wanted to get the facts correct about the argument. Stockton apologized to the writer, saying he couldn't divulge such information, that it was a team matter. "It made my job tougher, but I respected him for that," Hemphill said. It was always among teammates and coaches, in his comfort zone, where Stockton would come most alive, where he would demonstrate a sense of humor and take some chances. He would dunk, sometimes, behind closed doors in practice, just to prove he could—never, ever, in games. "He could imitate me, imitate my voice," Layden said. "I'd hear him mimicking me at the back of the bus. . . . 'If you're not ready when I push your button, then you're not going to be a player in this league. . . . You're going to play in the grocery league . . . '" There was another day, Hemphill remembered, when the Jazz was waiting for a commercial flight at the airport and Dantley asked Stockton to watch his stuff while he went to eat something. Here was another opportunity to play impressionist. Stockton put on Dantley's long fur coat, providing another comedy routine.

Among these trusted teammates, Stockton would laugh. Stockton would talk. Stockton would sob, too, as he did from sheer relief and joy in the locker room when the Jazz beat Houston in a six-game series to finally reach the NBA Finals. That was the night, May 29, 1997, when Stockton freed himself on a Malone pick that stopped defender Clyde Drexler in his tracks. Stockton buried the three-point shot at the buzzer, as the Jazz came back in Houston from 10 points down for a 103–100 victory over Olajuwon, Barkley, and Drexler, an All-Star cast. Stockton cried that night in the locker room, still trying to keep such emotions out of public sight, letting only his teammates witness them.

Steve Luhm, Hemphill's replacement on the Jazz beat in 1986, watched Stockton become even more circumspect once talk radio invaded the region. The player just would not whine about anything. "For two and a half years at the start of his career, he sat and kept his mouth shut, even though it became obvious he should be starting in front of another All-Star guard," Luhm said. Surely Stockton wanted a bigger role; he just didn't demand it. Back home in Spokane, his father waited and wondered along with him. Jack

Stockton would drive to the city's outer limits at night with his wife, Clemmie, trying to tune in KSL, the Salt Lake City radio station that carried Jazz games. This was before Jack and Dan's Tavern got the big satellite dish that made it a favorite sports bar in town. "We'd park our station wagon by the entrance to the old bridge, where the reception was best," Jack Stockton said. "We'd have to move the car sometimes, point it south toward Salt Lake." The waiting and listening paid off for everybody. Slowly, improbably, Stockton to Malone became the NBA's Montana to Rice.

They never won a championship. Like Barkley and Ewing, two other superstars without rings, Stockton's hopes would be throttled by Michael Jordan and the Bulls. Utah would fall in successive, competitive, six-game Finals. "It's never pleasant to think about," Stockton said. "That was our goal and it didn't happen. I talked to Karl after our last NBA Final and said, 'I just know this is going to happen. I just know it.' And he felt the same way. I knew it was an opportunity for us and it was slipping away. . . . We just weren't good enough."

Still, Stockton's own numbers accumulated impressively, for 19 seasons in the same city, until they were so large as to border on the ridiculous. He proved to be strong and durable, just as Frank Layden figured when he tested those biceps in that Chicago hotel. The little playmaker was an extraordinary iron man, missing just 4 games in his first 13 seasons and only 54 games in his entire career—averaging more than 79 games played per season. He led the league in assists for 9 straight seasons, setting the all-time NBA career mark of 15,806. He had the most assists in a single season, 1,164, in 1990–91. He had the most career steals, 3,265. He averaged 14.5 assists in 1989–90, the highest per game mark ever in the league. Stockton played 1,504 regular season games with the Jazz and 182 playoff games. On June 10, 1998, he had 8 assists in one quarter. He had 24 assists in a playoff game on May 17, 1988, against the Lakers.

Those were just numbers. Everybody had his own special memories of Stockton, beyond the stats. For Luhm, two episodes came to mind, because the spotlight was not turned so bright on these performances. There was a regular season night at Madison Square Garden, when Stockton totally took apart the Knicks. A fan was running around, screaming, "It's Bob Cousy! It's Bob Cousy! I've seen Bob Cousy!" The second night was even more telling, an exhibition game between the Jazz and Pistons in October 2000, at Lansing, Michigan, which was supposed to be a homecoming of sorts for the Detroit rookie Mateen Cleaves from Michigan State. Stockton was now thirty-eight, starting to feel the seepage of relentless age in his joints. A couple of hours before game time, his knee locked up. Stockton somehow got it moving again. Then he played in this meaningless exhibition and ran circles around Cleaves. "Most guys would have blown off that game in the regular season," Luhm said. "Here he goes out in a preseason game at Michigan State, it was almost like he had to prove himself every time out there." When Stockton finally quit in the spring of 2003, his final game was a playoff loss in Sacramento where the fans graciously cheered his exit, as Stockton and Malone were pulled from the blowout loss by Jerry Sloan with five minutes left. When he spoke later to his dad, Jack Stockton wanted to know why John hadn't acknowledged the crowd. "We were down 17," John said. "I'm not going to wave at anybody."

It was Stockton's work ethic that drove Malone, at least until the big man learned to drive himself. Stockton and Malone were never close friends, never went out for beers or pizza after a game. But they were always the closest of teammates. Malone liked to say he would get up and work out on the Stairmaster, knowing that Stockton was across town doing the same thing. They had separate lives, especially after they married and were raising their own families. But they never bolted Utah, never quit on each other, in an era of free agency that had parted budding partnerships like the one in Orlando, with Penny Hardaway and Shaquille O'Neal. And when it was time for their official, honorary nights in Salt Lake City, for their jerseys to be retired and for their statues to be unveiled, each of them understood his place was next to the other.

Stockton's evening came first. On November 23, 2004, he traveled to the Delta Center for a halftime ceremony to retire his number 12. Old tapes were played on the scoreboard, with highlights that included the three-pointer against the Rockets. There were his former coaches—Dan Fitzgerald from Gonzaga, Frank Layden and Jerry Sloan from the Jazz. U.S. Senator Orrin Hatch was on hand. He couldn't resist the photo op. Stockton's wife, Nada, declared that John was "the greatest thing that ever happened to me." Dantley came, proving that Stockton was a bridge between factions on that old Jazz team. And of course Malone was there, wearing a cowboy hat. "You appreciate a guy who shows up for work every day," Malone said. "I knew what I was going to get every night." Stockton was dressed that day formally in a black suit for a change, not in his usual collared T-shirt. Fitzgerald joked that Stockton must have bought himself a mortuary in Spokane. Layden, again referencing the culture wars, compared Stockton's quiet dignity to the shenanigans of the more recent Pistons-Pacers brawl. To Layden, Stockton was the ultimate role model. "I wonder how many mothers said, 'You think John Stockton won't eat his dinner? You think John Stockton won't go to Mass?' John Stockton and what we're doing tonight is about all the good things in sport," Layden said. Finally, it was Stockton's chance to speak, which is always a nervous time for everybody. "I feel like a dead guy, hearing my eulogy in advance," he said. He didn't have to say much, through all the applause.

Stockton dutifully returned in March 2006, for Malone's celebration. Malone's jersey number 32 was retired and his statue was unveiled right next to Stockton's, on the southeast plaza of the Delta Center. Stockton attended an invitation-only luncheon at the arena,

closed to the public and to the media. David Stern was in attendance, and the commissioner thought it was a shame that more people didn't hear Stockton's speech about his ex-teammate. "I got up
and spoke for two minutes, like we were told," Stern said. "John
spoke for a full five minutes, more than I'd heard him talk altogether
in 20 years. He was really eloquent." Stockton's eyes watered a bit,
by his own account. When he finally faced the press later, he said he
was in no mood to cry again.

And that was that, the last sighting of Stockton at an NBA arena
in the spring of 2006. Like Olajuwon and Bowie, Stockton preferred
to live his life outside of professional basketball. During his career he
turned down endorsement deals that might have netted him millions
but would have cost him valuable personal time. He settled back into
Spokane, with his wife and their six children. He watched his kids
play in their sporting events on a considerably smaller scale than the
NBA Finals. He kept working out at Gonzaga, in the gym and weight
room, sometimes playing in pickup games with varsity players.

"It's been great having him and his family around," Jack Stockton
said. "He still has a lot of fun at the dinners, and he comes around
the bar once in awhile. But if I had to depend on his business, I
would starve."

EPILOGUE

The 2006 NBA draft took place on Wednesday night, June 28, at Madison Square Garden—the same theater as in 1984. A month earlier, the NBA had held its draft lottery inside a television studio in Secaucus, New Jersey. Fourteen mediocre-to-lousy teams that had failed to qualify for the playoffs participated, though not on equal footing. The number of Ping-Pong balls assigned to each team was carefully weighted. The worse the team's regular-season record, the greater was its chance at a better pick. The Portland Trail Blazers, now the dregs of the league, had a 25 percent shot at winning the top pick. But bad clubs had a history of bad luck. The team with the worst record had finished atop only four of the previous twenty lotteries. And on this Tuesday, it happened again to the Blazers. Toronto captured the number 1 pick, beating odds greater than eleven-to-one. The second pick went to the Knicks, who had a 19.9 percent chance at the top choice. But there was a catch. The dismal New York franchise had traded away this draft pick to the Chicago Bulls in 2005 for Eddy Curry, a promising young big man who had learned almost nothing under that famous teacher, Larry Brown.

The two worst teams, the Blazers and Knicks, were stuck with the fourth and twentieth picks, respectively. The end result was not all that different from the many crazy, upside-down draft orders throughout NBA history, the ones with predatory deals and coin flips that preceded this statistically jiggered drawing. But the inequities were now the result of a random-chance system, not the purposeful tanking of games down the stretch of a season. This was the twenty-first year for this system, which was put into place as a direct result of those 1984 shenanigans.

The broadcast of the draft itself was significantly more polished than in 1984; now it was a prime-time presentation both on stage and on ESPN, brought to you very conspicuously by the corporate sponsor du jour, Sprite. The background set was snazzy; the seats were packed with resentful Knicks fans; the graphics and video highlights on television were so comprehensive they were very nearly incomprehensible. There were now network reporters everywhere. Dan Patrick anchored a team of five on-site analysts. Others were chiming in on remote feeds or roamed around with complete access to any of the twenty prospects who were present at the Garden and were expected to be chosen in the first round. The new league-mandated age minimum of nineteen years (and one year removed from high school) prevented kids from coming out very early, so these were college players and international stars, most of them known quantities to discerning fans in attendance.

One of the draftees, Adam Morrison from Gonzaga, already had agreed on a deal with Topps to cut up his draft-day jacket into little pieces for inclusion in his trading cards. ESPN trumpeted an anticlimactic satellite feed from inside the Toronto Raptors' draft room (courtesy of Visual Communications Technology by Sony, everyone was reminded), where general manager Bryan Colangelo would soon announce his well-known decision to select Andrea Bargnani from Italy with the first overall pick. A moustache-free commissioner

Stern was still the master of ceremonies, as clumsily upbeat as ever. But the TV analysts were no longer such hopeless Pollyannas. They complained that big men like Bargnani and LaMarcus Aldridge were too soft, while reporters posed tough questions to the prospects. Right there on camera, they were bugging J. J. Redick from Duke about his recent DUI arrest, asking Morrison about his diabetes, and interrogating Bargnani about the jeers he received from the crowd.

There was also a clumsy moment inside the theater, reminiscent of Mel Turpin's erstwhile humiliating confusion. This time, the Chicago Bulls drafted Aldridge only in order to trade him to Portland, yet Aldridge was forced to march to the stage wearing a Bulls' cap. Then Tyrus Thomas made the same, long walk with a Blazers' cap, even though his move to Chicago had been finalized. The biggest drama of the day was also filled with great irony. The Charlotte Bobcats were now co-owned and operated in large part by Michael Jordan. Charlotte was picking at number 3, the identical spot in the draft order where Jordan had once been plucked by Rod Thorn twenty-two years earlier. Jordan was searching for the same secret qualities in these college kids that he possessed in 1984, when he became such an unexpected breakout superstar. There was a greater, more frustrating pressure now, because he could not simply slash to the basket and make everything right. And like Thorn back in 1984, Jordan had some unfortunate decisions already engraved on his resume. He was at least somewhat responsible, after all, for the Wizards' selection of high schooler Kwame Brown in the 2001 draft with the number 1 overall pick, ahead of Pau Gasol and Tony Parker.

The Bobcats had seriously considered drafting one of three players: Morrison, the forward with the hard-nosed game and soft touch; shooting guard Brandon Roy from Washington, who was judged by some scouts as the best all-around talent in the draft; and forward Rudy Gay from University of Connecticut, a big man expected to contribute immediately. Despite early indications he preferred Gay,

Jordan eventually went with the more conventional choice, Morrison, who would surely sell some tickets even if the second-year Bobcats continued to lose games. Before the draft, Jordan said that he had learned his lesson in Washington and he would make his opinion known louder than all others, as part of a collaborative decision in Charlotte involving about twenty coaches, scouts, and officials. After the Morrison selection, Jordan appeared at a news conference in Charlotte, sporting a thin moustache and admitting he had not really paid much attention to this draft class until he became part owner:

> I had to play catch-up. I had to gather as much information as I could to better myself and the needs of this franchise. I made a lot of phone calls and watched a lot of tape. We narrowed it down every hour, taking a vote, taking a vote, voicing our opinions. Everybody had a vote. But the final decision was a different story. There wasn't one controlling view about a particular player. I came in with an open mind, with the option of listening to what was being put on the table with possible trades and some names that were being considered. Then you think about what this franchise needs to get better and narrow it down from that direction. Looking at the team, we desperately need some fourth-quarter scoring. What I see most is [Morrison's] desire to win. He's got an innate feeling that he's going to work hard to make himself a better basketball player.

Jordan was asked if he were disturbed by Morrison's emotional breakdown after his NCAA tournament loss, when the Gonzaga forward sobbed publicly on the court. He didn't mind at all, Jordan said. He might well have been remembering his own tearful reaction to Bobby Knight's rebukes, after the West Germany game at the Olympics. "That was more about a showcase for his passion for the game," Jordan said. "All great players want to win, where they've gone through those periods of being tearful or they've felt low, myself included. It's not a distraction. It's a sign this kid cares about the game of basketball."

The man who once selected Jordan at that number 3 spot was very much involved in this draft, as well. Thorn became an executive with the New Jersey Nets in June 2000, soon remaking the team into a contender with the acquisition of Jason Kidd. This 2006 draft was very different for Thorn from the one in 1984. Thorn, the franchise president, was not picking third, for one thing. He had aspired for just such a spot when he acquired the Los Angeles Clippers' first round pick in July 2004 as part of the Kenyon Martin deal with the Denver Nuggets. But the historically woeful Clippers turned themselves around in unexpected fashion, and Thorn owned only the twentieth pick, which was his own, and the twenty-second pick, belonging to Los Angeles. "Lower than I was hoping for, let me say that," Thorn commented. It was not just the drafting position that had changed dramatically. The whole landscape and process had shifted.

For starters, the Nets now employed a full-time European scout, Rob Meurs, based in Belgium. Meurs would travel to see younger players all over the world, in South America and even in Africa to monitor the annual Basketball Without Borders game—an All-Star showcase that did not exist when Hakeem Olajuwon first emerged. Ed Stefanski, the team's general manager with a keen eye for talent, would also go to Europe several times a year. The Nets relied on several scouting services, not just on Marty Blake's continued assistance. "It's very difficult for a player to be missed now," Thorn said. "It used to be that virtually every year somebody got missed, even in this country. Now it's impossible to be missed here. You may not be evaluated properly. But somebody is seeing you." Internationally, one or two players could still slip through, but not often. "You're not going to see that anymore," Thorn said.

Thorn and officials from other teams had other options available, too, beyond the game films and live scouting missions. Players were traveling great distances for pre-draft workouts and interviews with interested NBA franchises. At these auditions, team officials would measure the players' jumping ability from a standstill position and with a step; measure their lateral quickness; test their ball-handling skills; put them through a variety of shooting drills; and, finally, match them with other players in one-on-one and two-on-two situations. Four players on the court at the same time was the league-mandated maximum.

For various reasons some players opted out of this ritual. In 2005 high schooler Gerald Green announced through his agent he would only work out for a few select teams, and then he would only shoot for them, not play against anybody. In 2006 several top prospects, such as Adam Morrison, Brandon Roy, and Randy Foye, said they were up for anything. They would take on all comers. But with a team picking at number 20, Thorn could not coax some of the blue chippers to visit New Jersey. If they expected to go higher in the draft, they did not want to encourage lesser projections. Marcus Williams, the University of Connecticut point guard, refused to audition for the Nets. Josh Boone, UConn's six-foot-ten, 237-pound center, was considered more of a project. He came to East Rutherford, New Jersey, to work out twice with the Nets, once against Solomon Jones, another big man.

Thorn knew the odds were stacked against him. Historically, only about 6 percent of players chosen between numbers 20 and 30 in the draft made a real impact with their team. Still, he also knew that virtually every year there was one player in that range of selection who broke through as a solid contributor. He cited Tony Parker, Josh Howard, Leandro Barbosa, and Nenad Krstic as recent examples. "We have to make sure we don't miss that player, so I think the scouting and evaluation part is more critical when you're drafting in that area," Thorn said.

Thorn had tried to pull off some trades before the 2006 draft. He wouldn't deal one of his core players—Jason Kidd, Vince Carter, or Richard Jefferson—without getting a superstar in return. That didn't happen. But there was another possible exchange with Seattle, which owned the number 10 pick overall. The Nets planned to send their two first-round picks and another future choice to the Sonics, and then draft Hilton Armstrong at number 10. The Sonics were interested in Shannon Brown from Michigan State and hoped they could still select him at number 20. Thorn kept trying to convince Seattle officials they could get Brown that low, and in the end Brown slipped all the way to Cleveland at number 25. But that was not really why the Sonics balked. "We were in the draft before they said they weren't going to do it," Thorn said. "They were considering it. The reason they stuck with the pick was because of this 6–11 guy with a 9–5 reach, Armstrong. How could they pass on him, even though they already had two young centers? He's going to have value."

By the time the draft reached the twentieth pick, the players left in this range were certain to have some negative marks against them. Marcus Williams was an obvious talent, but he had a pockmarked portfolio, and so he dropped unexpectedly right down to the Nets at number 20. While at UConn, Williams had been nailed for trying to sell two laptops stolen by a friend. He was charged with four counts of third-degree larceny, sentenced to eighteen months probation, ordered to perform twenty-five hours of community service, and was banned from campus dining facilities and dorms. He was suspended from the team for more than a month, missing 11 games.

Williams was only six-foot-three, and there were also questions about his defensive abilities. Thorn was still thrilled to take a chance on him. The Nets were looking for a backup to Jason Kidd and had figured Williams would go in the top fifteen, maybe even in the top seven. "The guys who go higher normally are big players who people take shots at, just in case," Thorn said, citing seven-foot center Patrick O'Bryant at number 9 as a player who went higher than the Nets projected. "Guys who go lower, it's usually something to do with character or size: This guy's a terrific college player, but he's 6–5, can he play guard? Or can he play a small forward as he did in college. Or here's a 6–8 pivot man who might not have skills to play out on the floor. You see a lot of that. There's a lot of mistakes that are made that way." Just in case, the Nets had run significant background checks on Williams and talked to all the UConn coaches. Thorn was convinced the kid was not the second coming of Quintin Dailey, his famous draft gaffe. "Everybody was very high on him as a player and leader," Thorn said of Williams. "He ended up taking most of the biggest shots for UConn."

The Nets also needed depth in the frontcourt and selected Boone at number 22. He did fine in the summer league for rookies in Orlando, Florida, where he averaged 10.6 points, 7.8 rebounds, and 2 blocks a game. But on the final day of that brief summer season, Boone suffered a torn labrum in his shoulder and required surgery that would leave him sidelined for months. The Nets were caught short again in frontcourt depth and were forced to scour the market. Williams became Thorn's great rookie hope heading into the autumn of 2006. As Thorn explained:

> He has a remarkable affinity for passing the ball, he can handle the ball well enough to do that in the half and fullcourt. What he did that surprised us in Orlando is he shot the ball well from outside. He was always a good free throw shooter, but he shoots three-pointers very easily. It gives you the opportunity to at least think you can play him with Jason Kidd, because he can make shots. As with most young players, defensively, it's such a different game here than it is in college. What you find in college a lot is you don't want your kids fouling out, it's just like starting over again for most. With Marcus,

there are two things. He's got to make sure he gets himself in top-flight condition. The second thing is the effort and concentration you have to put in on the defense.

Work ethic, luck, serendipity, karma, destiny, intuition, skill: you can believe in one or all and still not quite figure out how things would turn out in 2006 or why they turned out the way they did back in 1984. Stu Inman at Portland, known among his peers as a master at scouting and personnel decisions, made that one drastic mistake with Sam Bowie. Yet by the second round of the same draft, he was back on his remarkable game, stealing Jerome Kersey with the forty-sixth overall pick. The previous spring of 1983, Inman had chosen Clyde Drexler with the fourteenth pick. In 1985 Inman would pluck Terry Porter, a future All-Star point guard out of little Wisconsin–Stevens Point, with the twenty-fourth pick in the 1985 draft. These were all very successful decisions, all of them overshadowed by the one choice that would forever haunt him. Did that make Inman a failure? "Anybody who says they'd have taken Jordan over Bowie is whistling in the dark," said Ray Patterson, who was president and general manager of the Houston Rockets in 1984. "Jordan just wasn't that good." Would Jordan ever have won a title, for that matter, if the Bulls hadn't managed to acquire Scottie Pippen in 1987? That deal was made possible not only by the foolish Sonics but also by the desperate Knicks, who had traded their pick to Seattle for the rights to an aging Gerald Henderson.

Standard deviation—what we non-statisticians might call good or bad fortune—is often underestimated in the analysis of sport. It is at the core of most results, determining the ramifications of many draft picks. Even with all the scouting and technological advantages available in the late twentieth and early twenty-first centuries, some of the NBA's greatest stars were passed over by seemingly smart general managers. In the 1996 draft, Kobe Bryant was chosen thirteenth by the Charlotte Hornets, who selected him only as part of a predetermined deal with the Lakers. In that same draft, future league MVP Steve Nash was selected fifteenth by the Phoenix Suns. A year later, Tracy McGrady was the ninth pick in the draft by the Toronto Raptors. The two biggest stars of the sparkling 2006 NBA Finals had also been foolishly neglected by several franchises. Dirk Nowitzki was selected ninth in 1998, while Dwyane Wade went fifth overall in 2003.

That 2003 draft was in many ways similar to the one in 1984. This was an extraordinary batch of impact stars, and the first five picks were further proof that scouting was hardly an exact science. The Cavaliers chose LeBron James at number 1, but then the Pistons selected Darko Milicic, a big mystery man out of Serbia and Montenegro, at number 2. Carmelo Anthony went number 3 to Denver, followed by Chris Bosh to Toronto and Dwyane Wade to Miami. If the draft were held again today, the order likely would be James or Wade at number 1, then Anthony or Bosh at number 3. They are four truly remarkable players. But Milicic, an early bust, would likely go somewhere in the second round. Detroit blew it big time yet won a title anyway as an unjust reward.

If thirty playing cards were allowed to represent the thirty NBA franchises, and if they were blindly drawn to anoint a champion for each season, then some cards would be pulled more often than others over the relatively short haul. That's standard deviation. And there you have it: dumb luck created a couple dynasties, perhaps, and a couple of perennial cellar dwellers. Of course, human design and error were also major factors in this grand scheme. But sometimes NBA franchises failed to capture titles not only because of managerial incompetence but also because they were in the wrong place in the wrong era. While Jordan was at his peak, the contending Knicks, Jazz, Sonics, and Blazers were all victims of a timeline as much as anything.

On it goes, these seemingly random events that created the ordered universe of Jordan, Olajuwon, Barkley, and Stockton. When he looked back at 1984, his first year as commissioner of the NBA, David Stern was still a bit confused about how it all came together for the league so very fast. It was more a balmy breeze than a perfect storm, because here were welcome winds blowing from a new direction. A mom and pop sports league suddenly became commercial, fashionable, international. It also made a ton of money. "The future sneaks up on you," Stern commented.

There isn't one event that happens. It's all these forces. It felt like we were in a horror movie, in this little rowboat being crashed about. You just don't want the rowboat to capsize. And then, all of a sudden, somebody's lifting up the lake.

We had no sense this would be transformational. You have to remember what was happening. The gestalt every year was Boston-L.A. Magic and Larry were in their prime, and in some ways the league was better situated geographically than it would be in Michael's prime. But there were probably four things that were about to change our league: First of all, it was sports marketing. Nike and Michael, with an assist from Spike Lee. They changed the conventional wisdom that a black athlete could not be a major endorser, that there was no crossover. Second, there was the television explosion. When Bird and Magic were at their peak, there were still no regional sports stations. Now there's more than 120 million households reached with regional sports networks. Third, there were building renovations. Since 1984, with the exception of the Meadowlands, every arena is new or has been rebuilt. The Palace of Auburn Hills was the first, then came the others.

And finally, there was the Class of '84.

The legacy of that class is complicated, because these players did not merely sow one evolutionary seed. Jordan changed the way that basketball was played and perceived in both good and bad ways.

Before Jordan arrived, it was the playmaker who was worshipped for his unselfish genius. Back then, also, the center was coveted for his sturdy, necessary presence in the middle. Somebody needed to block the shot, wrestle for the rebound, provide the scowl, and elbow in the paint. Before Jordan, there was Bob Cousy and Bill Russell, Magic Johnson and Kareem Abdul-Jabbar. After Jordan, though, the scorer would become king of all he surveyed, regardless of his position. Jordan begat gunners and superstars of all shapes and sizes: Kobe Bryant, Shaquille O'Neal, Vince Carter, LeBron James, Dwyane Wade. . . . The three-second highlight film was now a requisite sugar rush on television sports programming, and it mattered most of all that a basket was invented in spectacular fashion. In this way, the league lost a great deal of its innocence and sacrificed many of its more endearing values for a shallow shot of adrenaline. Everything about the game had looked and sounded different back in 1984—from the media sitting courtside (to be replaced by celebrities and high rollers) to the length of the shorts and the sounds inside the arenas. Cheerleaders were the exception in 1984, not the rule. Organists once played lilting old tunes at halftime, and the background noise rarely obscured conversations. Stern shrugged his shoulders in this regard, admitting that his hearing had suffered long-term damage over the years from the roar of the artificial, scoreboard-produced cacophony. He insisted the noise level was capped at 94 decibels, though that sometimes seemed hard to believe.

Blame this on Jordan, if you will. But there were other members of that Class of '84, and each of them provided his own lessons, sometimes contradictory. Stockton was a throwback, one last ledge to grab hold, for old schoolers who wanted their basketball played "the right way." He demonstrated not only selflessness but also loyalty to a single organization. Jordan would come back to play for a second team in Washington. Olajuwon had a similar, silly ending in

Toronto. Barkley, true to his vow of opportunism, played for three different franchises. Not Stockton: it was hard enough to get him out of Spokane, let alone Salt Lake City.

Olajuwon represented the foreign invasion, the internationalization of the sport. Here was a superstar hatched from Africa, from a place few American fans had visited or even considered. There was no turning back anymore from an outside world that could produce such a dominant athlete. Soon enough, other nations would be trouncing NBA stars regularly at the Olympics and at World Championships. There would be eighty-two international players from thirty-eight countries and territories on NBA rosters at the close of the 2005–06 season, including seven such players on the San Antonio Spurs. Bargnani would become the third foreign player—after Olajuwon and Yao Ming—to be drafted first overall in the draft.

Barkley, meanwhile, was all sass and power, a new breed of player taking control of his own words and image, unafraid to create waves. Did Barkley's outrageous behavior indirectly lead to Dennis Rodman's head butting, then finally to the November 2004 brawl between the Pacers and Pistons? It's tough to make the case. When Barkley came around, the Bad Boys existed in Detroit and were on the ascendancy. Players like Micheal Ray Richardson already suffered famous drug setbacks. Barkley was merely an effective variation on a theme, a mutation. He was more verbal, more engaged with his audience. Barkley was playing to and with the crowd, not just with his teammates and against opponents. While others were suspended or lost face because of their insubordination, Barkley would cash in on his mischief. Barkley sold shoes, jerseys, and TV ratings. Celebrities and celebrity interviewers enjoyed his company. Suddenly, you weren't anybody unless you were talking hoops with a hoopster.

"The landscape wasn't just changing, it was exploding," Stern said.

Every talk show, Arsenio Hall, whoever, wanted to affirm their relevance by bringing on an NBA player. On her sitcom, Murphy Brown would joke: 'You want to use my Wizards' tickets to see the Celtics, or wait 'til the Clippers come to town?' And it kept escalating. Michael Jordan the rookie played in relative anonymity compared to Michael Jordan, the veteran. The individual was being magnified by the media. This was the athlete as personality. Dennis Rodman became the anti-authority guy. I knew it was over when his book was translated into Hebrew. That was the end of civilization as we know it.

If there was a common thread to the Class of '84, beyond the players' transcendent talents and commercial value, it might have been their pursuit of the challenge. That kind of passion was evident in what they brought to the court every night. Jordan and Stockton never rested on their laurels, on their uncommon instincts. Instead, both worked very hard to improve their perimeter games as their careers advanced. The lean-in, fall-back jumper became Jordan's primary weapon in his later years, when his dashes to the basket required too much energy and were no longer so numerous. In this way, Jordan remained a viable offensive threat, while other famous high-wire acts like Julius Erving and David Thompson never quite adapted as well to their own aging bodies.

The rewards were innumerable for Jordan, and they spilled over to everyone. Money was flying everywhere, at such ridiculous levels that it was almost impossible to compare NBA finances to real world economics. By the 2005–06 season, the league salary cap per team (which had been $3.6 million in 1984–85 and $23.0 million in 1995–96) was $49.5 million, representing just under half the league's basketball-related income. The highest paid players active in the league that season were O'Neal in Miami, at $20 million; Chris Webber in Philadelphia, $19.1 million; Kevin Garnett in Minnesota,

$18.0 million; Stephon Marbury in New York and Allen Iverson in Philadelphia, both $16.5 million. The Knicks had a $120 million player payroll, demonstrating exactly how soft the cap really was. The minimum salary in 2006–07 for a player with no prior NBA experience would rise to $412,718. This was no wonder, considering the amount of television revenues shared by the thirty teams (there were just twenty-three franchises in 1984). The NBA signed a two-year, $11 million cable deal with USA Network and ESPN in 1982 through the 1983–84 season. Exactly two decades later, the league struck a $2.2 billion, six-year cable deal with TNT through the 2007–2008 season. During the 1983–84 season, CBS was in the middle of a four-year, $91.9 million network deal with the NBA and was showing a total of thirty-two games during the season, including the All-Star game and playoffs. Again, two decades later, ABC/ESPN was paying $2.4 billion over six years in a network deal that would expire in 2008, showing fifteen regular season games plus the playoffs and Finals.

At the same time all these riches were cascading down from satellite signals, however, ratings had plateaued or slipped a bit. Critics complained about a lack of soul and substance to the league. Ticket prices were way out of hand, escalating to nearly $2,000 per seat for a courtside place at a Knicks game. There were concerns about image problems, about the brawl in Auburn Hills and about life after Jordan. Stern would insist that he was not the least bit worried. Television ratings were down for all sports. That was the nature of the diversified entertainment market. The players were fine, just a very few bad apples. And as for superstars to replace the Class of '84, Stern said they were coming out his ears. "I never, ever worry about the next star," Stern said.

Dwayne Wade and LeBron James were the latest models. Wade, a fluid small man able to dominate entire games, looked like the closest thing to Jordan since Jordan, and he was well situated in

Miami with O'Neal. James was arguably more Magic Johnson than Jordan, stuck in the non-glamorous market of Cleveland, not far from his Ohio home. This was a problem for Stern, even if he didn't care to confirm it. In the 1980s and 1990s, marquee teams from large markets like Los Angeles, New York, Boston, Philadelphia, and Chicago were the backbone of the league. In this way, through no fault of its own, the NBA had run out of luck, just like Inman in 1984. Standard deviation, planned parity, and the cyclical nature of the sport had created a league that allowed the San Antonio Spurs to rise and James to toil for the Cavaliers, a franchise that had plucked the right Ping-Pong ball in the revised, weighted lottery.

There were no Ping-Pong balls back in 1984. Even if there had been, the Cavs probably would have traded their first pick to Dallas or Philadelphia. Olajuwon, Jordan, Barkley, and Stockton reshaped the basketball world with drop steps, impossible acrobatics, bruising rebounds, and perfect passes. Nothing is as it was, when Portland selected Sam Bowie and Rod Thorn chose a shooting guard with the third pick in the draft.

ACKNOWLEDGMENTS

I first covered the NBA for the now-defunct *Paterson News* as a New Jersey Nets beat writer in 1979, after an editor, Joe Edwards, moved me from city side to the sports section. The league was a perfect breeding ground for well-rounded sports reporters, with a stimulating mix of outrageous quotes and trade rumors.

In those early years, I was treated fairly and graciously by such team public relations directors as Matt Dobek, John Hewig, Kevin Kennedy, Ted Pase, Kevin Sullivan, Jim Foley, Harvey Pollack, and Jeff Twiss. I enjoyed the company and competition in New York of reporters and columnists like Harvey Araton, Gary Binford, the late Bill Barnard, the late Dan Blumenthal, Curtis Bunn, Bryan Burwell, Dave D'Alessandro, the late Sam Goldaper, Nat Gottlieb, Roy S. Johnson, Fred Kerber, Kevin Kernan, the late Leonard Lewin, John Rowe, Carrie Seidman, Dave Sims, George Vecsey, and the late Mike Weber.

On the road, I met talented and helpful reporters like Elton Alexander, Fran Blinebury, the late Jeff Denberg, Tom Enlund, Randy Galloway, Buck Harvey, Lex Hemphill, Johnette Howard,

Jan Hubbard, Phil Jasner, Steve Luhm, the late Corky Meineke, Charlie Pierce, Bob Sakamoto, Dan Shaughnessy, George Shirk, Mark Vancil, and David Remnick, who probably doesn't want to remember now his nights at the Cap Centre, covering Jeff Ruland and grumbling about tight deadlines at the *Washington Post*. There were also born-to-be-NBA-writers, whose love of the sport and for reporting always brought the game to life: Mark Heisler, Terry Pluto, Bob Ryan, Sam Smith, and Aileen Voisin.

The access to players was remarkable back then, and I came to know and appreciate unique personalities, including Otis Birdsong, Darwin Cook, Darryl Dawkins, Len Elmore, Mike Gminski, Eddie Jordan, Albert and Bernard King, Maurice Lucas, Mike Newlin, Mike O'Koren, Micheal Ray Richardson, Buck Williams, and Super John Williamson. I also learned the game, and the strategies, from some of the sharpest coaches, general managers, and officials: Stan Albeck, Larry Brown, Dave DeBusschere, Red Holzman, Phil Jackson, Bob MacKinnon, and Joe Taub. There were wonderful characters in different roles: Fritz Massmann, the eternally upbeat trainer of the woeful Nets; Dick Bavetta, referee and NBA lifer; Sid Bronsky, the ultimate fan, who had a way of sneaking his way into any basketball game; and the late Jim Karvellas, a broadcaster of renowned passion.

Here's to Kevin Hanover, my editor at Da Capo Press, who did everything right for this book, signing it up, editing it, marketing it, practically turning the wood pulp into pages. And here's to my agents, David Black and David Larabell, who were the ones who lured Kevin into this project in the first place. Also, a nod to Shana Murph and Beth Wright for their work on the manuscript.

I received enormous help setting up key interviews and acquiring materials from Brian McIntyre of the NBA, Jeff Pomeroy at Turner Sports, and Rick Brewer at the University of North Carolina.

I would also like to thank Barry Werner, a sports editor who back in the day was operating primitive fax machines, sending copy back from the arenas to newspaper offices; Dave Kaplan, a friend and former editor; and the current group at the *New York Daily News* who have made my body of work appear greater than its weight: Leon Carter, Teri Thompson, Adam Berkowitz, Jim Rich, and a sterling desk that features none other than John Gruber, eraser of excess commas.

Finally, I would like to thank my family. Without the distractions and demands of my wife, my children, and my grandson, this project probably would have been much easier. But then, I would have had no reason in the world to complete it.

BIBLIOGRAPHY

BOOKS

Barkley, Charles. *I May Be Wrong, But I Doubt It.* Edited by Michael Wilbon. New York: Random House, 2002.

Boling, Dave. *Tales from the Gonzaga Hardwood.* Champaign, Ill.: Sports Publishing, 2005.

Delsohn, Steve, and Mark Heisler. *Bob Knight: The Unauthorized Biography.* New York: Simon & Schuster, 2006.

Hubbard, Jan, editor. *Official NBA Basketball Encyclopedia.* Introduction by David J. Stern. 3rd ed. New York: Doubleday, 2000.

Naughton, Jim. *Taking to the Air: The Rise of Michael Jordan.* New York: Warner Books, 1992.

MAJOR MAGAZINE, WIRE SERVICE, AND NEWSPAPER ARTICLES

Anderson, Dave. "An Olympian Task." *New York Times*, March 27, 1984.

Barnard, William. "NBA Notes." Associated Press, December 12, 1984.

Bernstein, Ralph. "Sports News: 76ers—Erving." Associated Press, June 22, 1984.

_____. "76ers—Barkley." Associated Press, September 26, 1984.

Daley, Steve. "Bulls Close out a Weird Season." *Chicago Tribune*, April 27, 1985.

De Leon, Virginia. "New Arena Exhilarates Zag Fans." *Spokane Spokesman Review*, October 24, 2004.

Drum, Keith. "Jordan's Final Decision to Come Today." *Durham Morning Herald*, May 5, 1984.

Elderkin, Phil. "Rookie Sam Bowie No Smash Hit, But Blazers Like His Potential." *Christian Science Monitor*, November 13, 1984.

Feinstein, John. "Olajuwon Is Expected to Enter NBA Draft." *Washington Post*, March 25, 1984.

_____. "For Wildcats, Seeing Is Believing." *Washington Post*, April, 1, 1984.

_____, and Michael Wilbon. "Waiting for Verdict Was Hardest Part of the Trials." *Washington Post*, April 21, 1984.

Hafner, Dan. "Akeem Throws Punch, Jazz KOs Rockets." *Los Angeles Times*, April 29, 1985.

Howard-Cooper, Scott. "Despite All of His Falls, Bowie Is Grateful He Still Has Two Legs to Stand On." *Los Angeles Times*, April 30, 1989.

Jerardi, Dick. "Barkley on Entering Hall: 'That's Pretty Cool.'" *Philadelphia Daily News*, April 4, 2006.

Johnson, Roy S. "The Union of Akeem and Ralph." *New York Times*, October 21, 1984.

Keech, Larry. "Eleventh Hour Arrives for Jordan's Decision." *Greensboro News & Record*, May 5, 1984.

Kirkpatrick, Curry. "A Towering Twosome." *Sports Illustrated*, November 28, 1983.

_____. "The Liege Lord of Noxzema." *Sports Illustrated*, November 28, 1983.

_____. "It Was Trial by Fire." *Sports Illustrated*, April 30, 1984.

Long, Ernie. "Katz and Croce Are Similarly Different." *Allentown Morning Call*, March 21, 1996.

Luhm, Steve. "Retiring John Stockton's Jersey." *Salt Lake Tribune*, November 23, 2004.

Mifflin, Lawrie. "A Lesson in Gold-Medal Economics." *New York Times*, September 24, 1984.

Mitchell, Fred. "Enough of This Boorish Behavior!" *Chicago Tribune*, July 21, 1995.

Picker, David. "Olajuwon Says He Gave in Good Faith." *New York Times*, February 16, 2005.

Quirk, Kevin. "Worthy Advice Helps." *Charlotte News*, May 7, 1984.

Recio, Maria E. "Michael Jordan Scores Big—On and Off the Court." *Business Week*, December 3, 1984.

Ulman, Howard. "Quiet Sam Perkins Fills Shooting Niche." Associated Press, June 4, 1991.

Verdi, Bob. "Bird Is Sold on Jordan, NBA's Future." *Chicago Tribune*, February 7, 1985.

White Jr., Gordon S. "Knight's Triumph Was One of Tactics." *New York Times*, March 24, 1984.

_____. "Sam Bowie in Portland for Physical." Associated Press, May 24, 1984.

_____. "Mavericks' Draft." Associated Press, June 13, 1984.
_____. "Olympic Tribute." Associated Press, June 21, 1984.

OTHER ARTICLES

An effort was made to cite and credit within the text substantive interviews or fac-
tual material believed to be exclusive. Other articles from the following publica-
tions and services were also utilized as background material or as sources for
quotations from group interviews:

Allentown Morning Call
Anchorage Daily News
Associated Press
Baltimore Sun
Boston Globe
Charlotte News
Chicago Sun-Times
Chicago Tribune
Dallas Morning News
Deseret News
Durham Morning Herald
Greensboro News & Record
Hartford Courant
Houston Chronicle
Houston Post
Lexington Herald-Leader
Los Angeles Times
New York Daily News
New York Times
Oregonian
Philadelphia Daily News
Philadelphia Inquirer
Raleigh-Durham News & Observer
Salt Lake Tribune
Spokane Spokesman Review
Sports Illustrated
United Press International
Washington Post

INDEX

ABC/ESPN, 261
Abdul-Jabbar, Kareem, xii, xiii, 56, 63,
  105, 116, 195, 198, 258
ACC. *See* Atlantic Coast Conference
Agents, xii, 26, 62, 63, 72, 73, 81, 110,
  194, 204, 217, 230
Aguirre, Mark, 131–132, 138, 139,
  141, 220
Ainge, Danny, 234
Alarie, Mark, 88
Albert, Al, 167, 171, 172, 178,
  179
Alcindor, Lew, xiii, 46, 102
Aldridge, LaMarcus, 249
Alford, Steve, 18–19, 89–90, 92, 94,
  97, 156
Allen, Paul, 199
Anderson, Greg, 57
Anderson, Ken, 77, 81–82
Anderson, Ladell, 155–156
Anger, Victor, 80
Anthony, Carmelo, 256
Appalachian League, 122
Armstrong, Hilton, 253
Atlanta Hawks, 176

Atlantic Coast Conference (ACC), 4,
  16, 128
Auburn Tigers, 65, 67, 68–69, 71–72,
  73, 74
Auerbach, Red, 107, 183
August, Joey, 75–76

Bailey, Thurl, 158, 159, 163, 186
Baldwin, Don, 79
Baltimore, 113
Banks, Ernie, 210
Ban the Soviets Coalition, 95
Barbosa, Leandro, 252
Bargnani, Andrea, 248, 249, 259
Barkley, Charles, x, 28, 40, 53, 65–74,
  127, 131, 141, 145–147, 148,
  149–154, 168, 173–174, 201, 206,
  221, 225–236, 259, 262
  decision to turn pro, 72–74
  in Hall of Fame, 235–236
  Olympic trials, 86, 87, 88–90, 91,
    92, 93, 94, 95–96
  retirement of, 229, 235
Barkley, Frank, 66
Bartelstein, Mark, 81

Basketball Without Borders, 251
Battistone, Sam, 162, 163, 241
Bayless, Skip, 143
Baylor, 143
Beal, Dicky, 36, 39, 40, 41
Bedford, William, 57
Bellamy, Walt, 134
Benhamu, Carlos, 48, 49
Bennett, Winston, 39
Benton, Ray, 26
Berry, Walter, 86
Bettman, Gary, xi
Bickerstaff, Bernie, 207
Bird, Larry, xi, 116, 120, 207,
    209–210, 215
Blab, Uwe, 18, 97
Black, Jimmy, 12, 22
Blackman, Rolando, 125, 138, 139,
    141, 178
Blackmon, James, 39
Blackwell, Cory, 28
Blair, Bill, 202, 212
Blake, Marty, 120, 167–169, 170,
    179, 251
Blinebury, Fran, 104, 182, 188,
    189
Bliss, Dave, 143
Boise State, 80
Boone, David, 80
Boone, Josh, 252, 254
Bosh, Chris, 256
Boston Celtics, xi, xii, 107, 108, 109,
    116, 129, 148, 169, 185, 188,
    209, 228, 262
Boston Herald, 95
Bouler, Slim, 213
Bowie, Cathy and Ben, 32
Bowie, Heidi, 201
Bowie, Sam, x, 3, 28, 31–43, 57, 58,
    69, 71, 114, 116–119, 129, 133,
    168, 193–198, 220, 255
  cracked rib injury, 195

fractured shin bones, 33–34, 85,
    116–117, 127, 130, 171, 172,
    197
  selected by Portland Trail Blazers,
    171–172
Bowie, Samantha, 31
Bratz, Mike, 136
Brewer, Rick, 14
Brown, Fred, 61
Brown, Hubie, 160, 209
Brown, Kwame, 214, 249
Brown, Larry, 2, 247–248
Brown, Shannon, 253
Bruton, Mike, 87
Bryant, Kobe, 129, 255–256, 258
Buckwalter, Bucky, 113, 117
Buffalo, 113

Cage, Michael, 91, 143, 168, 178
Calandruccio, Dr. R. A., 34
Campbell, Tony, 168, 179
Canada, 98
Caray, Harry, 205
Carnesecca, Lou, 167, 170, 171, 172,
    173, 175, 176, 178, 179
Carr, Antoine, 88, 92, 96
Carr, Kenny, 115, 196
Carroll, Joe Barry, 106
Carter, Donald, 223
Carter, Fred, 212
Carter, Vince, 212, 253, 258
CBS, xi, 261
Ceballos, Cedric, 234
Central African Republic, 47
Chambers, Tom, 125, 234
Chaney, John, 16, 17
Charles, Lorenzo, 55
Charlotte Bobcats, 215, 249–251
Charlotte Hornets, 256
Cheeks, Maurice, 93, 147, 176
Chicago Bulls, 123, 124, 128–129,
    138, 149, 152, 153, 172,

179–180, 184, 200, 203–215, 243,
    249, 262
purchased by Jerry Reinsdorf,
    211–212
China, 98
Christian Science Monitor, 195
Cleaves, Mateen, 244
Cleveland Cavaliers, 103, 113, 126,
    136, 137, 143, 157, 174,
    176–177, 184, 256, 262
Cocaine, x, 158, 185
Cohen, Alan, 109
Colangelo, Jerry, 235, 248
Cooper, Joe, 119
Cooper, Michael, 82
Cooper, Wayne, 115
Corzine, Dave, 212
Cousy, Bob, 169, 244, 258
Craighill, Frank, 26
Crossman, Herb, 6, 8, 9, 10–11
Crum, Denny, 38, 40
Cummings, Pat, 142
Cummings, Terry, 152, 153, 178
Cunningham, Billy, 2, 32, 131, 146,
    148, 152, 227, 228, 229, 233
Curry, Dell, 91
Curry, Eddy, 247

Dailey, Quintin, x, 124, 126, 208, 212,
    254
Dakich, Dan, 18
Dallas Mavericks, 26, 126, 131,
    135–144, 149, 173, 178, 196,
    217–223
Dantley, Adrian, 138, 162–163, 237,
    239, 241, 242, 245
Daugherty, Brad, 6, 11, 15–16
Daugherty, Walter, 11
Davis, Brad, 138, 142
Davis, Walter, 177
Dawkins, Darryl, 32, 97, 148, 158
Dawkins, Johnny, 92

Dees, Benny, 66–67
Dell, Donald, 26
Dennehy, Patrick, 143
Denver Nuggets, 114, 169, 251, 256
Detroit Pistons, 244, 256, 259, 262
Dickau, Dan, 78, 81
Dixon, Fitz Eugene, Jr., 150, 232–233
Doherty, Matt, 6, 17
Donaldson, James, 218
Donoher, Don, 85
Doucette, Eddie, 167, 170
Draftniks, 165–166, 174, 176, 178,
    179
Draft picks. *See under* National
    Basketball Association
Drew, John, 158, 159, 163
Drexler, Clyde, 49–50, 54–55, 56, 61,
    63, 108, 114, 115, 119, 125, 129,
    166, 194–195, 196, 242, 255
Duke University, 16
Dumars, Joe, 87, 96
Duncan, Tim, 43

Eaton, Mark, 159, 163, 186, 239
Eaves, Jerry, 157, 238
Edwards, Franklin, 226
Edwards, Johnnie, 66, 73
Ehlo, Craig, 188
Elacqua family, 9–11
Ellis, Cliff, 73
Ellis, Pat, 110
Endorsements, xii, 89, 90, 206,
    208–209, 231, 236, 257
Erving, Julius, 128, 146–147, 212, 227,
    233, 260
ESPN, 261
Esquinas, Richard, 213
Ewing, Patrick, ix, 5, 25, 28, 41, 42,
    58, 60, 85, 86, 87, 91, 92, 98,
    106, 109, 110, 119, 129, 142,
    152–153, 176, 181, 234
Exum, Cecil, 12

Falk, David, 26, 63, 129, 204, 205, 206, 217
Falkoff, Robert, 185
Far West Classic, 80, 82
Fentress, Lee, 26, 222, 223
Ferry, Bob, 128
Fields, Kenny, 168, 177
Fitch, Bill, xv, 1–2, 101, 102, 104–106, 107–108, 114, 132–133, 140, 149, 171, 181–182, 183–184, 185, 186, 188
Fitzgerald, Dan, 76–77, 79, 159, 245
Fleisher, Larry, 62–63, 118, 194
Fleming, Vern, 92, 93, 169
Fleming, Victor, 179
Foley, Jim, xiii, xiv
Ford, Phil, 3, 30
Foye, Randy, 252
France, 98
Franklin, Alvin, 60
Fredman, David, 156, 157
Free, Lloyd (World) B., 148, 173
Furlow, Terry, 158

Galloway, Randy, 143
Gardner, Jack, 156
Garnett, Kevin, 261
Gasol, Pau, 249
Gavitt, Dave, 90
Gay, Rudy, 249
Georgetown Hoyas, 41–43, 60–61, 62
Gettys, Reid, 57–58
Gilmore, Artis, 183
Glenn, Charcey Mae, 66, 225
Glickman, Harry, 110, 111–112, 113, 117
Gminski, Mike, 231
Goldberg, Jay, 50, 189
Golden State Warriors, 106, 141, 169, 196
Gomelsky, Alexander, 95

Gonzaga University, 75, 76–78, 155, 157
   Gonzaga Bulldogs, 78–82, 159
Goode, Wilson, 153
Goodrich, Gail, 158
Goporo, Fred, 48
Gordon, Lancaster, 86, 92, 97, 169, 175
Graham, Michael, 61
Granger, Stewart, 137
Granik, Russ, 136
Grant, Horace, 212
Gray, Stuart, 28
Green, Gerald, 252
Green, Kenny, 58
Green, Rickey, 157, 160, 238
Green, Sidney, 125, 212
Greene, Herbert, 66
Greenwood, David, 124, 212
Grevey, Kevin, 38
Griffith, Darrell, 158, 163, 179
Gund, Gordon and George, 137
Gundy, Jeff Van, 181
Guokas, Matt, 229, 231

Hale, Steve, 17
Hall, Joe B., 33, 34, 35, 36, 37–38, 39, 42–43, 118, 127
Halsel, Mark, 88
Hamilton, Leonard, 214
Hansen, Bob, 159
Hardaway, Penny, 141, 245
Harper, Derek, 221
Harris, Lusia, 161
Hartford Courant, 217
Hatch, Orrin, 245
Hayes, Elvin, 53, 102, 104–105, 108, 140
Hemphill, Lex, 163, 239, 241
Henderson, Gerald, 255
Henson, Lou, 41
Herald-Leader (Lexington), 34, 37

Higgins, Rod, 212
Hillock, Jay, 76–77, 78, 82, 157, 160
Holland, Terry, 15, 20, 59
Hollins, Lionel, 185
Holzman, Red, 113
Houston Baptist University, 48
Houston Chronicle, 47, 104, 182
Houston Cougars, 39, 46, 52–63
Houston Rockets, xii, xiii, xiv, 63,
    103–104, 110, 114, 133, 149,
    166, 170–171, 181–192, 218, 219,
    239, 242
  dumping games at end of season,
    101–102, 104, 106, 140
Howard, Josh, 252
Humphries, Jay, 169, 177
Hurt, Bobby Lee, 65, 66
Huston, Geoff, 136

Iavaroni, Marc, 174, 228
Idaho, University of, 77
Idaho State, 80
Illinois, University of, 40–41
I May Be Wrong, But I Doubt It
    (Barkley), 89
Indiana, University of, 86
Indiana Hoosiers, 17–19
Indiana Pacers, 111, 200, 259
Inman, John, 21
Inman, Stu, 2–3, 28, 112–117,
    119–120, 129, 130, 163–164, 196,
    200, 255
Italy, 84
Iverson, Allen, 261

Jack and Dan's Bar and Grill
    (Spokane), 75, 76
Jack Levy & Associates, 208
Jackson, Bo, 67, 71
Jackson, Phil, 181, 212
James, LeBron, 256, 258, 261–262

Jasner, Phil, 225, 227
Jefferson, Richard, 253
Jehovah's Witnesses, 7
Johnson, Dennis, 177
Johnson, Frank, 235
Johnson, Magic, xi, 82, 103, 116, 123,
    124, 158, 176, 181, 207, 258
Johnson, Robert, 215
Johnson, Steve, 126, 212
Jones, Arch, 168
Jones, Bobby, 146, 147, 228, 229
Jones, Caldwell, 103
Jones, K. C., 185
Jones, Solomon, 252
Jones, Steve, 167
Jordan, Deloris, 5, 6, 11, 23–24,
    29–30, 205
Jordan, James, 5, 11, 23–24, 29, 205,
    213
Jordan, Larry, 23
Jordan, Michael, x, 2, 3, 4–6, 7, 11–12,
    13–14, 15, 17, 18, 21–30, 55, 83,
    86, 87, 92, 93, 94, 96, 97, 98,
    99–100, 106, 107, 108, 115, 116,
    126, 128, 129, 130–131, 132,
    133, 135, 138, 140, 145, 152,
    153, 166, 183, 184, 197, 200,
    201, 203–215, 260, 262
  and Charlotte Bobcats, 215,
    249–251
  competitiveness of, 22, 99, 213,
    214
  decision to join NBA, 28–30, 211
  endorsements, 206, 208–209, 215,
    257
  and gambling, 213
  and golf, 21, 22–23, 213, 214
  photo portfolio of, 206
  retirement of, 213–214
  selected by Chicago Bulls, 172, 177,
    179–180

Jordan, Roslyn, 13
Joyce, Jack, 110

Kansas City Kings, 176
Karl, George, 142
Katz, Harold, 150, 151–152, 153, 226, 230, 232, 233–234
Keeling, Harold, 80, 81
Kelley, Rich, 237, 239
Kellogg, Clark, 124
Kentucky Wildcats, 31, 32, 39, 40, 57, 71, 117
Kersey, Jerome, 120, 150, 179, 198, 255
Kidd, Jason, 212, 251, 253, 254
King, Bernard, 158
Kirkpatrick, Curry, 51, 69
Kleine, Joe, 91, 92, 95
Knight, Bob, 17–18, 19, 20, 24, 28, 89, 90–91, 92–94, 97–100, 115, 150, 172, 174, 177
    personal problems of, 83–84
Koncak, Jon, 91, 92, 94, 95
Kongawoin, Bruno, 48
Kovler, Jonathan, 130, 153, 204–205, 211
Krause, Jerry, 138, 209, 212
Krstic, Nenad, 252
Krystowiak, Larry, 91
Kupchak, Mitch, 2, 187, 188

Lasorda, Tommy, 75
Lavodrama, Anicet, 48
Layden, Frank, 106, 155–161, 179, 187, 237, 238–239, 241, 242, 245
Layden, Scott, 156–157, 163, 238
Lechman, Gary, 78
Lee, Keith, 57, 86
Lee, Spike, 206, 257
Lester, Ronnie, 125
Lever, Lafayette (Fat), 115, 119, 164
Lewis, Carl, 133
Lewis, Dena, 45–46, 51

Lewis, Guy V., 45–47, 48–49, 50, 51, 52–53, 55, 56, 57, 60, 61
Lloyd, Lewis, 185, 188
Los Angeles Lakers, xi, xii, 104, 105, 116, 123, 124, 129, 138, 148, 187, 195, 197, 222, 223, 228, 256, 262
Loughery, Kevin, 125, 128, 130, 172, 177, 203, 207, 209, 211, 212
Love, Davis III, 21, 22–23
Lovelady, J. P., 168
Lucas, John, 185, 187, 188
Luchnick, Lance Jay, 73, 151, 226, 230
Luhm, Steve, 242
Lynam, Jimmy, 149
Lynch, George, 2

McAdoo, Bob, 4
McCarthy, James, 230
McCarthy, Neil, 155
McClendon, John, 141
McCormick, Tim, 91, 92, 97, 168, 174, 177
McCray, Rodney, 103, 104, 108, 114, 171, 185, 187, 188
McGinnis, George, 111
McGrady, Tracy, 256
McGuire, Al, xiii
McHale, Kevin, 98, 106, 107, 116, 158
McKenzie, Forrest, 80, 81
McKenzie, Michael, 109, 110, 111
MacLeod, John, 241
McMahon, Jack, 150
McQueen, Cozell, 57
Macy, Kyle, 38
Mahorn, Rick, 174, 207
Majerle, Dan, 168, 234
Malone, Karl, 91, 92, 96, 156, 220, 234, 240–241, 243, 244–245, 245–246
Malone, Moses, 54, 103, 107, 147, 148, 152, 171, 184, 227, 233, 235

Manning, Danny, 86, 88
Manning, Ed, 88
Maravich, Pistol Pete, 161
Marbury, Stephon, 261
Marin, Jack, 102
Martin, Kenyon, 251
Martin, Maurice, 91, 92, 94
Mashburn, Jamal, 141
Master, Jim, 36, 39
Matthews, Wes, 212
Memphis State, 57
Meurs, Rob, 251
Micheaux, Larry, 55
Milicic, Darko, 256
Miller, Larry, 241
Milwaukee Bucks, 208, 210–211,
    229
Moe, Doug, 2
Moncrief, Sidney, 125, 175
Montana, University of, 77
Morgan, Winston, 17
Morrison, Adam, 81, 248, 249, 250,
    252
Motta, Dick, 26, 102, 104, 131, 138,
    139, 140–141, 142, 149, 178,
    217–218, 219, 220
Mullin, Chris, 86, 92, 94, 98
Mumphord, Alvin, 70
Murphy, Calvin, 161

Nash, Steve, 256
National Basketball Association
    (NBA), 82, 210
  All-Star teams, 85, 92, 96, 98, 138,
      167
  background noise at games, 258
  birth of modern NBA, x
  draft picks, xii–xv, 2–3, 25–26, 63,
      85, 89, 91, 101, 102–103, 104,
      105, 106, 107, 108, 109, 110,
      111, 112, 116, 117, 119, 120,
      123–133, 135–144, 148, 149, 152,

    157, 158, 159, 161, 165–180,
    193, 212, 214, 217, 240,
    247–256
  height standards in, 146
  international players in, 259
  lottery system used by, 106,
      247–248, 262
  pre-draft workouts and interviews,
      252
  Rule 6.05, 111
  U. S. dream teams, 84, 86
  See also Salary issues
National Collegiate Athletic
    Association (NCAA), 2, 53
  tournaments, ix, 4, 40, 46, 52, 55,
      57, 60, 61, 69, 72, 83, 250
National Hockey League, 146
Natt, Calvin, 115, 119, 196
NBA. *See* National Basketball
    Association
NCAA. *See* National Collegiate
    Athletic Association
Nelson, Don, 139
Newell, Pete, 18, 84
New Jersey Nets, 109, 129, 148, 230,
    254
Newman, Johnny, 72
New Orleans Jazz, 161. *See also* Utah
    Jazz
Newton, C. M., 85, 95
New York Knicks, 110, 113, 126, 169,
    209, 238, 244, 247, 248, 255,
    261, 262
New York Nets, 147, 179
New York Post, 63, 110
New York Times, 183, 206
Nike, 206, 208–209, 231, 236, 257
North Carolina State Wolfpack, 48,
    55, 57
North Carolina Tar Heels, 1, 6, 15,
    16, 17, 52, 83, 224
Norton, Sam, 28

Nowitzki, Dirk, 256
NutriSystem, 232

Oakley, Charles, 212
O'Brien, Lawrence, x, 110, 162, 165, 166
O'Bryant, Patrick, 254
Olajuwon, Alhaji Salaam Olude and Alhaja Abike, 48, 50
Olajuwon, Hakeem, ix–x, xii, xiii, xiv, 25, 28, 39–40, 41, 47–63, 106, 107, 108, 109, 110, 117, 125, 132, 140, 166, 167, 181–184, 186, 187, 194, 204, 218, 258, 259, 262
    announcement of turning pro, 63–64
    elbowing of Olden Polynice, 59
    and Guy Lewis, 52–53
    as Hakeem vs. Akeem, 189–190
    and Islamic Da'Wah Center, 191–192
    move to Jordan, 190–191
    on Nigerian national team, 47
    as party animal, 182
    performances in 1983 NCAA tournament, 56
    religious awakening of, 188–189
    selected by Houston Rockets, 170–171
Olczyk, Eddie, 204
Olson, Lute, 159
Olympics
    Moscow Olympics (1980), 84
    Soviet boycott of, 95, 96
    U. S. team, 24, 28, 33, 83, 84–100, 144, 156, 167, 174, 175, 177, 190, 204, 232
O'Neal, Shaquille, 245, 258, 260
Oregon Arena Corporation, 199
Oregonian, The, 110
Owens, Tom, 111

Packer, Billy, 41
Parish, Robert, xii, 106, 107, 116, 183
Parker, Tony, 249, 252
Pate, Harvey, 49
Patrick, Dan, 166, 248
Patterson, Liz, xiii
Patterson, Ray, xii–xiii, xiv, 101, 104, 171, 188, 255
Patterson, Steve, xiv
Paulz, Billy, 186–187, 239
Paxson, Jim, 114–115, 118, 129, 194, 196, 235
Perdue, Will, 212
Perkins, Martha, 7
Perkins, Sam, x, 3, 6–11, 12, 17, 19, 20, 26, 30, 86, 92, 93, 94, 98, 99, 127, 138, 140, 142, 143, 144, 149, 168, 173, 178, 215, 217–224
    as restricted/unrestricted free agent, 222, 223
    retirement and marriage, 223–224
Person, Chuck, 69, 71, 86, 91, 92, 97
Peterson, Buzz, 13–14, 20–21, 22, 26–27
Philadelphia Daily News, 732
Philadelphia 76ers, xii, 25, 32, 102, 103, 111, 145–154, 169, 173, 225–234, 262
Phillip, Andy, 134
Phoenix Suns, 115, 177, 234, 235, 241, 256
Pickett, Paul, 80
Pierce, Charlie, 87, 95
Pinckney, Ed, 91
Pippen, Scottie, 107, 168, 212, 255
Pollard, Jim, 112–113
Pollin, Abe, 214
Pollock, Bill, 221
Polynice, Olden, 59, 212
Pond, Christopher, 47–49
Porter, Terry, 90–91, 92, 94, 96, 255

Portland Trail Blazers, xii, xiii, xiv, 3, 63,
    109–120, 129, 133, 164, 171–172,
    179, 193–201, 221, 247, 248
    attendance and media relations, 200
    fined by NBA, 111
Press conferences, 19, 24–25, 26, 29,
    63, 87, 205, 225
Price, Mark, 91
Princeton, West Virginia, 121–122

Racial issues, 10, 157–158
Raleigh News and Observer, 26
Ramsay, Jack, 103, 113, 117, 118–119,
    171, 195
Ransey, Kelvin, 125
Rautins, Leo, 226
Raveling, George, 85
Rawlings, Lenox, 26
Redick, J. J., 249
Referees, 61
Reid, Robert, 82, 103, 185
Reinsdorf, Jerry, 211
Reuss, Anthony, 80
Rice, Russell, 34, 41
Richardson, Micheal Ray, x, 148, 209,
    259
Richmond Spiders, 72
Riley, Pat, 181
Robert Morris University, 80
Roberts, Fred, 239
Robertson, Alvin, 92, 93, 98, 169, 175,
    178
Robertson, Oscar, 107
Robey, Rick, 38
Robinson, Cliff, 174
Robinzine, Bill, 158
Rodgers, Guy, 134
Rodman, Dennis, 168, 212, 259, 260
Rogers, Paul, 81
Rose, Lauren, 230
Rothenberg, Alan, 109–110, 111, 194
Roundfield, Dan, 176

Roy, Brandon, 249, 252
Rucker Tournament (New York City),
    10
Ruland, Jeff, 174, 207
Rupp, Adolph, 37
Russell, Bill, 116, 183, 258
Rust, Art, Jr., 166–167
Ryan, Bob, 207

Salary issues, 3, 100, 152–153, 194,
    204, 222, 226, 237, 239
    salaries in 2005–07 seasons,
    260–261
    salary caps, xi, xii, 5, 62–63, 109,
    110, 118, 145, 151, 194, 199,
    226, 227, 260, 261
Salt Lake City, 157, 238
Sampson, Ralph, xiii, xiv, 12, 38, 59,
    63, 103, 104, 105–106, 107–108,
    132, 133, 140, 142, 171, 181,
    182, 183–184, 187, 188, 194,
    204, 218, 219
    legal problems of, 191
San Antonio Spurs, 175, 208, 259, 262
San Diego Clippers, 148, 149, 152,
    173, 175, 178, 194, 251
San Francisco, University of, 80
Sangodeyi, Yommy, 28, 49
Scandals, 34, 109, 143, 213
Schrempf, Detlef, 139, 220
Seattle Sonics, 138, 169, 174, 253, 255
SEC. *See* Southeast Conference
Sewell, Tom, 226
Shackleford, Charles, 233
Shaker High School (Albany, New
    York), 9, 10
Shelton, Lonnie, 198
Shidler, Jay, 34
Shue, Gene, 175
Sichting, Jerry, 108
Sloan, Jerry, 125, 245
Sloan, Norm, 48

Smith, Dean, 1–2, 2–3, 3–4, 4–6, 10,
    16–17, 19, 24–25, 29, 30, 55, 93,
    94, 97, 128, 132, 152, 159, 173,
    175, 204–205, 217, 222
Smith, Keith, 80, 81
Smith, Kenny, 6, 12–13, 15–16, 19, 20,
    22, 27, 85, 86
Smith, Sonny, 65–66, 67–68, 69–70,
    70–71, 72–73, 95
Smith, Tubby, 31
Sobers, Ricky, 174
Sonju, Norm, 114, 135–139, 140, 141,
    143, 220, 221
Southeast Conference (SEC), 67, 69,
    70, 71, 72, 73
Spain, 84, 98, 99
Sports Illustrated, 4, 51, 69
Stansbury, Terence, 16–17, 142,
    143–144, 169, 178, 217, 221
Stefanski, Ed, 251
Steinbrenner, George, 129
Stepien, Ted, 136–137, 176
Stepp, Blake, 78
Stern, David, x, xi, xii, xiv, 111, 112,
    133, 136–137, 166–167, 170, 171,
    230, 246, 249, 257, 258,
    259–260, 261
Stipanovich, Steve, xiv
Stirling, Scotty, 106
Stockton, Jack, 76, 79, 242–243, 246
Stockton, John, 28, 76–82, 88, 91–92,
    94, 96, 119–120, 142, 143, 150,
    155–164, 169, 237–246, 258, 259,
    260, 262
  assists of, 243
  at Karl Malone's retirement
    celebration, 246
  selected by Utah Jazz, 178–179
Stockton, Nada, 245
Stuff magazine, 73
Substance abuse, penalties for, x. *See
    also* Cocaine

Sullivan, Kevin, 140, 143
Sund, Rick, 131, 132, 136, 139–140,
    142, 188, 221–222, 222–223
Superstars, 169, 183, 197, 212, 259,
    261
Sutton, Eddie, 91

Tarpley, Roy, 220, 223
Teagle, Terry, 102
Television, xi, xii, 74, 165, 208, 248,
    257, 258
  revenues from, 261
Temple Owls, 16–17
Tennessee, University of, 71
Thomas, Charles and Tracy, xiii, 170
Thomas, Tyrus, 249
Thompson, Bernard, 120
Thompson, David, 260
Thompson, John, 110, 119
Thompson, Mychal, 115, 119, 172
Thorn, Joe, 121, 122, 251
Thorn, Rod, 3, 87, 116, 121–134, 147,
    203–204, 205, 211, 212, 252–253,
    254–255
  and big-man philosophy,
    126–127
Thorpe, Otis, 150, 168, 176
Thurmond, Nate, 134
Tilden High School (Brooklyn), 8
Tisdale, Wayman, 7, 28, 86, 92, 93
TNT, 261
Todd, Rolland, 113
Tomjanovich, Rudy, 190
Toney, Andrew, 93, 131, 147, 152
Toronto Raptors, 247, 248, 256
Tudor, John, 15
Turner, Booker, 61
Turner, Jeff, 92, 95, 168, 179
Turpin, Mel, x, 26, 35, 36, 38, 39, 40,
    41, 42, 43, 57, 71, 86, 127, 131,
    141, 149, 168, 173, 174–175
Tyler, Jeb, 230

UCLA, 46
Unseld, Wes, 105, 150
Uruguay, 98
USA Network, 165, 167, 169, 261
Utah Jazz, 120, 149, 155–164,
    178–179, 186–187, 238–246

Valentine, Darnell, 115, 119
Valvano, Jim, 48, 55–56, 159
Vanderbilt, 71
Vandeweghe, Kiki, 119, 125, 136, 196
Vanos, Nick, 80, 81
Vincent, Jay, 139, 141
Virginia Cavaliers, 59–60

Wade, Dwyane, 256, 258, 261–262
Wake Forest, 58
Walker, Chet, 134
Walker, Kenny, 35, 39, 42, 43, 71, 201
Walsh, Donnie, 2
Walton, Bill, 115, 130, 172, 175
Washington, Pearl, 88, 91
Washington, Richard, 136
Washington Bullets, 105, 174, 177,
    207, 229
Washington Generals, 167
Washington Wizards, 214, 249
WCAC. *See* West Coast Athletic
    Conference
Webb, Spud, 57
Webber, Chris, 260–261
Webster, Keith, 161
Webster, Marvin, 126
Weinberg, Larry, xiv, xv, 110, 112, 118
Weiss, Bobby, 26, 142
West, Jerry, 2, 107, 121, 122–123
West, Mark, 234
West Coast Athletic Conference
    (WCAC), 80–81

West Germany, 84, 99
Weston, Jimmy, xiii
Whatley, Ennis, 212
White, Gerald, 71
Whitehead, Jerome, 136
Whitmarsh, Mike, 80
Whittenburg, Dereck, 55
Wiggins, Mitchell, 185–186, 188
Wilcox, Bill, 194
Wilkins, Dominique, 159
Williams, Buck, 198
Williams, Freeman, 159
Williams, Gus, 174
Williams, Marcus, 252, 253–255
Williams, Pat, 102, 123, 148–149,
    150–151, 153, 163, 225, 226,
    229
Williams, Reggie, 61
Willis, Kevin, 156, 176
Wilson, Othell, 60
Winslow, Ricky, 57, 60
Winston-Salem Journal, 26
Wirtz, William, 129
Wohl, Dave, 109
Wood, Leon, 86, 87–88, 92, 93, 94,
    97, 176, 220, 226, 228
Wooden, John, 46
Woolridge, Orlando, 126, 209, 210,
    212
Worthy, James, 3, 5, 6, 11–12, 21, 188,
    222

Yardley, George, 113
Young, James Earl, 60, 61
Young, Michael, 53–54, 55, 57, 58, 59,
    60, 168, 179
Yugoslavia, 84

Zaslofsky, Max, 134